T0391882

Poetry, Sound, and the Matter of Prosody
1800–2000

Poetry, Sound, and the Matter of Prosody 1800–2000

PETER MILLER

OXFORD
UNIVERSITY PRESS

OXFORD
UNIVERSITY PRESS

Great Clarendon Street, Oxford, OX2 6DP,
United Kingdom

Oxford University Press is a department of the University of Oxford.
It furthers the University's objective of excellence in research, scholarship,
and education by publishing worldwide. Oxford is a registered trade mark of
Oxford University Press in the UK and in certain other countries

Published in the United States of America by Oxford University Press
198 Madison Avenue, New York, NY 10016, United States of America

British Library Cataloguing in Publication Data
Data available

Library of Congress Control Number: 2024946801

ISBN 9780198937180

DOI: 10.1093/9780198937210.001.0001

Printed and bound by
CPI Group (UK) Ltd, Croydon, CR0 4YY

The manufacturer's authorised representative in the EU for product safety is
Oxford University Press España S.A. of El Parque Empresarial San Fernando de Henares,
Avenida de Castilla, 2 – 28830 Madrid (www.oup.es/en or
product.safety@oup.com). OUP España S.A. also acts as importer into Spain
of products made by the manufacturer.

for James and Clara

blithe newcomers

who teach me to listen

Acknowledgments

This book began as a dissertation at the University of Virginia, and my first and deepest debt of gratitude goes to the members of my dissertation committee. Chip Tucker demonstrated in word and deed how much fun prosody can be. Jerry McGann showed me that poems are made objects, patchworks of details bearing the owner's name someway in the corner. Jahan Ramazani opened my eyes to the global reach and formal memory of the genre, modeling a level of scholarship and professionalism I doubt I'll encounter again. Beyond my committee, Vicki Olwell offered teaching support when I needed it most, while serving as a consistently helpful and responsive director of graduate studies. Andy Stauffer and the NINES team let me dip my toes in the digital humanities. The members of my dissertation writing group—Jordan Buysse, Ali Glassie, Karen Huang, and Samantha Wallace—were a source of good ideas and good cheer, and my bandmates in Better Off Read—at last tally Tom Berenato, Jesse Bordwin, Annie Galvin, and Brandon Walsh—kept my cello from collecting too much dust. Caleb Agnew, Jordan Burke, Evan Cheney, and Anne Marie Thompson were helpful interlocutors on matters poetical. Sam Lemley was my correspondent from the land of bibliography. A Battestin Fellowship from the Bibliographical Society of the University of Virginia nurtured early inklings that Ezra Pound's books betray phonographical ambitions. The university's Society of Fellows sustained this line of inquiry by supporting research in the Pound Papers at the Beinecke Library, Yale University, while a Buckner W. Clay Award in the Humanities made possible research in the Langston Hughes Papers, also at the Beinecke.

Our five years in Charlottesville were sweetened by the fast friendship of Luke and Janie Beck Kreider, Kate Lichti and Caleb Hendrickson, the happiest windfall of our time there. Let's roll dice again soon.

Joining the faculty at Goshen College meant arriving where I started, and so getting to know the place, if not for the first time, then in a new way. Early jitters were calmed by a truly big-hearted set of English Department colleagues: Ann Hostetler, Skip Barnett, Beth Martin Birky, Kyle Schlabach, Pamela Carralero, and most of all Jessica Baldanzi, my tireless chair, mentor, and advocate during my first four years at Goshen. Thanks are due as well to Dean Ann Vendrely for a pair of well-timed course releases, to Jan Bender Shetler for support and encouragement as I developed a global literature course in London, and to John D. Roth, who showed that scholarship can be a form of compassion. We shall not cease from exploration, but Goshen will always be home turf.

My transition to Reed College was smoothed by an unfailingly friendly group of English colleagues: Jin Chang, Jay Dickson, Michael Faletra, Maureen Harkin, Sara Jaffe, Joan Naviyuk Kane, Nathalia King, Laura Leibman, Lucía Martínez Valdivia, Kritish Rajbhandari, Pete Rock, John Sanders, Pancho Savery, Dustin Simpson, Sarah Wagner-McCoy, and Simone Waller. Dean Kathy Oleson provided funding to secure permissions for text and images reproduced in this book. Professors Nigel Nicholson and Margot Minardi made teaching in Reed's freshman Humanities program anything but onerous, as did my cheerful inaugural cohort of "Hum" students.

Returning to Oregon has put me back in the good company of Mike Chasar, fellow inquirer into poetry's media, who years ago went above and beyond to offer encouragement to a twenty-something college grant writer with a poem in his heart and grad school on the horizon. Mike offered valuable feedback on bits and pieces of this book, as did three other friends and mentors: Rebecca Rush, Nathan Suhr-Sytsma, and Bobby Meyer-Lee.

Staff at Oxford University Press have good-naturedly helped steer the project to completion. My biggest thanks go to Eleanor Collins, who responded with remarkable speed to my initial book proposal and then found two highly perceptive anonymous readers for my manuscript, one of whom was later revealed as Matthew Rubery. Jack McNichol and Henry Clarke provided editorial guidance during the final phases of the project.

Portions of the book have appeared in journals whose permission to reprint I gratefully acknowledge. An early version of Chapter 1 appeared as "William Wordsworth and the Invention of Culture," in *Studies in English Literature 1500–1900*, 58/4 (Autumn 2018): 809–31. A version of Chapter 2 appeared as "Prosody, Media, and the Poetry of Edgar Allan Poe," in *PMLA*, 135/2 (March 2020): 315–28. Much needed tough love on still earlier versions of this chapter came from Marshall Brown and Rita Felski. Snippets from my introduction appear in my article "Patience Agbabi, *The Canterbury Tales*, and Polyhistorical Form," in *English Literary History*, 91/1 (Spring 2024): 263–84.

To my parents Lee and Susan, brothers Chris and John and sister-in-law Anna, grandparents John and Pauline, Phyllis and Bill: you've been valued encouragers since the beginning, and I'm the better for it. The same could be said of the wonderful cohort of in-laws I've gained along the way: John and Ruth, Sarah and Luke, Hannah and Jake, Mary and Katie. The lines have fallen to me in pleasant places.

Thanks, finally, to Leah, my partner in marriage fifteen years this month, my closest friend for longer still. The arrival of our children James and Clara during the writing of this book was the luckiest thing I could have hoped for. Like all prosodic ventures, the study ahead inverts the normal process by which sounded words gain human meaning. It reads for tones and textures rather than messages sent and received. But if there's one thing I've learned from our kids these past few years, it's that the smallest, most mundane prosodic materials have a way of bending, as if by magic, toward coherence. One day there's a handful of notes and then, suddenly, as the poet says, the clear vowels rise like balloons.

P. M.
Portland
July 2024

Contents

List of Figures

Permissions Credits

Introduction

The Matter of Prosody, 1800–2000

In the preface to the first (1906) volume of his *History of English Prosody*, George Saintsbury recalls an impactful early experience with poetry:

> More than forty years ago, I was reading the *Odyssey* one evening in a set of Oxford rooms, on the ground-floor looking into Merton Street. Somebody had a wine not far off; and the respectable "Slap" (whom Oxford men of my generation will remember) had brought his "noise" to the spot according to custom. Just as I came to the Song of the Sirens, they were playing a certain waltz of the day, well known to me . . . as *The Cornflower*. And it struck me, as I listened to the slow voluptuous music, and read the famous line with the clinging *u* sound pervading it, and rendered poignant by the sharper *i*'s and *o*'s and *a*'s—
>
> Δεῦρ᾽ ἄγενῦν, πολύαιν᾽ Ὀδυσεῦ, μέγακῦδος [Ἀχαιῶν],
>
> with how little truncation (of the last word only) it could be adjusted—*spaced*—to the waltz-time itself, different as it is from that of the natural hexameter. I do not mean to say that I elaborated a theory of prosody at the age of eighteen. But I had, even before that, been accustomed to scan (and if possible to scan in different ways) the poetry of which I was, and ever have been, an unsatiated and insatiable lover.[1]

Part of the poignancy of Saintsbury's account derives from what we know happens next in literary history. Just three years after the third and final volume of his *History* appeared, a twenty-eight-year-old Ezra Pound, writing in *Poetry* magazine, would advise modern poets against "[chopping] your stuff into separate *iambs*." "As regarding rhythm," Pound suggested, "compose in the sequence of the musical phrase, not in sequence of a metronome."[2] What Saintsbury names as the crux of poetic experience—the metrical foot—Pound categorically discards, and in doing so appears to enact a clean break

---

[1] George Saintsbury, *A History of English Prosody: From the Twelfth Century to the Present Day*, vol 1. (London: Macmillan and Co., 1910), ix–x.
[2] Ezra Pound, *Literary Essays of Ezra Pound* (New York: New Directions, 1935), 6, 3.

Poetry, Sound, and the Matter of Prosody 1800–2000. Peter Miller, Oxford University Press. © Peter Miller (2025). DOI: 10.1093/9780198937210.003.0001

with the prosodic tradition the elder scholar held so dear.[3] Yet *Poetry, Sound, and the Matter of Prosody* revises this account by showing that meter was just one of many sound media that poets on either side of 1900 used to structure their poems. Even Saintsbury, we should note, locates his youthful pleasure not in meter's autonomy but in its compelling interaction with other mediating forms, most notably the rhythms of the accompanying waltz but also the phonetic particularities of Homer's vowels and even the wine wafting from across the Oxford room. Across the nineteenth century and beyond, as new technologies unsettled print modes of representing sound, language, and voice, poets likewise emphasized the sonic plurality of their work. Enlisting printed ballads and talking birds, illuminated manuscripts and books shaped like vinyl LPs, poets in Britain and America mixed new media with old to revitalize the lyric tradition and explore the cultural stakes of sound reproduction. Examining key moments of prosodic innovation from Romanticism to hip-hop, this book correlates the fall of meter with the rise of modern sound technology to revitalize prosodic analysis for a multimedial age.

The heady array of sounds that so captivated the college-aged Saintsbury comprise what we might call the "matter" of prosody: the physical materials used to record poetic sound but also, in a related but distinct sense, the customs, discourses, and tools used to parse that sound.[4] For although prosody is often associated specifically with meter, the *Princeton Encyclopedia of Poetry & Poetics* is right to include in its definition any of the "measurable structures of sound in language and in poetry."[5] The breadth of this definition is an asset because it invites us to contextualize more narrowly literary efforts to analyze sound within their broader cultural and technological landscape. Before turning to literary prosody, then, let us consider three adjacent modes of sound writing developed across the long nineteenth century.

---

[3] Saintsbury, *A History of English Prosody*, vol. 1, names "feet or 'spaces' . . . the integers, the grounds, the secret, of English prosody" (ix). As Charles Hartman, *Free Verse: An Essay on Prosody* (Evanston: Northwestern University Press, 1980), observes, after modernism "the 'science' of prosody was at stake" (7); "few have tried seriously to study English prosody in any way that could include poetry written after 1912" (8). Pound's rejection of meter casts off a religious heritage as well. Writing in 1499, the Italian humanist Polydore Vergil, *On Discovery*, ed. and trans. Brian P. Copenhaver (Cambridge: Harvard University Press, 2002), suggested that "The origin of meter, then, is from God Almighty, who set out the globe of the earth and all it contains in fixed order, as if by meter, for surely no one doubts that there is harmony in heaven and earth, as Pythagoras taught" (99).

[4] Jason Camlot's illuminating study *Phonopoetics: The Making of Early Literary Recordings* (Stanford: Stanford University Press, 2019) demonstrates the value of maintaining a distinction between physical or acoustic texts and historical prosodic discourses. "One of the major assumptions that will allow my chapter [on T. S. Eliot] to proceed," Camlot explains, "is that the key voices in which Eliot spoke his poetry . . . were articulated against Victorian ones" (138).

[5] R. Winslow, "Prosody," *Princeton Encyclopedia of Poetry and Poetics*, ed. Roland Greene, Stephen Cushman, Clare Cavanagh, Jahan Ramazani, and Paul Rouzer (Princeton: Princeton University Press, 2012), 1117.

The first is a book published in 1779 by the British linguist Joshua Steele titled *Prosodia Rationalis: An Essay Towards Establishing the Melody and Measure of Speech, to be Expressed and Perpetuated by Peculiar Symbols*. Seeking to establish an analogy between the tones of English speech and music, Steele observes that:

> Whilst almost every one perceives and admits singing to be performed by the ascent and descent of the voice through a variety of notes, as palpably and formally different from each other as the steps of a ladder; it seems, at first sight, somewhat extraordinary, that even men of science should not perceive the rapid slides of the voice, upwards and downwards, in common speech. But the knowledge of the various distinct notes of ordinary music is not only laid open to those multitudes who learn that art; but also, being rendered visible and palpable to the unlearned, by the keys of organs and such like instruments, it happens that almost every one knows, the variety of music to arise, in part, from the difference of acute and grave tones.
>
> In traveling through a country, apparently level, how few people perceive the ascents and descents that would astonish them, if the man of art were to demonstrate them by his instrument, and to bring the sluggish stream to form a cascade! In like manner, when the modulation of the melody of speech shall be ripened into method by art, even the vulgar may be taught to know what the learned can now scarce comprehend.[6]

Steele's utopian rhetoric of harnessing science to unlock the sonic structures of language reappears in many modern attempts to write the sounds of speech. His account pinpoints a key challenge as well. Namely, while the Western chromatic scale is made up of a series of posited tonal intervals (thus Steele's reference to the discrete "steps of a ladder" and the "keys of organs"), English speech is comprised of far more subtle, sinuous parts. Its tonal modulations, like those of a gradually undulating terrain or a slowly swelling river, are almost impossible to chart without the aid of mechanical tools that did not yet exist in 1779. The set of "peculiar symbols" Steele develops toward this end therefore represent a remarkable fusion of theoretical ambition and practical limitation (Figure 0.1).

What Steele could only approximate—an acoustically precise form of sound writing—was achieved near the middle of the following century. In 1857, a Parisian typesetter named Édouard-Léon Scott de Martinville patented

---

[6] Joshua Steele, *Prosodia Rationalis: Or, an Essay Towards Establishing the Melody and Measure of Speech, to be Expressed and Perpetuated by Peculiar Symbols* (London: J. Nichols, 1789), 4–5.

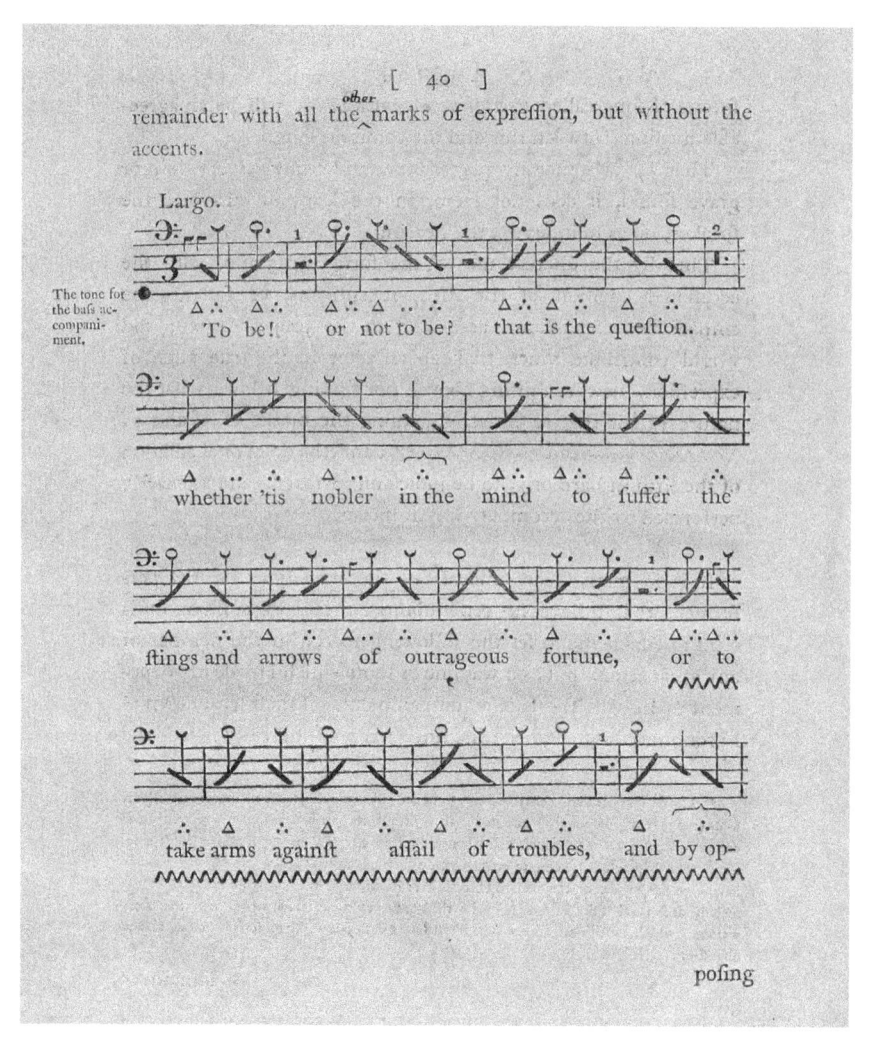

Figure 0.1 Some of the "peculiar symbols" employed in Joshua Steele's *Prosodia Rationalis* (London: J. Nichols, 1779), p. 40. Bodleian Library, Oxford University

a device he called the phonautograph. By capturing sound waves with a vibrating diaphragm and transferring them to a stylus, Scott's phonautograph could translate real-time sound into etchings on sheets of soot-blackened paper. Because of their fragility and near-two-dimensionality, these recordings could not be played back acoustically but existed only as graphical transcriptions of sound. For Scott, reproduction was beside the point. He simply wanted to develop a new form of writing that bore a strictly analog, indexical relation to sound. "Is it possible," wondered Scott, "to achieve for sound a result analogous to that attained presently for light by photography? Can one hope that the day is near when the musical phrase escaping the lips of the singer will come to write itself?... Could one conserve for future generations some trains of diction of our eminent actors, who now die without leaving after them the feeblest trace of their genius?"[7] Decades later when the fanfare surrounding Thomas Edison's phonograph reached Scott, he deemed the device a gimmick because it "merely reproduced sound—it was not a *sound-writer*."[8] As Jonathan Sterne observes, Scott's "monomaniacal focus on writing" seems odd, given how transformative the phonograph would prove.[9] Nevertheless, Sterne explains, Scott's device remains significant because it was among the first to demonstrate how "auditory and visual phenomena could first be isolated and then mixed or made to stand in for one another."[10] Like contemporaneous literary scansions that sought to more accurately visualize the sounds of verse, Scott's phonautograms, as he called them, opened new possibilities for linguistic sound writing that would be further exploited in the decades ahead.

The third mode of sound writing is the tool most often credited with launching the age of modern sound recording: the phonograph. Edison's phonograph worked much like Scott's device, but because it inscribed its recordings into wax, a comparatively rigid material, it allowed users to play back the sounds they had recorded. In 1899, one New York City couple hosted a "phonograph party," sending invitations to friends that included "the mystifying words, 'Please bring your voice.'"[11] The party's hosts later reflected on the event in a promotional essay published by the National Phonograph Company:

Our bass and baritone artists made highly successful records. Our tenor sang "The Holy City" most beautifully, but his voice lacked that peculiar quality necessary for Phonograph record making. The tones of his voice were like the invisible rays of the spectrum beyond the violet; it seemed impossible to record them. Charlotte discoursed learnedly about the number of vibrations per second caused by his high C—about a thousand I think she said ...

The talking records were mostly all good too. The performers were cautioned to speak very distinctly, sounding the S's and soft C's with particular

---

[7] Édouard-Léon Scott, qtd. in Jonathan Sterne, *The Audible Past: Cultural Origins of Sound Reproduction* (Durham: Duke University Press, 2003), 45.

[8] Édouard-Léon Scott, qtd. in Sterne, *The Audible Past*, 46.

[9] Sterne, *The Audible Past*, 46.

[10] Sterne, *The Audible Past*, 50.

[11] "How We Gave a Phonograph Party" (New York: National Phonograph Company, 1899), in *Music, Sound, and Technology in America: A Documentary History of Early Phonograph, Cinema, and Radio*, ed. Timothy D. Taylor, Mark Katz, and Tony Grajeda (Durham: Duke University Press, 2012), 48.

emphasis. Some of them caused lots of merriment when they were reproduced, owing to the funny and irrelevant side remarks of the speakers; most of whom had never talked into a Phonograph, and seemed to forget that the machine would catch and repeat all that was said.[12]

Though neither hosts nor guests likely understood the phonograph party as an exercise in prosodic thinking, the participants nevertheless gained a heightened sensitivity to issues of phonetics and elocution ("S's and soft C's"), pitch and acoustics ("vibrations per second"), which the author of this passage interprets by reference to the science of optics. Though the phonograph produced acoustic rather than visual texts, these sound-written texts nevertheless allowed the party-goers to isolate, reproduce, and reflect on the prosodic elements of their spoken and sung recordings.

Many more examples could be summoned, but these three illustrate some of the ways that prosodic inquiry developed outside expressly literary spaces across the nineteenth century. Alongside these developments occurred more narrowly poetic efforts, which emerged from, and fed back into, their broader cultural moment. Joshua Steele's ideas were taken up by the speech therapist John Thelwall, a key interlocutor for William Wordsworth and Samuel Taylor Coleridge during the pivotal decade surrounding the publication of *Lyrical Ballads*. Wordsworth's famous claim that his poetry captures "the real language of men," though in part an argument about poetic diction, is also an argument about prosodic accuracy.[13] Édouard-Léon Scott's ambition to solve the problem of sound writing once and for all finds a host of literary counterparts in the visual notation systems developed by poets and theorists across the nineteenth century. And toward the end of the century, the phonograph was receiving test runs from major poets. During the last year of his life, Robert Browning spoke his verse into Edison's device and found the experience more than a bit unsettling. Like the participants in the phonograph party, Browning was struck by the device's indiscriminate capture of acoustic material. Unnerved by this new degree of high fidelity, he forgot the words to his own poem: "I forget it— er . . . I—I am most terribly sorry that I can't remember my own verses."[14] As a younger man, Browning had made his name writing poems in which

[12] "How We Gave a Phonograph Party," 50–51.

[13] William Wordsworth and Samuel Taylor Coleridge, *Lyrical Ballads: 1798 and 1802*, ed. Fiona Stafford (Oxford: Oxford University Press, 2013), 95.

[14] Robert Browning, "How They Brought the Good News from Ghent to Aix," *The Spoken Word, Poets: Historic Recordings of Poets Born in the Nineteenth Century* (British Library Board, 2003).

a lyric speaker's exuberant desire for autonomy lays bare, in an ironic reversal, the social forces tethering that speaker to reality. To produce this effect,
Browning inserted into his speakers' texts verbal tics and asides that emulated
within the visually static medium of print the kinds of hesitations and second
thoughts that beset people during real-time conversation:

> She had
> A heart—how shall I say?—too soon made glad,

remarks the ego-tripping Duke Ferrara in "My Last Duchess."[15] Browning's
real-life encounter with the phonograph, in an ironic reversal of its own, produced just this effect in the author: hoping for a continuous lyric performance,
the actual Robert Browning was beset by context-induced verbal hiccups.[16]

Such examples suggest a level of consonance, if also some friction, between
literary and technological forms of sound writing. Yet the media theorist
Friedrich Kittler presents the two as diametrically opposed. In his influential study *Gramophone, Film, Typewriter*, Kittler argues that at the dawn of
the twentieth century poetry's traditional prosodic features were effectively
rendered obsolete by new forms of sound recording:

> At the origin of poetry, with its beats, rhythms (and, in modern European
> languages, rhymes), were technological problems and a solution that came
> about under oral conditions. Unrecognized by all philosophical aesthetics,
> the storage capacity of memory was to be increased and the signal-to-noise
> ratio of channels improved. (Humans are so forgetful and the gods so hard
> of hearing.) The fact that verses could be written down hardly changed this
> necessity. Texts stored by the medium of the book were still supposed to find
> their way back to the ears and hearts of their recipients in order to attain . . .
> the indestructibility of a desire.
>
>   These necessities are obliterated by the possibility of technological sound
> storage. It suddenly becomes superfluous to employ a rhythmical tick-tock (as
> in Greece) or rhyme (as in Europe) to endow words with a duration beyond

[15] Robert Browning, "My Last Duchess," *Robert Browning: Selected Poems*, ed. Daniel Karlin
(London: Penguin Books, 1989), 25.
[16] Reflecting on a visual illustration ("phonogram") of the Browning cylinder produced in the late
nineteenth century, Yopie Prins, "Robert Browning, Transported by Meter," in *The Traffic in Poems:
Nineteenth-Century Poetry and Transatlantic Exchange*, ed. Meredith L. McGill (New Brunswick: Rutgers University Press, 2008), observes that, "In different ways, both the illustration of the wax cylinder
and the recording itself provoke new questions about reading the 'voice' of Browning's text, as a figure
generated by the printed word, the phonogram, the engraving, and, of course, the meter" (217).

their evanescence. Edison's talking machine stores the most disordered sentence atoms and its cylinders transport them over the greatest distances . . . Technology triumphs over mnemotechnology. And the death bell tolls for poetry, which for so long had been the love of so many.[17]

Kittler's account is clearly polemical, but his diagnosis is nevertheless compelling. If poetry isn't quite "obliterated," its traditional prosodic features—rhyme and especially meter—are indeed singled out for extermination after roughly 1910 by modernist tastemakers such as Pound. The experimental, visually innovative poetry that Pound and other modernists produce, moreover, seems to back up Kittler's claim that, in an age of sound recording, serious poetry must abandon its pretensions to real-time vocal capture and instead embrace its material aspects, becoming in the most extreme case "a form of typographically optimized blackness on exorbitantly expensive white paper."[18]

Accounts such as Kittler's can spur us to think in broad terms about the differences between oral media, print media, and newer media such as the phonograph. But in practice these media ecosystems overlap and interpenetrate one another. Recent work in sound studies has emphasized the ways that modern sound reproduction technologies crystalized, as much as inaugurated, changes in discourses about sound and hearing already well underway in the nineteenth century. Lisa Gitelman suggests that Edison's phonograph should be understood within "a cluster of mutually defining literacy practices, texts, and technologies."[19] Scholars of literary modernism have also challenged Kittler's account by detailing ways that poets worked in productive tandem with modern sound technology. In *The Great American Songbooks: Musical Texts, Modernism, and the Value of Popular Culture*, T. Austin Graham asks "whether the crisis of language that Kittler describes was really so pressing . . . and whether recording technology might not have had quite the opposite effect, enriching the sensory possibilities of language."[20] In readings of T. S. Eliot, Langston Hughes, and others, Graham explores how modernist poets invited readers to sing or play along with their poems via textual allusions to current popular music, thereby enlisting readers in the cultural phenomenon

---

[17] Friedrich Kittler, *Gramophone, Film, Typewriter*, trans. Geoffrey Winthrop-Young and Michael Wutz (Stanford: Stanford University Press, 1999), 80.

[18] Kittler, *Gramophone, Film, Typewriter*, 80

[19] Lisa Gitelman, *Scripts, Grooves, and Writing Machines: Representing Technology in the Edison Era* (Stanford: Stanford University Press, 1999), 1.

[20] T. Austin Graham, *The Great American Songbooks: Musical Texts, Modernism, and the Value of Popular Culture* (Oxford: Oxford University Press, 2013), 22.

of sound reproduction. Jason Camlot, meanwhile, listens closely to actual audio recordings to develop what he terms "audiotextual" criticism, which he defines as "an expansion of the sociology of texts, introduced by textual critics and book historians, into the realms of media history, sound studies, performance studies, format theory, and other related approaches to the production and circulation of audible literary works."[21] Extending ideas put forth by the textual scholars Donald McKenzie and Jerome McGann, Camlot approaches literary recordings not simply as linguistic texts but as historically dynamic, sensory-rich media objects.[22]

Another branch of literary studies, known as historical poetics, has likewise nuanced Kittler's account, in part by pluralizing meter, diversifying its cultural operations and thereby making it less susceptible to the modernist accusation of aesthetic rigidity and homogeneity.[23] Meredith Martin excavates a dynamic history of metrical practice and prosodic debate in the nineteenth century to caution against "[taking] meter's meaning for granted as merely the measure of the line."[24] Instead, Martin argues, "'Meter' in the nineteenth century meant different things to different communities . . . By stabilizing, attempting to define, or grappling with their use of meter, poets and prosodists were often attempting to define, transform, or intervene in an aspect of modern culture."[25] Such work extends a longer historicizing trend in poetry studies away from the abstractive reading practices of the mid-century New Criticism. In her influential 2005 book *Dickinson's Misery: A Theory of Lyric Reading*, Virginia Jackson surveys the standardizations of punctuation, spelling, syntax, and medium that Emily Dickinson's poetry underwent following her death in 1886, arguing that such standardizations are simply the more visible markers of the larger transformative process by which all poetic writings, generically indeterminate or not, become legible *as* poems. A key aspect of

---

[21] Camlot, *Phonopoetics*, 6.

[22] See, for instance, D. F. McKenzie, *Bibliography and the Sociology of Texts* (Cambridge: Cambridge University Press, 1999): "The ostensible unity of any one 'contained' text—be it in the shape of a manuscript, book, map, film, or computer-stored file—is an illusion. As a language, its forms and meaning derive from other texts; and as we listen to, look at, or read it, at the very same time we re-write it" (60). Jerome McGann, *The Textual Condition* (Princeton: Princeton University Press, 1991), calls for an historical mode of literary interpretation that considers the text "not as an object but as an action" (183). Derek Furr, *Recorded Poetry and Poetic Reception from Edna Millay to the Circle of Robert Lowell* (New York: Palgrave Macmillan, 2008), applies McGann's framework to argue that "the recorded poem often troubles the shape and sounds of the poem as we've received it in print" (3).

[23] Antony Easthope, *Poetry as Discourse* (London: Routledge, 1983), laid early groundwork for this historicizing effort: "If the material basis of poetry is recognized in metre, in the 'parallelism of the signifier,' the ensuing question must be how different metres are historically specific" (52).

[24] Meredith Martin, *The Rise and Fall of Meter: Poetry and English National Culture, 1860–1930* (Princeton: Princeton University Press, 2012), 5.

[25] Martin, *Rise and Fall of Meter*, 4.

this transformation is publication in book form, which sorts potentially miscellaneous textual materials into coherent aesthetic objects worthy of critical interpretation. As Jackson writes, "as variously mimetic poetic subgenres collapsed into the expressive romantic lyric of the nineteenth century, the various modes of poetic circulation—scrolls, manuscript books, song cycles, miscellanies, broadsides, hornbooks, libretti, quartos, chapbooks, recitation manuals, annuals, gift books, newspapers, anthologies—tended to disappear behind an idealized scene of reading progressively identified with an idealized moment of expression."[26] Jackson terms this historical process "lyricization," and much subsequent work in historical poetics has presented itself as a critique of such idealizing reading practices.[27]

Insofar as this work has restored to view forgotten poetic practices that have, in turn, opened readers to new ways of experiencing poetry, historical poetics has been a boon to literary studies. Yet excavating obscure poetries has also, somewhat ironically, meant further compartmentalizing periods, coteries, and sub-genres, arguing for ways that poetry does *not* cross spatial or temporal boundaries. Indeed, the premise from which these scholars often proceed—that modern readings are predominantly *mis*readings—can have the effect of casting contemporary readers as wrongheaded or naïve for seeking transhistorical resonance from poems. Two important recent studies thus pursue alternatives to what they see as an overly narrow historicism: Jonathan Culler's *Theory of the Lyric* (2015) and Jahan Ramazani's *Poetry in a Global Age* (2020). Culler's book, while drawing chiefly on poetry from the past two centuries, ranges back in time to the ancient Greeks and consults poems in at least five languages to develop a transhistorical definition of lyric. "A greater foregrounding of rhythm," Culler proposes, "might enable the teaching of

---

[26] Virginia Jackson, *Dickinson's Misery: A Theory of Lyric Reading* (Princeton University Press, 2005), 7.

[27] Important meter-attuned studies in historical poetics include Jason Rudy, *Electric Meters: Victorian Physiological Poetics* (Athens: Ohio University Press, 2009), the collection *Meter Matters: Verse Cultures of the Long Nineteenth Century*, ed. Jason David Hall (Athens: Ohio University Press, 2011), and Hall's *Nineteenth-Century Verse and Technology: Machines of Meter* (London: Palgrave, 2017). As this list suggests, much seminal historical poetics work studies the nineteenth century, but its rhetoric of reconstructing reading and writing practices obscured during later periods shows up in a variety of recent monographs treating other historical periods. See, for instance, Eric Weiskott, *Meter and Modernity in English Verse, 1350–1650* (Philadelphia: University of Pennsylvania Press, 2021), which argues that "the medieval/modern periodization as instituted in the nineteenth century clarifies but also distorts critical understanding of metrical practice" (3), and Rebecca Rush, *The Fetters of Rhyme: Liberty and Poetic Form in Early Modern England* (Princeton: Princeton University Press, 2021), which argues that "analogical reading, which was central to ancient, medieval, and early modern theories of music and poetry, has become less common since the Romantics and therefore often seems alien and backward" (14). Ben Glaser, *Modernism's Metronome: Meter and Twentieth-Century Poetics* (Baltimore: Johns Hopkins University Press, 2020), examines the persistence of meter during modernism.

poetry to regain some of the ground lost in recent years and also might lead to a different sort of poetics."[28] Ramazani's book narrows its focus to English-language poetry from the twentieth and twenty-first centuries to develop a "polytemporal, polyspatial" poetics.[29] Both studies mount eloquent formalist defenses of transhistorical approaches to lyric. Yet their interest in poetry's spatial and material capacities remains largely figurative. Ramazani, for instance, leaves matters of "ink, paper, binding, [and] glue" to the book historians to focus instead on "words, forms, rhythms, tropes, and genres."[30] While illustrating the interpretive limits of historical poetics, then, these scholars leave a key question unasked: on what grounds might we trace a prosodic continuity between nineteenth- and twentieth-century poetry, between metrical and post-metrical verse? What, in other words, is the matter of prosody?

The present study answers this question by reframing prosodic analysis as a form of media studies. Drawing alike on formalism, textual studies, historical poetics, and critical sound studies, I neither document a transhistorical lyric genre nor excavate a period- or place-based challenge to lyric's hegemony but rather explore how poems and poets have navigated precisely these terms over the past two centuries. That is, I track how poets placed Romantic ideals of unmediated voice in a productive tension with the shifting historical facts of mediation. In the chapters ahead I therefore sometimes zoom in, aiming for a high degree of historical or material particularity when considering *this* book review, *this* audio recording, *this* printed edition. But equally often I zoom out, observing the transhistorical staying power of common meter, for instance, from the ballads of Wordsworth to the hymn-like poems of Dickinson to the lyrics of today's pop artists.[31]

[28] Jonathan Culler, *Theory of the Lyric* (Cambridge: Harvard University Press, 2015), 173.

[29] Jahan Ramazani, *Poetry in a Global Age* (Chicago: The University of Chicago Press, 2020), 3.

[30] Ramazani, *Poetry in a Global Age*, 3, 4. Other important formalist responses to the historicist trend in poetry studies include Herbert F. Tucker, "Unsettled Scores: Meter and Play in Two Music Poems by Browning," *Critical Inquiry*, 41 (Autumn 2014): 24–52, and Stephanie [Stephen] Burt, "What Is This Thing Called Lyric?" *Modern Philology* 113.3 (2016): 422–440. Richard Taruskin, *Text and Act: Essays on Music and Performance* (Oxford: Oxford University Press, 1995) offers a critique of historicism from a musicologist's perspective: "The invention of sound recording has obviously been a tremendous spur to this tendency [of attempting to escape personality], since it offers the possibility of permanence to a medium that had formerly existed only 'at the moment' . . . No less than the score, the performance is regarded as a 'text' rather than as an activity, and this creates another pressure toward the elimination from it of anything spontaneous or 'merely' personal, let alone idiosyncratic" (61).

[31] Meredith L. McGill, "What Is a Ballad? Reading for Genre, Format, and Medium," *Nineteenth-Century Literature*, 71/2 (2016), explores the benefits of adopting a variety of generic and materialist reading strategies: "My aim is not to arrive at a comprehensive definition of the ballad, but rather to show what kinds of reading become possible and what considerations of necessity get shifted to the margins when critics . . . think of the ballad primarily as a text, when they take print format into consideration, and when they broaden their sights to consider the role of print in a larger media ecology" (157).

What definition of media will best support such a project? As is probably already apparent, *media* and *medium* refer in this book not to channels of mass communication or new media as such but to something more like "an intervening substance through which . . . impressions are conveyed to the senses; any substance considered with regard to its properties as a vehicle of light or sound" (*OED*). The primary "substance" concerning us here is language, but because language is more complex than, say, ink or wax, its "properties as a vehicle of . . . sound" are likewise complex. As the editor and textual scholar G. Thomas Tanselle observes,

> the medium of language is the most mysterious of all media. It would not be so if it were unquestionably oral, with tangible texts being only the records (like musical scores) by which the vocal work is recreated. Not only is it possible, however, to have languages without oral components but also . . . it is common for authors to expect their works to be read silently, without the spoken sounds of the words being formed imaginatively in the mind. Of course, some writers (and not only poets) do wish the sounds to be heard internally; but even in those cases, or most of them, the authors feel that the works have been experienced in their intended medium whether read silently or aloud. Whatever may be said about the origins of language, in practice it is a medium that can exist apart from speech. But its written presentation on a physical surface is not its primary form either: most writings, from the point of view of their creators, are not visual works, for the works still exist when presented in different handwriting or typefaces on different papers.[32]

Because the scholarly editor's primary task is to accurately discern and transmit the words of a given work, rather than the visual or physical idiosyncrasies of a given document, Tanselle ultimately concludes that language is best understood as an intangible medium. Indeed it is only by granting the intangibility of the literary medium that readers of two different copies of *Pride and Prejudice* or *Hamlet* can rightly claim to have read the same work. Yet for the poet, as for the prosodist, physique is everything, which is why the range of material issues Tanselle surveys en route to his intangibility thesis are exactly the kinds of issues that will occupy us in the chapters ahead, where poets routinely probe the difference between oral and written modes, between musical and linguistic form, and between scripted, printed, audio-recorded, and otherwise mediated work. While language's semantic and grammatical codes may well be intangible, its prosody takes shape in particular physical and social spaces.

---

[32] G. Thomas Tanselle, "The Textual Criticism of Visual and Aural Works," *Studies in Bibliography*, 57/1 (2005): 3–4.

For this reason, three priorities guide the readings ahead. First, I examine not just a poem's language but the various paralinguistic media that embody its language, particularly in cases where a poem's media format(s) change dramatically over time. The manuscripts Dickinson left locked in her desk at the time of her death are visually quite different from the first edition of her poems published in 1890, and still more different from the poetry as depicted in the recent Apple TV series *Dickinson*. I therefore approach a poem's prosody not as a stable textual or historical feature but, following Gitelman, as a "cluster" of mediating substances—a matrix of text, technology, and literary practice that reproduces sound while making evident its modes of reproduction. I draw as well on Caroline Levine's notion of aesthetic "affordances," a term she borrows from design theory and defines as "the potential uses or actions latent in materials and designs."[33] Some of the materials I examine are physical objects (e.g. books, postcards, musical scores, phonograph records), while others are conceptual forms (e.g. meter, genre). The first group can be readily pinned down to specific documents or recordings, while the second group is more elusive. (Where, exactly, is a poem's meter?) What all such materials have in common, however, is their ability to store and measure time.[34] An iamb proposes a temporal relationship between two syllables in which the first syllable receives roughly half the duration of the second syllable. A phonograph creates a temporally indexical ("analog") relationship between a physical text and its acoustic content. And a book contains pages and alphabetic scripts that are themselves tools for reproducing sound, each with its own pacing protocols. My book is not a history of modern sound media, then, or of early literary recordings, or of poetry's place within popular culture, though I consult these histories along the way. Mine is rather a study of how poets from Romanticism to the present have grappled with the question of sonic reproducibility, as both a trope within their poems and a matter of personal, authorial concern.

Second, I gravitate toward aspects of a poet's work that elicit creative remediation and performance. Wordsworth's ballads evoke song but leave their educated readers feeling bashful. Edgar Allan Poe builds his famous "Nevermore!" refrain out of meaningless phonetic matter ("the long *o* as the most sonorous vowel, in connection with *r* as the most producible consonant") so as to make the poem an open-source, editable document.[35] Dickinson's manuscripts develop an intricate set of visual conventions that (perhaps?)

---

[33] Caroline Levine, *Forms: Whole, Rhythm, Hierarchy, Network* (Princeton: Princeton University Press, 2015), 6.

[34] See Hartman's helpful definition in *Free Verse*: "*The prosody of a poem is the poet's method of controlling the reader's temporal experience of the poem, especially his attention to that experience*" (13).

[35] Edgar Allan Poe, "The Poetic Principle," in Stuart Levine and Susan F. Levine, eds., *Edgar Allan Poe: Critical Theory, the Major Documents* (Springfield: University of Illinois Press, 2009), 64.

provide elocutionary cues for recitation. Pound writes an opera libretto in Old French featuring odd time signatures like $^7/_8$ and $^{11}/_{16}$ that make it virtually impossible to perform. And Hughes's 1961 book *Ask Your Mama: 12 Moods for Jazz* presents itself as both a vinyl record and musical score, complete with performance instructions, musical scoring, liner notes, and other paratextual elements that invite collaborative remediation. In all of these cases, poets open their work to prosodic variance at the scene of readerly engagement, indeed all but mandate it. Attuned to such instances, this book explores how poetry's sounds are transformed and repurposed, rather than obscured or misread, when taken up by later readers and media platforms. I take seriously, for instance, the American singer Taylor Swift's allusion to Wordsworth on her 2020 track "The Lakes" ("I've come too far to watch some namedropping sleaze / Tell me what are my words worth") as an instance of a contemporary form of lyrical balladry.[36] My chapter on Poe, similarly, sees *The Simpsons'* 1990 parody of "The Raven" as a witty fulfillment of Poe's hopes for the poem.

Third, rather than abandoning traditional prosodic concepts (e.g. iambs, trochees, blank verse), I approach them as one class of sound media among others. My readings of poems often begin with traditional prosodic concepts before proceeding to demonstrate how these concepts exist in tension with other mediating elements or with aspects of themselves.[37] By downgrading meter as the normative or sole object of prosodic analysis, my book seeks to provide a richer account of the array of media that structure a poem's language, while also enabling comparisons of poets across periods and cultural traditions that might otherwise seem incompatible. For instance, although Dickinson, whose poems often feature a four-beat common meter, is in one sense prosodically quite different from the modernist Pound, whose poems eschew meter in favor of free verse, the two poets are bound together by their shared interest in the prosodic information communicated by the visual elements of a book or manuscript page. The English Romantic poet Wordsworth is likewise bound to the Harlem Renaissance poet Hughes, across differences of nationality, race, and much else, in their shared interest in folksong as a source of poetic material.

What does a media-oriented prosody look like in practice? Let me offer an illustration by comparing two texts that might initially seem rather dissimilar. In the spirit of Saintsbury's waltzing Homer, one of my texts is literary, the

---

[36] Taylor Swift, "The Lakes," track 17 on *folklore* (Republic Records, 2020).
[37] Camlot takes a similar approach in *Phonopoetics*. Analyzing a recording of a poem titled "The Phonograph's Salutation," Camlot notes that, "The punctuation of the sentences rather than the poem's lineation is honored in performance with pauses, with an effect that underplays the ABAB rhyme scheme, a generic feature of the printed poem, and gives a sense of gravity in caesura as it moves from one assertion to another" (42).

other musical, and they are separated by more than a few centuries. The first is a sonnet written by the English poet Edmund Spenser in 1595. Scanned using traditional prosodic terms, the poem offers a textbook case of iambic pentameter:

> One **day** | I **wrote** | her **name** | up**on** | the **strand,**
> But **came** | the **waves** | and **wash** | ed **it** | a**way**[38]

What this visual markup, or scansion, helps us see and hear is that the lines are composed of five two-syllable units, or feet, in which the rhythmic emphasis falls on the second, bolded syllable. The same iambic pattern shows up in the opening lines of the American singer Beyoncé's 2016 song "All Night," though in lines that contain only four feet:

> I **found** | the **truth** | be**neath** | your **lies**
> And **true** | love **nev** | er **has** | to **hide**[39]

There are of course other differences. Spenser wrote for a relatively small cohort of educated English readers and published his work in books. Beyoncé is a global pop star who releases her music via CDs, streaming services, and other audio platforms. Given these differences of genre and medium, we might therefore choose to represent the sounds of "All Night" using a different visual markup language, that of musical notation:

This notation makes evident what we already know: Beyoncé's song contains non-verbal acoustic material that Spenser's poem does not. Its key signature (E major), time signature ($^4/_4$), pitched notes (ranging from C# to G#), and rhythmic subdivisions (straight eighth notes until the final

---

[38] Edmund Spenser, "Amoretti 75," in Margaret Ferguson, Tim Kendall, and Mary Jo Salter, eds., *The Norton Anthology of Poetry, Sixth Edition* (New York: Norton & Co., 2018), 202.

[39] Beyoncé, "All Night," track 11 on *Lemonade* (Columbia Records, 2016). Beyoncé's second line arguably contains a spondaic substitution in its second foot ("love nev"); in performance the song's highly percussive beats push the foot back toward an iamb. For a discussion of four-beat forms in English poetry, see Derek Attridge, "The Rhythms of the English Dolnik," in Ben Glaser and Jonathan Culler, eds., *Critical Rhythm: The Poetics of a Literary Life Form* (Fordham University Press, 2019), 153–73. Attridge offers the helpful reminder that "an emphasis on historical change can obscure the remarkable longevity of some verse-forms" (153).

beat of the bar) all provide performance information that Spenser's text lacks. At the same time, the score confirms the finding of our initial prosodic analysis: Beyoncé's rhythmically prominent syllables (*found, truth, neath, lies*) fall directly on the score's musical beats. While any number of aesthetic, cultural, and historical forces could be identified that separate Spenser from Beyoncé, the artists are allied, in this case, by their use of iambs.

So far this comparison, while establishing a common iambic ground between the two texts, has suggested that Beyoncé's "All Night" contains musical and paralinguistic elements that Spenser's sonnet lacks, since the sonnet is composed only of words. Yet the prosodic structure of a poem, even an ostensibly simple poem, is never fully contained or determined by its linguistic text. Poems exist in specific social and material contexts, which alter the effects they produce on readers. A love poem shouted from a rooftop is different from the same poem whispered in an ear. A haiku on a billboard is different from one sent via text message. And a sonnet typed into Microsoft Word is different from one published by a Renaissance print shop, as a glance at Spenser's first edition confirms (Figure 0.2). Some of the 1595 text's oddities of spelling (e.g. "Vayne" and "vaine" spelled differently within the same line) do not cause too much of a problem. But the typographically interchangeable *u*'s and *v*'s, and the long form *s*'s that look quite a lot like *f*'s, produce phonetic hiccups for the modern reader. The 1595 text also lacks quotation marks, which momentarily disguises the fact that the poem is spoken by two different people and thereby sustains the impression that the sonnet (like many sonnets) is a thoroughly first-person lyric. The catchword at the bottom of the page ("Fayre"), which previews the first word of the following page in order to help bookbinders group leaves in the proper order, feels equally odd within a modern critical climate that places a premium on the unadorned printed text surrounded by ample white space. It would be obtuse to suggest that we pronounce Spenser's *u*'s as *v*'s, or include the catchword in a reading of the poem, but neither should we be too eager to discard these paralinguistic elements, particularly in a poem about poetry's dependence on both tangible and intangible media. In her recent study of early modern rhyme, Rebecca Rush uncovers a trove of Renaissance prosodic theory that turns regularly to printed infographics to back up its claims about the sonic structures of language. "Poetic theorists of the period," Rush explains, "not only discussed the binding function of rhyme but made its connective power visible on the page by providing diagrams of rhyme schemes in which rhyming lines are connected by curved lines."[40] That such tactics were deemed necessary should remind us that prosodic effects are never wholly contained *by* written language, but rather emerge *from* language through a complex, audio-visual process of performative remediation.

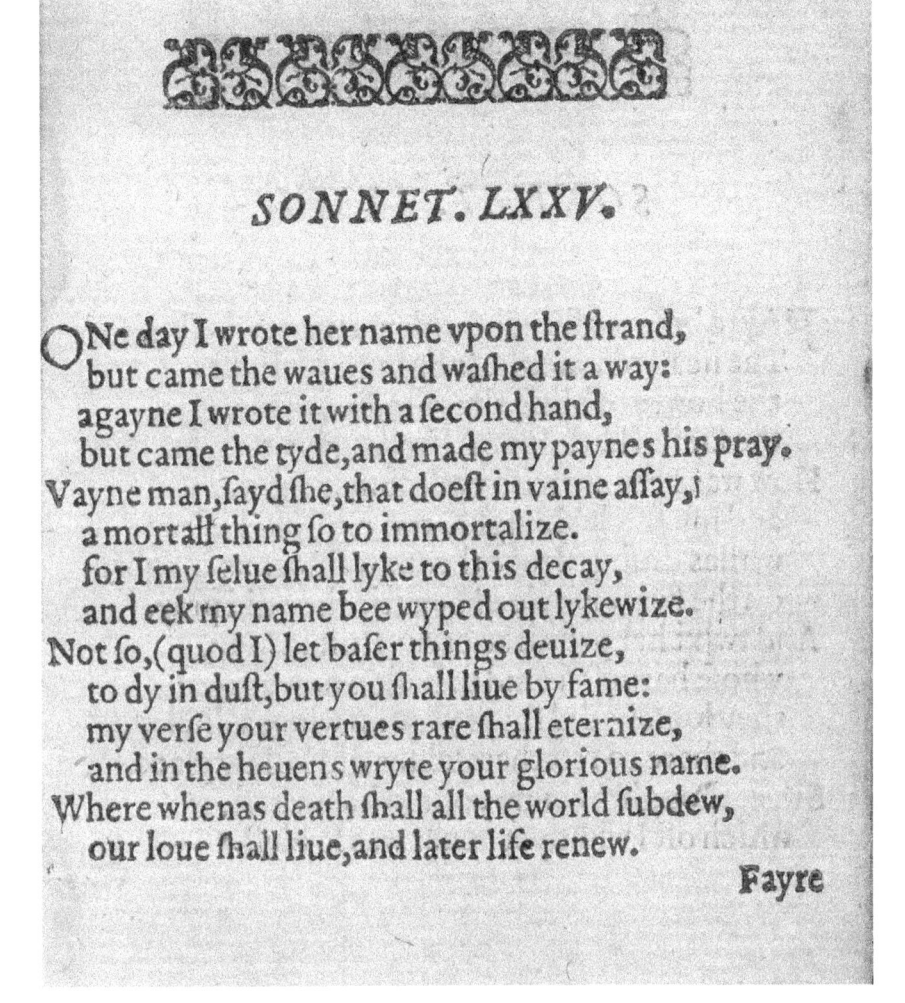

SONNET. LXXV.

ONe day I wrote her name vpon the ſtrand,
  but came the waues and waſhed it a way:
agayne I wrote it with a ſecond hand,
  but came the tyde, and made my paynes his pray.
Vayne man, ſayd ſhe, that doeſt in vaine aſſay,
  a mortall thing ſo to immortalize.
for I my ſelue ſhall lyke to this decay,
  and eek my name bee wyped out lykewize.
Not ſo, (quod I) let baſer things deuize,
  to dy in duſt, but you ſhall liue by fame:
my verſe your vertues rare ſhall eternize,
  and in the heuens wryte your glorious name.
Where whenas death ſhall all the world ſubdew,
  our loue ſhall liue, and later life renew.

                                    Fayre

Figure 0.2 Edmund Spenser's "Amoretti 75," from *Amoretti and Epithalamion* (London: William Ponsonby, 1595). Bodleian Library, Oxford University

[40] Rush, *Fetters of Rhyme*, 3. Rush notes that pre-modern readers regularly approached prosody not only as a function of "local meaning" but a function of "patterns formed by rhyme, meter, line length, and so on," as well as "patterns . . . outside the poem" (14).

That poems are not merely linguistic objects but the products of habitual upkeep by their human users is the theme of Spenser's sonnet, which we can consult now in its entirety:

> One day I wrote her name vpon the strand,
>> but came the waues and washed it away:
>> agayne I wrote it with a second hand,
>> but came the tyde, and made my paynes his pray.
> Vayne man, sayd she, that doest in vaine assay,
>> a mortall thing so to immortalize,
>> for I my selue shall lyke to this decay,
>> and eek my name bee wyped out lykewize.
> Not so, (quod I) let baser things deuize
>> to dy in dust, but you shall liue by fame:
>> my verse your vertues rare shall eternize,
>> and in the heuens wryte your glorious name.
> Where whenas death shall all the world subdew,
>> our loue shall liue, and later life renew.[41]

We might begin our analysis by noting the variation to the iambic pentameter norm at the beginning of line 5, in the spondaic phrase "Vayne man," the first words spoken by the speaker's beloved. Emphasizing "Vayne" helps mark the female speaker's entrance into the poem and underscores just how much rhyme and assonance Spenser packs into the opening octave: *day, name, came, waues, away, agayne, paynes, pray, Vayne, sayd, vaine, assay, decay*. When the *v* from "vaine" appears again in line 11, it cues a new set of vowel and consonant sounds in the words "verse your vertues . . . eternize." Allied sonically, these words are further allied in their association with the male poet-speaker's idealized conception of poetry, which contrasts with the female speaker's materialist rejoinder in lines 5–8. The rhyme words linking the sonnet's closing couplet (*subdew, renew*) thus recapitulate this contrast while suggesting a synthesis of sorts: just as the perpetual ebb and flow of tides shape and reshape the sand of a beach, so is a marriage continually reshaped within the covenant that sanctioned it, and so is a poem reshaped by the manuscripts, books, and mouths that see it on its way.

The prosodic analysis just offered began at the small scale of syllables and phonemes and then linked these effects to the sonnet's larger themes. But our

---

[41] Edmund Spenser, *The Shorter Poems*, ed. Richard A. McCabe (New York: Penguin Books, 1999), 425.

analysis might equally begin with what is arguably the sonnet's most distinctive prosodic feature: its two voices, one male and one female, whose speech is reported directly. In contrast to what is sometimes understood to be the inward, monologic mode of lyric poetry, Spenser's poem is dialogic, a literal debate between two individuals. If we were to cast two actors in a dramatic reading of the poem, its most consequential prosodic feature would likely be the tone and cadence of these actors' voices, rather than a posited metrical schema. This vocal information, short of an actual performance, can only be imagined, but the same could be said about the iambic reading of Spenser's lines, which remains theoretical until actuated in some form of performance or another. Nor are these two options, call them the iambic and the theatrical, mutually exclusive: our two actors could accentuate the iambic character of their lines. Or they could bring out the long *a* sounds. Or they could produce a rubato performance of the text, dwelling on certain key words or phrases in a manner that weakens a sense of regular metrical pulse. Because a poem's prosody emerges as a function of its various sonic elements, different prosodic effects will be produced by foregrounding different elements. Some effects may be mutually reinforcing: every long *a* sound, for instance, occurs in a syllable emphasized by the iambic pattern. Other effects could be seen to work against each other: Spenser's original rhyme scheme produces three alternately rhymed quatrains, but also blurs their boundaries by embedding a rhyming couplet between each quatrain: *abab bcbc cdcd ee*. The sensation produced is a kind of interference effect between two overlapping coherencies, each with their own integrity outside the sonnet form (e.g. rhymed quatrains, heroic couplets), but each made answerable to its new context.

As my comparison of Beyoncé and Spenser suggests, the claim underwriting this book—that a poem's prosody is its sound media—is at root theoretical. But I narrow the historical frame to the past two centuries because that is the span in which the concept of lyric and the concept of media achieve their modern forms. As John Guillory observes, "The emergence of the media concept in the later nineteenth century was a response to the proliferation of new technical media—such as the telegraph and phonograph—that could not be assimilated to the older system of the arts"; these new media "thus seemed to reposition the traditional arts as ambiguously both media and precursors to the media."[42] Guillory concludes "that the concept of a medium of communication was absent but *wanted* for the several centuries prior to its appearance, a lacuna in the philosophical tradition that exerted a distinctive pressure, as if from the

[42] John Guillory, "Genesis of the Media Concept," *Critical Inquiry*, 36/2 (2010): 321–2.

future."[43] Reversing the historical vantage, we can observe a complementary process: looking back the centuries at Romanticism, we find ourselves wanting a lyric genre that, though perhaps a modern invention, nonetheless speaks to us, as if from the past. Most broadly, then, this book reveals the mutual entanglement of two broad conceptual narratives that have shaped our understanding of verbal expressivity over the past two centuries. One narrative sees poetry codified in terms of the increasingly capacious, idealized genre of lyric. The other narrative runs something of the inverse course and sees sound after roughly 1850 as something that, with the aid of new technical media, could be recorded, reproduced, and analyzed as an object of study in its own right. Drawing together these two narratives, this book reads for moments in which the lyricization of poetry runs up against the mediatization of sound, where the promise of voice runs into the matter of prosody.

Each of the following chapters adopts a slightly different lens depending on the nature of the poetry at hand, meaning that the book can be read as a series of formalist case studies but also as a broadly sketched historical argument. My opening chapter considers the prosodic implications of genre difference, specifically as regards the terms *lyric* and *ballad* as they operate in Wordsworth's epochal 1798 collection *Lyrical Ballads*. Though Wordsworth's poetry has often been seen as paradigmatically and even categorically lyrical, a judgment that has led some to consider prosody a minor or secondary feature of his work, many early readers of *Lyrical Ballads* found the collection oddly bifurcated into poems in unrhymed blank verse and poems in rhyming four-beat lines. These early readers, moreover, tended to interpret this prosodic difference in terms of the difference between a "higher species" of versification and a more primitive folk form.[44] Yet even as they sorted poems into these categories, readers encountered poems whose prosody and subject matter seemed to invert or reject the binaristic model of blank verse lyrics and common meter ballads. Recovering the ethnographic tensions bound up in Wordsworth's prosody, this chapter approaches lyricism and balladry as co-constitutive generic modes in the poet's work. After testing this claim against Wordsworth's *Prelude*—whose narrative structure and epic ambition ally it with balladry even as its first-person, blank verse introspection allies it with lyric—the chapter concludes by considering an allusion to Wordsworth in the work of the singer-songwriter Taylor Swift.

---

[43] Guillory, "Genesis of the Media Concept," 321.
[44] Charles Burney, unsigned review, *Monthly Review*, 29 (June 1799), rprt. in Robert Woof, ed., *William Wordsworth: The Critical Heritage, Volume I: 1793–1820* (New York: Routledge, 2001), 74.

The American poet Poe was highly skeptical of the idealist theory of poetry Wordsworth had by the 1830s come to represent, and Poe's poetry therefore draws constant attention to issues of prosodic reproducibility as opposed to psychological authenticity. In poems such as "The Raven" and "The Bells" and essays such as "The Rationale of Verse," Poe presents prosodic structure as a cluster of jostling sound media—phonetic script, meter, scansion, page turns, bells—which obey different prosodic logics when engaged in real time by different readers. The emblem of Poe's prosody-oriented poetics is his famous raven. Introduced as "a non-reasoning creature capable of speech," Poe's raven functions much like a phonograph, capable of reproducing speech without comprehending it.[45] By presenting language as the product of purely mechanistic operations, Poe offers one of the earliest historical deconstructions of the Romantic fiction of unmediated lyricism. What he presents in its place, however, is not historicism as such. While drawing attention to the physical media and literary conventions that shape prosodic form, Poe's work ultimately affirms the importance of prosodic variability from one reader to the next, both within and across historical periods. Highly musical, eminently reproducible, and enduringly popular, Poe's poetry anticipates debates about literary technique and popular culture that will recur during modernism, providing a toolkit of sorts for reframing prosodic analysis as a form of media studies.

Unlike the dogged self-publicist Poe, Dickinson published almost nothing during her lifetime, leaving nearly 1,800 poems in manuscript at the time of her death in 1886. Noting this fact, Virginia Jackson makes Dickinson the centerpiece of her lyricization thesis: because the poet did not publish, her writing became legible as poetry only after editors, readers, and critics packaged it as such. One strand of Dickinson criticism has therefore argued that her work should be read in manuscript or facsimile in order to avoid the impositions of posthumous editorial intervention. Another strand, by contrast, has wondered if this materialist approach, in John Shoptaw's words, "forfeit[s] the aural experience of her poems for the graphic delights of her manuscripts."[46] Dickinson herself does not provide a clear answer as to whether we are to prioritize her scripted forms or her audible language. But her poems contemplate this choice at the level of image and trope, frequently juxtaposing images of fluidity and gradience with images of materialist particularity: "tint—and spot" (*F* 367), "Thread & Needle" (*F* 681), and most significant for the present study,

---

[45] Poe, "The Philosophy of Composition," 64–5.
[46] John Shoptaw, "Listening to Dickinson," *Representations*, 86/1 (Spring 2004): 21.

"Sound" and "Syllable" (F 598).[47] Reading these oxymoronic pairings along-side Dickinson's textual history and alongside contemporaneous advances in sound recording, this chapter suggests that we engage Dickinson's prosody not in terms of scanning the words of a given text, nor of restoring a partic-ular document to its original discourse network, but as an act of remediation. No more or less than her earliest readers, modern readers are charged with determining what constitutes Dickinson's poetic media (e.g. syllabic structure, metrical convention, manuscript and/or print layout, punctuation), and then foregrounding certain elements within a given reading.

Between Dickinson's death and the advent of modernism, new sound tech-nologies transformed media landscapes around the world. Not everyone was pleased. "Our ears are passive before the onslaught of gramophones," writes Pound in 1917.[48] Pound's scorn for mechanical audio technologies goes hand in hand with his well-documented scorn for metronomic Victorian metrical practices. As we have seen Pound write in "A Few Don'ts by an Imagiste," "com-pose in the sequence of the musical phrase, not in sequence of a metronome."[49] Or as he puts it in his *ABC of Reading*: "You don't ask an art instructor to give you a recipe for making a Leonardo da Vinci drawing. Hence the extreme bore-dom caused by the usual professorial documentation or the aspiring thesis on prosody. The answer is: LISTEN to the sound that it makes."[50] Yet as both of these commands suggest, Pound is in fact deeply concerned with poetry's sonic and verbal structure. Moreover, despite his clear antipathy toward the gadgetry of popular culture, many of the poet's critical writings character-ize prosody and rhythm using technical language associated with modern sound recording. "Rhythm is a form cut into TIME," Pound suggests, evok-ing the spatial dynamics of early phonograph recordings that cut their analog sound files into wax.[51] Focusing primarily on Pound's *Cantos* and his opera *Le Testament de Villon*, this chapter argues that the poet's twinned commit-ment to acoustic and print forms appears throughout his work as a *groove*, a troping of verbal performance as the obverse of material inscription. Far from rejecting prosody, Pound's work transfigures it for an age of modern media.

---

[47] Emily Dickinson, *The Poems of Emily Dickinson: Reading Edition*, ed. Ralph Franklin (Cam-bridge: Harvard University Press, 1998), 167, 303, 269. Parenthetical references above indicate the poem numbers assigned by Franklin and are abbreviated *F*.

[48] Ezra Pound, *Ezra Pound and Music: The Complete* Criticism, ed. R. Murray Schafer (New York: New Directions, 1977), 49.

[49] Ezra Pound, *Literary Essays*, 3.

[50] Ezra Pound, *ABC of Reading* (New York: New Directions, 2010), 201.

[51] Pound, *ABC of Reading*, 198.

Scholarship on Harlem Renaissance poets like Hughes has tended to emphasize their turn away from English prosodic convention and toward a body of Black vernacular speech and folk sources. Hughes's biographer Arnold Rampersad praises the poet's 1927 collection *Fine Clothes to the Jew* for presenting a "barely mediated recording of the sounds . . . of black life."[52] Yet Hughes's final book of poetry, *Ask Your Mama: 12 Moods for Jazz*, is a conspicuously mediated work. The most visually ornate of Hughes's books, the 1961 collection includes a set of "Liner Notes" that suggest the work is also, paradoxically, a vinyl record. This audio-visual back-and-forth is captured by the "12" in the title, which refers variously to the number of sections in the book, the twelve-bar blues, the chromatic scale, and, perhaps most significantly, the Dozens, the game of vernacular one-upmanship traditional in African-American communities. Add to this pinkish-beige paper, blue and black ink, an all-caps typeface, and marginal cues describing specific musical effects, and one is left nearly at a loss about how best to read Hughes's book. On one hand, these paralinguistic features underscore the work's bookishness, its status as a silent printed object. On the other hand, these same features are what invite collaborative multimedial performance of a kind traditional prosodic analysis is ill-equipped to evaluate. With this dual operation, the chapter argues, Hughes is able to critique idealized notions of Black folk lyricism that his work often stands in for, while also expanding a reader's sense of Black performativity beyond the physical media and historical contexts of his book's original production.

My book's epilogue, "A Transmedial Poetics," brings my study into the present by considering two quite different pieces of contemporary prosodic culture—Amazon's voice-activated "virtual assistant" Alexa and the body of musical poetry known as rap or hip-hop—before suggesting some possible directions for the future of poetry studies.

A final note on prosodic notation: rather than offering a single system of scansion in this introduction and then applying it throughout the chapters ahead, I employ a range of audio-visual markup techniques depending on a poem's historical context or, alternatively, the formal elements I wish to highlight. As in the pages above, the same line of verse might be broken into poetic feet, scored using musical notation, or excerpted to indicate phrasal structure. Often I bold syllables to indicate relative stress, sometimes in combination with numerals above the line indicating the relationship of linguistic prosody to musical beats.

---

[52] Arnold Rampersad, "Langston Hughes's Fine Clothes to the Jew," *Callaloo*, 26 (Winter 1986): 146.

Where relevant I include facsimiles of specific documents (e.g. Dickinson's manuscripts, Hughes's 1961 book), since these present prosodic information not easily translated into print typographies. In all cases, the point to keep in view is that the myriad systems of visual scansion we use to parse poetic sound themselves help determine the shape and quality of that sound. Like the proverbial tree falling in the forest, prosodic analysis produces, even as it presupposes, certain acts of attention. This book will succeed if it begins to illustrate just how limited visual texts often are at writing sound in all its dazzling effervescence, and how mightily poets struggled with this fact. For in an age of media, poets both covet and disown the condition of sonic reproducibility, beguiled equally by the privacy of lyric and the siren song of an older art.

1

Lyrics/Ballads

In 1774, Thomas English purchased Belle Isle, an island on Lake Windermere, and built there a rotunda-style mansion that many local residents considered an eyesore. The lavish home and others built nearby helped establish England's Lake District as a tourist destination.[1] As William Wordsworth would later observe, the construction of Belle Isle House prompted a general gentrification of the area, which entailed sprucing up an old-timey inn, the White Lion, so that it boasted "chaises, grooms, and liveries, and within / Decanters, glasses, and the blood-red wine."[2] The inn, Wordsworth wistfully recalls, had surely "been / More worthy of a poet's love" before high culture was brought to the region. And yet:

> though the rhymes were gone which once inscribed
> The threshold, and large golden characters
> On the blue-frosted signboard had usurped
> The place of the old lion, in contempt
> And mockery of the rustic painter's hand,
> Yet to this hour the spot to me is dear
> With all its foolish pomp.[3]

Wordsworth likely never experienced the charm and comforts of the original White Lion. (He was only four when the Belle Isle House was built.) But the inn's pompous modern version is dear to him as a kind of cultural palimpsest, a blend of old and new that spurs the adult poet to nostalgic thought. One imagines him contemplating the layers of flaking paint, noting how they at once obscure and underscore the building's past lives. Even the "blood-red wine" is a hybrid thing, the phrase taken from the traditional ballad "Sir Patrick Spens" while the wine itself signifies a self-consciously modernizing taste. In a dynamic that would form the crux of Wordsworth's mature poetics, the

[1] Margery E. Brown, *A Man of No Taste Whatsoever: Joseph Pocklington 1736–1817* (AuthorHouse, 2010), 12.

[2] William Wordsworth, *The Prelude: 1799, 1805, 1850*, ed. Jonathan Wordsworth, M. H. Abrams, and Stephen Gill (New York: Norton, 1979), 72.

[3] Wordsworth, *The Prelude*, 74.

Poetry, Sound, and the Matter of Prosody 1800–2000. Peter Miller, Oxford University Press. © Peter Miller (2025).
DOI: 10.1093/9780198937210.003.0002

poet's felt sense of the value of the past arrives, paradoxically, the moment he perceives it to be gone.[4]

Wordsworth is describing changes in his local community, but he could equally be describing changes in English poetry around 1800. That year closed a century captivated by balladry and the folk customs associated with it, and opened one that would see the introspective first-person lyric installed as modern poetry's normative mode.[5] If renovating a homely inn in Cumberland involved trading rustic rhymes for markers of individual taste, renovating English poetry entailed a similarly fraught process of exchange. No one played a more decisive role in this process than Wordsworth himself, who in 1798 had published, with his friend Samuel Taylor Coleridge, a collection of poems that, like the White Lion, juxtaposed highbrow and lowbrow forms:

> Five years have passed; five summers, with the length
> Of five long winters! and again I hear
> These waters, rolling from their mountain-springs
> With a sweet inland murmur.[6]

The elaborate, self-sustaining sentence that opens "Tintern Abbey" contrasts markedly with a poem appearing earlier in the collection, "Goody Blake and Harry Gill," which opens rather more boisterously:

> Oh! what's the matter? what's the matter?
> What is't that ails young Harry Gill?
> That evermore his teeth they chatter,
> Chatter, chatter, chatter still. (*LB* 39)

---

[4] See Geoffrey Hartman's early assessment in *Wordsworth's Poetry 1787–1814* (New Haven: Yale University Press, 1964) that Wordsworth's poems are products "of two kinds of consciousness, old and new, ordinary and supervening, which gather in tension around the precipitating image" (16). "When Wordsworth depicts an object he is also depicting himself or, rather, a truth about himself, a self-acquired revelation" (5). See also M. H. Abrams, *Natural Supernaturalism: Tradition and Revolution in Romantic Literature* (New York: Norton, 1971): "the poet, seeking the elements of continuity between his two disparate selves, conducts a persistent exploration of the nature and significance of memory, of his power to sustain freshness of sensation and his 'first creative sensibility' against the deadening effect of habit and analysis, and of manifestations of the enduring and the eternal within the realm of change and time" (75).

[5] For an overview of lyric's generic ascendency across the nineteenth and twentieth centuries, see Virginia Jackson's entry on "Lyric" in the *Princeton Encyclopedia of Poetry and Poetics*, ed. Roland Greene, Stephen Cushman, Clare Cavanagh, Jahan Ramazani, and Paul Rouzer (Princeton: Princeton University Press, 2012), 826–34. On the history of the ballad revival, see David D. Buchan, *The Ballad and the Folk: Studies in the Balladry and the Society of the North-East of Scotland* (Aberdeen: Aberdeen University Press, 1966), and David Vincent, *Literacy and Popular Culture: England 1750–1914* (Cambridge: Cambridge University Press, 1993).

[6] William Wordsworth and Samuel Taylor Coleridge, *Lyrical Ballads: 1798 and 1802*, ed. Fiona Stafford (Oxford: Oxford University Press, 2013), 87. Subsequent references to this edition are cited parenthetically and abbreviated *LB*.

The first excerpt luxuriates in the subtle sonic terrain of enjambed blank verse, its three uses of "five" winkingly acknowledging the prosodic affordances of the Miltonic pentameter. Indeed, that the word "five" appears in metrically unstressed positions in line 1 and in a metrically prominent position in line 2 illustrates, in conjunction with the passage's varied phrase lengths and heavy enjambment, the degree of prosodic flexibility often associated with blank verse. The second excerpt, by contrast, with its heavy-footed rhymes, dense phonemic patterning, and insistent four-beat ballad meter, organizes its prosodic matter in quite a different way; what is heard in this poem is not the silent operation of thought but the "chatter[ing]" of human teeth and the human drama they stand in for.

Why does Wordsworth include poems that are so prosodically dissimilar within the same collection? Or to frame the question in literary historical terms, what have readers since Wordsworth's day made of this striking juxtaposition? These are questions that modern scholarship has left largely unaddressed, despite the fact that scholars over the years have expressed strong opinions about the differences between ballad meter and blank verse more generally. Summarizing a history of reading dating back to the English Renaissance, Antony Easthope observes that blank verse is often associated "with polish and reformed manners," while ballad meter is seen "as rude, homely, and in the modern sense, vulgar."[7] Early readers of *Lyrical Ballads*, as we shall see, made just this distinction, finding the book oddly bifurcated into sophisticated poems in blank verse (e.g. "Tintern Abbey") and lowly poems in rhyming four-beat lines (e.g. "Goody Blake"). Yet by 1910, when George Saintsbury published his monumental *History of English Prosody from the Twelfth Century to the Present Day*, he concluded of Wordsworth that "in no great poet does prosody play so small a part," sidestepping the question of any tension between the two prosodic forms.[8] Subsequent studies have revised this account by demonstrating the importance of prosodic form to Wordsworth, but the question of the structural relationship between blank verse and ballad meter in *Lyrical Ballads*, and the related question of how this relationship itself structures our understanding of the generic terms *lyric* and *ballad*, remains surprisingly open.[9] Recovering the ethnographic tensions

---

[7] Antony Easthope, *Poetry as Discourse* (London: Routledge, 1983), 65.

[8] George Saintsbury, *A History of English Prosody: From the Twelfth Century to the Present Day*, vol. 3 (London: Macmillan and Co., 1910), 74.

[9] Brennen O'Donnell, *The Passion of Meter: A Study of Wordsworth's Metrical Art* (Kent: Kent State University Press, 1995), documents in admirable detail the variety of Wordsworth's metrical practices. O'Donnell's broad grouping of the poet's verse forms into "stanzaic verse" and "varieties . . . of blank verse" (9) implies the ballad/lyric tension without explicitly exploring it. Simon Jarvis, *Wordsworth's Philosophic Song* (Cambridge: Cambridge University Press, 2006), argues that Wordsworth's metrical

bound up in Wordsworth's prosody, this chapter sheds light on a key early moment in the history of lyric's ascendency across the nineteenth century. Lyric, to the extent that the term denotes the obverse of balladry in a period of expanding literacy, indeed begins to be linked with traits such as solitude, introspection, and unmediated feeling. But by restoring to Wordsworth's ballads some of the acoustic shock value they delivered to their early readers, we can gain a clearer picture of the media conditions that gave rise to a poetics of immediacy.

Lyrical Ballads appeared at the end of a century that had witnessed a surge of interest in balladry and the English folk customs associated with it. By Wordsworth's day, ballads were sometimes shared orally in the manner they would have been centuries earlier, but the real impetus for the form's revival came from a burgeoning print culture and rising literacy rates.[10] Having been slighted for centuries by literary tastemakers, the ballad's fortunes began to rise in 1711 when Joseph Addison published three *Spectator* papers championing "the darling Songs of the common People."[11] Thomas Percy's 1765 *Reliques of Ancient English Poetry*, a collection of ballads from England and Scotland, secured the form's place in both literary and popular spheres. These printed ballads offered literate audiences "the allure of the archaic," in Daniel Tiffany's words, transporting readers back in time to a medieval world of knights and ladies, castles and potions, feasts and hunts.[12] Though this medieval, magical atmosphere best characterizes a ballad such as Coleridge's "Rime of the Ancient Mariner," many of Wordsworth's ballads incorporate similar tropes into the eighteenth-century English countryside. The impoverished Goody Blake, for instance, having been caught stealing firewood from Harry Gill's hedge, prays that he will "never more be warm!" and he is indeed stricken cold for life.[13]

verse is "a kind of cognition, with its own resistances and difficulties" (5), though he understands these resistances as operating largely within poems rather than between or among classes of poems (e.g. blank verse lyrics and tetrameter ballads).

[10] "A form of cheap print that endured for centuries," observes Meredith L. McGill, "What Is a Ballad? Reading for Genre, Format, and Medium," *Nineteenth-Century Literature*, 71/2 (September 2016), "broadside ballads shift the locus of oral performance from the minstrel or the ballad singer to the ballad seller, who sings not to transmit tradition but to hawk a cheap commodity" (163). See also Vincent, *Literacy and Popular Culture* (1993), who nuances the historical progression from orality to literacy that Buchan charts in *The Ballad and the Folk* (1966).

[11] Joseph Addison, *Spectator* 85, The Spectator Project: A Hypermedia Research Archive of Eighteenth-Century Periodicals, http://www2.scc.rutgers.edu/spectator/project.html

[12] Daniel Tiffany, *My Silver Planet: A Secret History of Poetry and Kitsch* (Baltimore: Johns Hopkins University Press, 2014), 63.

[13] For historical context on Wordsworth's turn to ballad meter, see Mary Jacobus, *Tradition and Experiment in Wordsworth's "Lyrical Ballads" (1798)*, (Oxford: Clarendon Press, 1976), 209–32, and Ian Newman, "Moderation in the *Lyrical Ballads*: Wordsworth and the Ballad Debates of the 1790s," *Studies in Romanticism*, 55/2 (Summer 2016): 185–210.

Readers paging through *Lyrical Ballads* for the first time would have depended as well on prosodic cues to identify the ballads, placing a poem like "Simon Lee" in the same category as "Goody Blake and Harry Hill" on the basis of its alternately rhymed four-beat lines:

> In the sweet shire of Cardigan,
> Not far from pleasant Ivor-hall,
> An Old Man dwells, a little man,
> I've heard he once was tall. (*LB* 150)

Conversely, a poem like "Lines Left Upon a Seat in a Yew Tree" would be placed in the same category as "Tintern Abbey" on the basis of its blank verse:

> Nay, Traveller! rest. This lonely yew-tree stands
> Far from all human dwelling: what if here
> No sparkling rivulet spread the verdant herb;
> What if these barren boughs the bee not loves;
> Yet, if the wind breathe soft, the curling waves,
> That break against the shore, shall lull thy mind
> By one soft impulse saved from vacancy. (*LB* 27)

In contrast to the starkly rhythmic, communal mode of balladry, this poem, like "Tintern Abbey," cultivates the private, metanarrative space of lyric. Its opening apostrophe interpolates us as the traveler, interrupting whatever plot or purpose we may have been pursuing with the command to tarry "[far] from all human dwelling." Nature even at its most "barren," this poem's lyric speaker promises, can salve a mind overburdened with the workaday demands of society.

Yet no sooner does *Lyrical Ballads* appear to sort its contents into lyrics and ballads than one encounters poems that frustrate this generic binary. Consider this stanza from "Lines Written at a Small Distance from My House":

> No joyless forms shall regulate
> Our living Calendar:
> We from to-day, my friend, will date
> The opening of the year. (*LB* 43)

Prosodically speaking, this stanza is textbook ballad meter. But a philosophical mood more associated with lyric now inhabits the form. The same thing happens in "The Tables Turned"—

> Sweet is the lore which Nature brings;
> Our meddling intellect
> Mishapes the beauteous forms of things;
> —We murder to dissect. (*LB* 82)

—and "Lines Written in Early Spring":

> I heard a thousand blended notes,
> While in a grove I sate reclined,
> In that sweet mood when pleasant thoughts
> Bring sad thoughts to the mind. (*LB* 51)

Meanwhile, rustic subject matter more associated with balladry has been repackaged in blank verse. The long poem "Michael," for instance, narrates the hardships endured by a father and son as they labor to retain ownership of the family farm. One particularly moving image sees the pair

> [Turn] to their cleanly supper-board, and there,
> Each with a mess of pottage and skimm'd milk,
> Sate round their basket pil'd with oaten cakes,
> And their plain home-made cheese. (*LB* 287)

Home-made indeed. If "Lines Written in Early Spring" is a lyrical ballad, "Michael" could be called a balladic lyric, a blank verse exposition of the rural lifeways of Cumberland in the late eighteenth century.

Rather than approaching *Lyrical Ballads* as a singular achievement, as we almost inevitably do given its historical importance, we might instead approach the collection as a kind of polarized generic field, in which readers are asked to classify poems either as one of the titular ballads or as one of the "other poems" named in the title's less-cited second half. Some poems sit squarely in the former category ("Goody Blake"), others in the latter ("Tintern"). Some play lyrical content off balladic form ("Lines Written in Early Spring"), while others gentrify rustic content with blank verse ("Michael"). And some poems hover near the center of the generic field, complicating the very idea of binary classification.[14] Consider the opening lines of "The Female Vagrant":

---

[14] As Herbert Tucker, "Balladry in Motion," *The Wordsworth Circle*, 52/1 (Winter 2021), observes in an analysis of "Simon Lee, The Old Huntsman," "Once again Wordsworth hybridizes balladic prosody in keeping with the volume's dual allegiance to both balladry and lyricality" (45).

> By Derwent's side my Father's cottage stood,
> (The Woman thus her artless story told)
> One field, a flock, and what the neighbouring flood
> Supplied, to him were more than mines of gold. (*LB* 32)

After just two lines, we might take this to be blank verse, though things feel a bit too iambic, too end-stopped, too narrative to be sure. Moreover, the rhyme word "flood" at the end of line 3 seems odd. (Where did our speaker say she is from again?) Suspicions that we're chatting with a balladeer in disguise are allayed temporarily by the heavy enjambment of "flood / Supplied," which buries the rhyme and the earlier faux pas. But no sooner are we back on cordial terms than "supplied" itself supplies another rhyme with "side" in line 1. The more we listen, the more the last two lines seem to rewrite themselves into tetrameter, against the visual grain, to better suit their sound and syntax:

> And what the neighbouring flood supplied,
> To him were more than mines of gold.[15]

In fact, "The Female Vagrant" is written in Spenserian stanzas of nine lines, of which I excerpted only the first four. Neither ballad meter nor blank verse, though reminiscent of both, Spenser's form burst onto the scene with commitments to both rhyming, action-packed narrative, on the one hand, and upper-crust Englishness itself, on the other, in its inaugural role in an allegorical epic glorifying Queen Elizabeth I.[16]

Wordsworth was well aware that his generic and prosodic experimentation would rub some readers the wrong way. As he writes in the "Advertisement" to the first edition of *Lyrical Ballads*:

> The majority of the following poems are to be considered as experiments. They were written chiefly with a view to ascertain how far the language of conversation in the middle and lower classes of society is adapted to the purposes of poetic pleasure. Readers accustomed to the gaudiness and inane phraseology of many modern writers, if they persist in reading this

---

[15] O'Donnell, *The Passion of Meter*, observes the tension between lineal and stanzaic prosody, but in the other direction, noting how the predominantly tetrameter lines of "The Sailor's Mother" "suggest rhythms more common in the heroic [i.e. pentameter] line" (56).

[16] Further evidence of prosodic contextualism might be found in Spenser's redeployment of his trademark stanza in his *Amoretti* sonnets (1596), whose interlocking rhyme scheme (*abab bcbc cdcd ee*) extends *The Faerie Queene*'s nine-line narrative stanza into lyric territory.

book to its conclusion, will perhaps frequently have to struggle with feelings of strangeness and aukwardness: they will look round for poetry, and will be induced to enquire by what species of courtesy these attempts can be permitted to assume that title. (*LB* 3)

Yet even as he predicts the collection's capacity to provoke, Wordsworth says little about its metrical superstructure. Though he invokes meter frequently in the longer "Preface" to the 1800 and 1802 editions, and though he attacks critics who "under-rate the power of metre in itself," Wordsworth makes no distinction between ballad meter and blank verse (*LB* 109). Instead he takes poetic diction as his chief concern in a more general comparison of poetry to prose, concluding that "except with reference to the meter ... some of the most interesting parts of the best poems will be found to be strictly the language of prose" (*LB* 101). To illustrate this claim, Wordsworth quotes a sonnet by Thomas Gray, italicizing its five most prosaic lines as "the only part ... of any value," before qualifying this linguistic claim even further (*LB* 102). Chiding Samuel Johnson's parody of a ballad included in Percy's *Reliques*, Wordsworth observes that the parody can be impugned "not from the metre, not from the language, not from the order of the words; but the *matter* expressed in Dr. Johnson's stanza is contemptible ... it is neither interesting in itself, nor can *lead* to any thing interesting; the images neither originate in that sane state of feeling which arises out of thought, nor can excite thought or feeling in the Reader" (*LB* 113–14). Poetry for Wordsworth must be, most basically, "interesting" by virtue of its closeness to authentic human feeling, whereas meter functions as a final touch, an ornament "superadded" to enhance pleasure and memory (*LB* 103). "Why trouble yourself about the species till you have previously decided upon the genus?" asks Wordsworth, suggesting Johnson had missed the forest of poetical feeling for the trees of metrical speech. "Why take pains to prove that an Ape is not a Newton when it is self-evident that he is not a man?" (*LB* 114).

The problem, for Wordsworth, was that his first readers kept finding the landscapes of *Lyrical Ballads* populated by both apes and Newtons, by both primitive and civilized poetic forms whose pasts had a way of catching up with them. "Would it not be degrading poetry, as well as the English language, to go back to the barbarous and uncouth numbers of Chaucer?" wondered Charles Burney in 1799. "Suppose, instead of modernizing the old bard, that the sweet and polished measures, on lofty subjects, of Dryden, Pope, and Gray, were to be transmuted into the dialect and versification of the [fourteenth] century? Should we be gainers by this retrogradation? ... None but savages have submitted to eat acorns after corn was found."[17] To Burney, Wordsworth's retrofitting of old-timey ballad meters is an affront to "a higher species of versification," namely blank verse, developed in England over hundreds of years, and so an affront to modernity itself.[18] Most perplexing to Burney is that the author of *Lyrical Ballads* is clearly capable of this higher species of composition. "Tintern Abbey" he calls "the reflections of no common mind," a tour de force rendition of "poetical, beautiful, and philosophical" sentiments unknown to the rustic folk featured in many of the collection's other poems.[19] Burney's assessment ties blank verse to a progressive, enlightened poetics and balladry to a retrograde barbarism. A figure like Goody Blake, though presumably just as English as Burney himself, is seen to suffer from a debilitating social backwardness, which "should have been relieved by the *two millions* annually allowed by the state to the poor of this country, not by the plunder of an individual."[20] Another reviewer, while enjoying "Goody Blake and Harry Gill," likewise grounds his enthusiasm in the poem's purported socio-physiological accuracy. In a near-quotation of Wordsworth, the reviewer calls it "a tale founded on a well authenticated fact, which happened in Warwickshire. Dr. Darwin relates it among other curious instances of maniacal hallucination in the second volume of his Zoonomia."[21] What might first seem to be a merely formal dichotomy in Wordsworth's collection, between ballad meter and blank verse, is confirmed by the early reception history to be an ideological one.[22] Prosodic and generic difference indexes readers' beliefs about economic, intellectual, and ethnic difference, and the ballads in particular either appeal or offend by virtue of being somehow underdeveloped.

More recent literary critics largely agree that Wordsworth's chief accomplishment in *Lyrical Ballads* was "to adapt the ballad to portraying precisely those states and feelings least susceptible to narrative presentation" while

---

[17] Charles Burney, unsigned review, *Monthly Review*, 29 (June 1799), rprt. in Robert Woof, ed., *William Wordsworth: The Critical Heritage, Volume I: 1793–1820* (New York: Routledge, 2001), 74.

[18] Burney, 74.

[19] Burney, 78. See also Charles James Fox, letter to Wordsworth, May 25, 1801, rprt. in *William Wordsworth: The Critical Heritage*, who confessed to the poet that "I am no great friend to blank verse for subjects which are to be treated of with simplicity" (106).

[20] Burney, 76.

[21] Unsigned review, *Analytical Review*, 28/6 (December 1798), rprt. in *William Wordsworth: The Critical Heritage*, 69.

[22] Robert Southey, unsigned review, *Critical Review* (October 1798), rprt. in *William Wordsworth: The Critical Heritage*, was far more taken by the "serious pieces" (67) in blank verse. "The 'experiment,' we think, has failed, not because the language of conversation is little adapted to 'the purposes of poetic pleasure,' but because it has been tried upon uninteresting subjects" (67).

simultaneously "democratizing . . . blank verse."[23] The action-centric ballad gains the psychological inwardness we identify with modern poetry, while the blank verse lyric is brought down to earth to smell the daffodils. But critics have not fully accounted for the degree of friction and indeed fiery debate caused by Wordsworth's juxtaposition of lyricism and balladry within the same collection. While some early readers distinguished lyrics from ballads on the basis of formal features that remain legible to us today, others did not, indeed could not, due to the degree of generic and prosodic experimentation that characterized the collection as a whole. In an 1801 review, John Stoddart complained that "The title of the Poems is, in some degree, objectionable; for what Ballads are not *Lyrical*? Besides, there are many compositions in blank verse, not at all Lyrical."[24] For Stoddart, lyrics and ballads are basically synonymous, whereas blank verse exists in a category of its own.

Such readerly confusion speaks as well to Wordsworth's confessed failure to articulate the unifying "theory upon which the poems were written" (*LB* 110). At the outset of the 1800 "Preface," Wordsworth explains that he has "altogether declined" to provide such a theory in order to avoid "[being] suspected of . . . the selfish and foolish hope of *reasoning* [the Reader] into an approbation of these particular Poems" (*LB* 95). Providing a full defense of his theory, moreover, "would require a space wholly disproportionate to a preface. For, to treat the subject with the clearness and coherence of which it is susceptible, it would be necessary to give a full account of the present state of the public taste in this country, and to determine how far this taste is healthy or depraved; which, again, could not be determined, without pointing out in what manner language and the human mind act and re-act on each other, and without retracing the revolutions, not of literature alone, but likewise of society itself" (*LB* 95-96). Coming from as notoriously egotistical a writer as Wordsworth, these remarks might be taken as a bluff, a cover for a collection of poems that is actually just about himself. But this is not the case. "Than the poets from Blake and Wordsworth to Shelley and Keats," observes Raymond Williams, "there have been few generations of creative writers more deeply interested and more involved in the study and criticism of the society of their day."[25] And yet, Williams continues, this historical fact "accords uneasily

[23] Jacobus, *Tradition and* Experiment, 233, and Susan J. Wolfson, "Wordsworth's Craft," in *The Cambridge Companion to Wordsworth*, ed. Stephen Gill (Cambridge: Cambridge University Press, 2003), 114.

[24] John Stoddart, *British Critic*, 17 (February 1801), rprt. in *William Wordsworth: The Critical Heritage*, 143n.

[25] Raymond Williams, *Culture and Society, 1780–1950* (New York: Columbia University Press, 1983), 30.

in our own time with that popular and general conception of the 'romantic artist' which, paradoxically, has been primarily derived from study of these same poets. In this conception, the Poet, the Artist, is by nature indifferent to the crude worldliness and materialism of politics and social affairs; he is devoted, rather, to the more substantial spheres of natural beauty and personal feeling."[26]

One way of resolving the paradox Williams identifies is to observe that the theory on which Wordsworth's poems were written, however underarticulated, appears to be no less than a theory of modern culture—that is, a theory that attempts to link broad social dynamics ("the present state of the public taste") to individual psycholinguistic processes ("language and the human mind") to national politics ("the revolutions . . . of society") to make a claim about the basis of human identity. In his masterful study *Wordsworth and the Enlightenment*, Alan Bewell argues that culture is indeed Wordsworth's great theme. "At the core of Wordsworth's poetry is an anthropological vision," Bewell writes, "a concern with how human beings, individually and as a species, made the transition from a state of nature to society."[27] For Bewell, Wordsworth's poems offer "narratives in which the imagination constructs scenes, situations, or modes of feeling that have the status of experiments."[28] In recent decades, professional anthropologists have made similar claims about their own work, emphasizing that culture denotes not simply the traits common to a group, but also the very process of discerning these traits in others. In his influential study *The Invention of Culture*, Roy Wagner suggests that the modern anthropologist "'participate[s]' in the subject culture not in the way a native does, but as someone who is simultaneously enveloped in his own world of meanings, *and these meanings will also participate*."[29] This framework could describe any number of Wordsworth's poems—surely "enveloped in his own world of meanings" could be a motto— but it recalls specifically the "Note" the poet added to "The Thorn" in 1800, which explains that the poem's seafaring protagonist is "not a native" of the rural village in which he finds himself and, having "become credulous and talkative from indolence" at sea, offers Wordsworth "a character . . . to exhibit some of the general laws by which superstition acts upon the mind" (*LB* 199).

[26] Williams, *Culture and Society*, 30.
[27] Alan Bewell, *Wordsworth and the Enlightenment: Nature, Man, and Society in the Experimental Poetry* (New Haven: Yale University Press, 1989), ix.
[28] Bewell, *Wordsworth and the Enlightenment*, 44.
[29] Roy Wagner, *The Invention of Culture* (Chicago: University of Chicago Press, 1981), 8.

What the anthropological framework makes clear is that the dialectic defining modern culture—the oscillation between subjects and objects, first-person experience and collective traits—functions much like the dialectic defining *Lyrical Ballads*. As Maureen McLane observes, "*Lyrical Ballads* as a collection navigates between a kind of documentary, ethnographic authority and that of represented subjectivity—between, say, 'The Complaint of a Forsaken Indian Woman' and 'Tintern Abbey.'"[30] Bewell offers a similar formulation: "what Wordsworth saw in the people he talked with, he also discovered in himself."[31] While these critics do not discuss this dynamic in terms of prosody, the connection between the collection's ethnographic-subjectivist binary and its balladry-lyricism binary is clear. The terms of these binaries, moreover, as McLane and Bewell suggest, are not antithetical as much as co-constitutive. Just as the poet's perceived difference from other people clarifies his own subject position, so do his lyrics and ballads define themselves in jostling relation to the other.

Lewis Carroll's trenchant parody of Wordsworth zeroes in on just this dynamic, presenting the poet as a laughably myopic ethnographer but an ethnographer all the same, who assiduously transcribes his field notes into the ballad meter proper to their rustic origins, only to realize he was never really paying attention:

> I'll tell thee everything I can;
>> There's little to relate.
> I saw an aged aged man,
>> A-sitting on a gate.
> "Who are you, aged man?" I said,
>> "And how is it you live?"
> And his answer trickled through my head
>> Like water through a sieve.[32]

The single prosodic hiccup in this otherwise smoothly iambic passage comes, tellingly, right where the aged man's response should be, where instead of his voice we find an anapestic substitution ("And his **an** | swer **trick** | led **through** | my **head**") that refocuses attention on the poet as craftsperson. Carroll's ballad,

---

[30] Maureen McLane, *Balladeering, Minstrelsy, and the Making of British Romantic Poetry* (Cambridge: Cambridge University Press, 2011), 196.

[31] Bewell, *Wordsworth and the Enlightenment*, 46. See also Alan Liu, *Wordsworth: The Sense of History* (Stanford: Stanford University Press, 1989): "Culture *is* the process of interpreting, knowing, and believing in referential truth" (42).

[32] Lewis Carroll, "A-Sitting on a Gate," in *The Child's Harvest of Verse*, ed. Mary Wilder Tileston (Boston: Little, Brown and Co., 1910), 269.

in other words, is a thoroughly lyricized ballad, evacuated of narrative content save that of the Romantic poet's own dreaming introspection. Precisely in its extremism, the parody highlights one of Wordsworth's chief insights: that we talk to other people to find out who we are. As a reader more sympathetic to Wordsworth's project put it near the end of the nineteenth century, "our poet recognized . . . [that] it is by touch with others, by knowing others, by taking and keeping in simple fidelity our due place with other lives, our full and frank relation to them, that 'the human heart by which we live' is unfolded and nourished in us."[33]

Three months after taking the first edition of *Lyrical Ballads* to press, Wordsworth began work on his great autobiographical epic, *The Prelude*. Known simply as "the poem to Coleridge" during his lifetime, published only after the poet's death in 1850, *The Prelude* charts "the growth of a poet's mind," beginning with Wordsworth's earliest memories in Cumberland and ending with his and Coleridge's collaboration toward *Lyrical Ballads* in the late 1790s. As a narrative genre concerned with collective origins and powered by bardic performance, epic has clear affinities with ballad. As Herbert Tucker observes, "it is the very idea of epic to tell a sponsoring culture its own story, from a vantage whose privilege transpires through the successful articulation of a collective identity."[34] Yet in the opening move of *The Prelude*, Wordsworth disappointedly concedes that the collectivist model will no longer serve, that there is

> No little band of yet remembered names
> Whom I, in perfect confidence, might hope
> To summon back from lonesome banishment.[35]

So instead of telling the story of, say, the English or the Romans, Wordsworth decides to tell "[some] tale from my own heart, more near akin / To my own passions and habitual thoughts"—that is, an autobiography.[36] The nearly 8,000-line poem is written entirely in blank verse and so might seem to sidestep the prosodic tension charted above. But this is only partly the case. For whereas *Lyrical Ballads* establishes a generic polarity between primitive balladry and

---

[33] John Fotheringham, *Wordsworth's "Prelude" as a Study of Education* (London: Horace Marshall & Son, 1899), 48–9.

[34] Herbert F. Tucker, *Epic: Britain's Heroic Muse, 1790–1910* (Oxford: Oxford University Press, 2008), 13. Tucker observes "a deep shift in epic's theoretical premises" in the decades immediately preceding Wordsworth's composition of *The Prelude*, which entailed "the replacement of a formal by a cultural criterion for epic unity" (13).

[35] Wordsworth, *The Prelude*, 36.

[36] Wordsworth, *The Prelude*, 40.

enlightened lyricism, between cultural objects and cultural agents, *The Prelude* attempts to synthesize this polarity within the bounds of a single poem and single mind, to translate a problem of bifurcated form into a parable of integrated consciousness.

Wordsworth describes the challenge at hand in a passage from Book 2:

> so wide appears
> The vacancy between me and those days,
> Which yet have such self-presence in my mind
> That, sometimes, when I think of them I seem
> Two consciousnesses, conscious of myself,
> And of some other being.[37]

In Geoffrey Hartman's pathbreaking study of Wordsworth, the poet's remembered child self is an intimate of an unfallen state of Nature to which the adult poet's modernity forbids return. Wordsworth's poetry, Hartman writes, is "apocalyptic," fueled by an "inner necessity to cast out nature, to extirpate everything apparently external to salvation."[38] The "other being" named here is displaced temporally from the adult poet, but some of the earliest lines Wordsworth composed for *The Prelude* figure his childhood self as racially and culturally displaced as well. Reminiscing in Book 1 about days spent splashing in rivers, running through fields, and tanning under the sun, Wordsworth says it was

> as if I had been born
> On Indian plains, and from my Mother's hut
> Had run abroad in wantonness, to sport,
> A naked Savage, in the thunder shower.[39]

In this and many other instances, it is as if the numerous "others" of *Lyrical Ballads*—vagrants, Indian women, convicts, children—are transported into *The Prelude* to serve as metaphorical proxies for Wordsworth's former self.[40] Roy

---

[37] Wordsworth, *The Prelude*, 66.

[38] Hartman, *Wordsworth's Poetry*, 49

[39] Wordsworth, *The Prelude*, 44. The poet was part of a society fascinated by Native Americans to a far greater degree than one might initially assume. "The Indian is a touchstone for a whole range of British perceptions concerning America during the long nineteenth century," argues Kate Flint, *The Transatlantic Indian, 1776–1930* (Princeton: Princeton University Press, 2009), "and plays a pivotal role in the understanding and imagining of cultural difference" (2). As Bewell observes, "Since the observer and the observed were part of the *same* history, 'others' were a primary means of self-reflection, a way of recovering aspects of the self that could no longer be easily recognized" (22).

[40] As Meredith Martin, "'Imperfectly Civilized': Ballads, Nations, and Histories of Form," *English Literary History*, 82/2 (2015), observes, "Ballad discourse . . . identified primitive groups of people

Wagner suggests that "an anthropologist 'invents' the culture he believes him-self to be studying . . . Before this he had no culture . . . since the culture in which one grows up is never really 'visible'—it is taken for granted, and its assumptions are felt to be self-evident. It is only through 'invention' of this kind that the abstract significance of culture (and of many another concept) can be grasped."[41] Wagner's analysis neatly summarizes the task Wordsworth sets himself in *The Prelude*, a "Hard task," he sighs, since "Not only general habits and desires, / But each most obvious and particular thought . . . Hath no beginning."[42] Read in anthropological terms, Wordsworth's self-fashioning as "naked Savage" is simply one of the more striking instances of the larger aes-thetic operation whereby the poet invents the cultural origin he is studying, his adult difference from which allows an enlightened identity to become visible in the present.

The Prelude, in short, attempts to transform a (public) matter of prosody into a (private) matter of cognition. The audible dissonance early readers detected in *Lyrical Ballads* is metaphorized in Wordsworth's autobiography as psychological dissonance, whose resolution is in turn offered as proof of the poetic sensibility:

> The mind of man is framed even like the breath
> And harmony of music. There is a dark
> Invisible workmanship that reconciles
> Discordant elements, and makes them move
> In one society.[43]

Wordsworth's metaphor for cognition attributes to music what critics have often attributed to the poet's blank verse, namely the power to "[rec-oncile] / Discordant elements" while deflecting external analysis. As the Wordsworth scholar Stephen Gill acknowledges, critics routinely struggle to articulate how *The Prelude*'s blank verse works, even as they acknowledge its central importance:

even in modern societies: the child, the uneducated working classes, the rural village-dweller, and the colonial subject, all of whom were not yet touched by Englishness and could be recruited to represent a powerful fantasy of poetic purity" (349). Some of *The Prelude*'s more significant examples of more or less primitive others would include the "infant Babe" in Book 2; the discharged soldier returning from the West Indies in Book 4; the Boy of Winander in Book 5; Wordsworth's partner in the alps, Robert Jones, in Book 6; the French soldier Michel Beaupuy in Book 9; and of course Dorothy Wordsworth and Coleridge.

[41] Wagner, *The Invention of Culture*, 4.
[42] Wordsworth, *The Prelude*, 76.
[43] Wordsworth, *The Prelude*, 46

It is not difficult to see why this should be so. First: medium and content are obviously indissoluble in lyrics by, for example, Marvell or Keats or Hopkins ... But though in theory this must also be true for *The Prelude*, we cannot in fact behave as if it is. Clearly it is possible to inspect the content of Book VIII, for example, without constant reference to the verse medium, whereas a discussion of *Ode to a Nightingale* that did not focus on rhythm, rhyme, and stanza formation would not be a literary discussion at all.

Second: there is the sheer difficulty of saying anything about a medium as elusive as blank verse ... It is easier to say what blank verse is not than to demonstrate what its properties and powers are. This chapter will fail to give a satisfactory account of Wordsworth's blank verse (even as an introduction), as all other attempts have done.

Third: there is the sense that it is somehow inappropriate to talk about Wordsworth as a verse technician ... A poem which celebrates freedom in its opening lines, which constantly opposes formal education to Nature's care, and which directly privileges sane, deep, personally intuitive response over "rules of mimic art transferred / To things above all art" (XI, 154–5), seems to direct attention away from art as such ... [At] its most memorable the verse affirms a state of pure being, when the tongue is still.[44]

In suggesting that blank verse suits Wordsworth because it is prosodically inconspicuous, Gill extends a line of criticism extending back to the poet's own day. "The best part of the human language," writes Coleridge in 1817, "is derived from reflection on the acts of the mind itself," and therefore the "supposed characteristics" of Wordsworth's poetry (e.g. simplicity, nature, rustic life) are not its "real characteristics."[45] John Stuart Mill echoes Coleridge in suggesting that a preference for true poetry over primitive balladry correlates with a preference for "the world within" over "outward things."[46] Nearer our own day, critics have tended to agree that the signature aspects of Wordsworth's poetry are lyrical, concerned with inward intellectual processes rather than external markers of human culture.[47] All of these critics are responding, in

---

[44] Stephen Gill, *Wordsworth: The Prelude* (Oxford: Oxford University Press, 1991), 20–1.

[45] Samuel Taylor Coleridge, *Biographia Literaria: Or, Biographical Sketches of My Literary Life and Opinions* (New York: Leavitt, Lord, 1834), 203, 250.

[46] John Stuart Mill, *Dissertations and Discussions: Political, Philosophical, and Historical*, vol. 1 (London: John W. Parker and Son, 1859), 1. It was a New Critical commonplace that the lyrical inflection of Wordsworth's ballads was what made them innovative, an assessment bolstered by the more properly lyrical longer poems that provided M. H. Abrams, "Structure and Style in the Greater Romantic Lyric," in *The Correspondent Breeze: Essays on English Romanticism* (New York: W. W. Norton, 1984), archetypes for what he called "the greater Romantic lyric" (80).

[47] The greatness mid-century critics located in Wordsworth's lyricism could also be read, a generation later, as an equally great misreading of history. See Marjorie Levinson, *Wordsworth's Great Period Poems: Four Essays* (Cambridge: Cambridge University Press, 1986) for a polemical reading

part, to the fact that Wordsworth himself often advocates for a verse medium whose suppleness matches that of human cognition. As he writes in an 1804 letter to the elocutionist John Thelwall, "the art of verse should not compell you to read in . . . emphasis etc that violates the nature of prose."

Yet in the following sentence Wordsworth offers an important caveat: "[this] rule should be taken with limitations," for "as long as verse shall have the marked termination that rhyme gives it and as long as blank verse shall be printed in lines, it will be Physically impossible to pronounce the last words or syllables of the lines with the same indifference, as the others, i.e., not to give them an intonation of one kind or an other, or to follow them with a pause, not called out for by the passion of the subject, but by the passion of metre merely."[48] A poem's prosody, Wordsworth acknowledges here, is not a strictly linguistic matter but is inevitably bound up in considerations of physical medium and literary convention, from something as trivial as a line break to something as significant as blank verse's proximity to ballad meter. Later Romantic figures such as Lord Byron and, as we will see in the next chapter, Edgar Allan Poe place these kinds of textual and prosodic contingencies at the center of their projects.[49] (Poe claims to have built his raven's famous "Nevermore!" refrain not from any narrative or thematic material but from "the long o as the most sonorous vowel, in connection with r as the most producible consonant."[50]) Wordsworth typically avoids this level of phonetic and prosodic detail, yet he remains deeply concerned with what might be called his poetry's interface, its means for engaging, and potentially improving, his readers' cognitive experience. As he writes in the "Preface":

the human mind is capable of being excited without the application of gross and violent stimulants . . . It has therefore appeared to me, that to endeavour to produce or enlarge this capability is one of the best services in which, at any period, a Writer can be engaged; but this service, excellent at all times, is especially so at the present day. For a multitude of causes, unknown to former times, are now acting with a combined force to blunt the discriminating powers of the mind, and, unfitting it for all voluntary exertion, to reduce it to

of "Tintern Abbey" as the poet's consummate attempt to deny socioeconomic history and then "hide [the poem's] omission of the historical" (39). For a critique of Levinson's approach, see Helen Vendler, "*Tintern Abbey*: Two Assaults," *The Bucknell Review*, 36/1 (1992): 173–90.

[48] Wordsworth, letter to Thelwall, qtd. in O'Donnell, *The Passion of Meter*, 179–80.

[49] See Jerome McGann, *Byron and the Poetics of Adversity* (Cambridge: Cambridge University Press, 2023), who observes that, "For Byron, the objective and socio-material character of language—its relation to the volatile world of fact and event—puts him at odds with both Coleridge's and Wordsworth's Romantic theories of poetry and Imagination" (11).

[50] Edgar Allan Poe, "The Philosophy of Composition," in Stuart Levine and Susan F. Levine, eds., *Edgar Allan Poe: Critical Theory, the Major Documents* (Springfield: University of Illinois, 2009), 64–5.

a state of almost savage torpor. The most effective of these causes are the great national events which are daily taking place, and the increasing accumulation of men in cities, where the uniformity of their occupations produces a craving for extraordinary incident, which the rapid communication of intelligence hourly gratifies. (*LB* 99)

Ironically, of course, many early readers found *Lyrical Ballads* itself to be full of gross stimulants and extraordinary incidents, and even as Wordsworth deplores the "idle and extravagent stories in verse" of ballad writers such as Gottfried August Bürger, the poet's landmark collection trades on the interest that Bürger and others had generated (*LB* 100). Keeping these ironies in view helps us see that even as certain poems, critics, and Wordsworth himself advocate for an inward-looking, lyrical, unmediated mode, his project as a whole depends on forces pushing in other directions, too.

One place this push-and-pull is particularly apparent is "Hart-Leap Well," a poem Wordsworth appears to have adapted directly from one of Bürger's ballads.[51] In the explicitly revisionary relationship of its two parts, "Hart-Leap Well" focalizes the tension between lyrics and ballads that Wordsworth exploited but never fully theorized. The poem's first part opens with narrative material that appears to honor its source text:

> The Knight had ridden down from Wensley moor
> With the slow motion of a summer's cloud;
> He turn'd aside towards a Vassal's door,
> And, "Bring another Horse!" he cried aloud. (*LB* 203)

No sooner is the poem's iambic pentameter measure established, however, than its protagonist's gait stalls in the irresistible languidness of line 2:

> With the **slow** | **mot**ion of | a **summ** | er's **cloud**

There is simply no good way to find five stresses in this line, which seems intent on confirming the four-beat norm of Bürger's ballad even as its Romantic imagery pulls Wordsworth's poem into more thematically lyrical territory. Lines 3 and 4 in turn restore the poem's iambic clip and kickstart its lagging plot, which follows the knight, Sir Walter, as he proceeds to exhaust three

---

[51] Geoffrey Hartman, *The Unremarkable Wordsworth* (Minneapolis: The University of Minnesota Press, 1987), notes of Wordsworth's revision of Bürger that "no ballad could be more parallel, and more opposed" (55).

horses and all of his hounds in his maniacal hunt for the titular hart. Finally he reaches the animal, itself exhausted to the point of death. Amazed at the distance of the dying hart's "three leaps" (*LB* 204), Sir Walter erects a memorial in the animal's honor, which he visits each summer "with his paramour" until, in old age, he dies and is buried "in his paternal vale" (*LB* 205).

Part 1 ends there, only for its closing lines to abruptly announce that "there is matter for a second rhyme, / And I to this would add another tale" (*LB* 206). This additional tale, Part 2 of the poem, opens with an explicit rejection of the ballad aesthetic of Part 1:

> The moving accident is not my trade:
> To freeze the blood I have no ready arts:
> 'Tis my delight, alone in summer shade,
> To pipe a simple song to thinking hearts. (*LB* 206)

Though stanza and prosodic structure remain identical—elegiac quatrains of alternately rhymed iambic pentameter lines—the poem's speaker now presents himself as a writer of lyrics rather than ballads, a poet of solitary musings for "thinking hearts" rather than supernatural tales. (The phrases "moving accident" and "freeze the blood" allude to *Othello* and *Hamlet*, as if to offer further evidence of the speaker's higher literary ambitions.) The relative frequency of first-person pronouns in Part 2—"I" appears eleven times in the first twenty-six lines as compared to just three times in the ninety-six lines of Part 1—further substantiates its lyrical orientation. "As I from Hawes to Richmond did repair," the speaker explains, in what we come to realize is an account of how he procured the narrative material of Part 1, he stumbled upon the Hart-Leap Well.

> I stood in various thoughts and fancies lost,
> When one, who was in Shepherd's garb attir'd,
> Came up the Hollow. Him did I accost,
> And what this place might be I then inquir'd.
>
> The Shepherd stopp'd, and that same story told
> Which in my former rhyme I have rehears'd.
> "A jolly place," said he, "in times of old!
> But something ails it now; the spot is curs'd." (*LB* 206)

This is Wordsworth playing ethnographer again, only this time he does a fairly decent job of transcribing his subject's speech, presenting verbatim in the following nine stanzas the shepherd's speculations about why the area around the well is cursed and why the dying hart may have sought it out. After the shepherd concludes, the poem's speaker responds that the two men share a common "lesson": "Never to blend our pleasure or our pride / With sorrow of the meanest thing that feels" (LB 208).

The question thus arises as to which voice is the "real" Wordsworth: the voice of Part 1 that presents a ballad, or the voice of Part 2 that favors lyric. To answer this question, critics sometimes consult a fragment of verse the poet composed in his sister Dorothy's journal that describes a visit to Hart-Leap Well. James Chandler observes that this fragment "has the signature marking of Wordsworthian blank verse in an autobiographical first-person narrative," whereas "Hart-Leap Well" features a "highly stylized ballad stanza."[52] Yet while the *abab* rhymes of "Hart-Leap Well" do evoke ballad meter, its pentameter measure does not. Similarly, while the *Home at Grasmere* fragment is indeed in blank verse, it appears alongside various of Dorothy's prose entries, making the journal itself a collaboratively authored, multi-generic, and arguably anti-lyric document. Rather than attempting to isolate individual texts or poetic features that are authentically Wordsworthian, then, we might instead approach lyricism and balladry as co-constitutive generic functions, alternately confirmed or complicated via prosody.

Our conventional history of prosodic innovation, hinging on Ezra Pound's modernist campaign "to break the pentameter," sees metrical verse supplanted by post-metrical ("free") verse sometime after 1910.[53] But Wordsworth's case offers another, earlier moment of prosodic friction or breakage in which the poet counterposes the perceived freedom of blank verse with the communitarian logic of balladry, a prosodic juxtaposition that would prove highly influential in the ongoing valorization of lyric immediacy. As Antony Easthope observes, "[by] eliding metricality in favor of 'the prosody of natural speech' the pentameter would render poetic discourse transparent, aiming to identify the speaking of a poem with the speaking of a represented

---

[52] James Chandler, *An Archaeology of Sympathy: The Sentimental Mode in Literature and Cinema* (Chicago: University of Chicago Press, 2013), 293.

[53] For a summary of this received account and its conceptual limitations, see Meredith Martin, *The Rise and Fall of Meter: Poetry and English National Culture, 1860–1930* (Princeton: Princeton University Press, 2012), 1–5.

speaker or a narrator."[54] That *Lyrical Ballads* remains pivotal in our literary histories suggests just how durable beliefs surrounding lyric poetry and balladry are. From Wordsworth we inherit a generic paradox of sorts in which lyric, despite the obvious musical associations of the term, comes increasingly to name a mode of poetry that downplays or metaphorizes its musical, metrical, and sonic characteristics. The modern ballad, in turn, becomes the "shadow image of the lyric," in Meredith McGill's phrasing, a form perceived as communal, audible, and for this reason less intellectually rigorous than page-based poetry.[55] If the literary academy has defined the modern lyric in terms of its ambivalent musicality, the modern ballad has been defined, in a reciprocal process, in terms of its dubious sophistication.

With the arrival of modernism, this distinction attached itself to a whole new set of cultural forms, the virtual orality of Wordsworth's printed ballads finding its modern counterpart in the real-time acoustic experience provided by the phonograph record, whose most popular musical artists would become the balladeers of their day. Daniel Tiffany goes as far as to suggest that "popular culture in its modern aspect (and the controversies surrounding it) may be said to have arisen in the context of the ballad scandals" of the later eighteenth century.[56] As the modern ballad became more literally audible via music recording technology, the modern lyric, through the reciprocal generic process this chapter has traced, became more firmly associated with its normative print context. Yet even as these broad patterns hold, what Wordsworth's example makes equally clear is that one can render introspective ("lyrical") content in ballad form, just as one can render low and rustic ("balladic") content in blank verse. Distinctions of genre, prosody, format, and much else, in other words, can indeed be correlated until they constellate into something as powerful as the modern Ur-genre of lyric. But these categories can also be untethered from one another, juxtaposed in novel ways to produce new cognitive and affective experiences.

In closing, let's test these claims against the work of one particular modern balladeer, the American singer-songwriter Taylor Swift. Any number of contemporary pop artists could serve this purpose, but Swift invites special

[54] Easthope, *Poetry as Discourse*, 75.
[55] McGill, "What Is a Ballad?" 160.
[56] Tiffany, *My Silver Planet*, 64. Newman, "Moderation in the *Lyrical Ballads*," observes that "By the time we reach the New Criticism, the ballad, though often explicitly contrasted with lyric, is also enshrined as the genre that initiates readers *into* lyric" (4).

analysis on the merit of her 2020 song "The Lakes." Her title refers to England's Lake District, whose most famous inhabitant she slyly names midway through her song:

> I've come too far to let some name-dropping sleaze
> tell me what are my words worth[57]

Like any pun, Swift's points in two directions. It claims an artistic confidence based not on outside approval (as might be granted by "some name-dropping sleaze") but on a felt sense of one's own powers. Yet with the very same words that declare this visionary freedom, Swift name-drops the canonical figure, William Wordsworth, most closely associated with this self-ramifying visionary mode. Swift's allusion to the poet, hidden in plain sight on a bonus track capping an album titled *folklore*, neatly captures the challenge facing all poets writing after Romanticism: how to make introspection new, again. As Swift puts it in the rhetorical question that opens the song, "Is it romantic how all my elegies eulogize me?"[58] From one perspective, yes, self-elegy is a textbook instance of Romanticism in the Wordsworthian mode. We might think of the Boy of Winander passage in Book 5 of *The Prelude* ("There was a boy; ye knew him well, ye cliffs / And islands of Winander!"), which Wordsworth wrote in the first person before revising into the third person for publication, in excerpted form, with the 1800 *Lyrical Ballads*.[59] *folklore*'s cover art features Swift alone in nature, surrounded by tall trees, head angled slightly upward as she gazes somewhere outside the frame. The wild secluded scene seems to impress on her thoughts of more deep seclusion. But from another perspective, no: Swift's self-elegies are not romantic because the Romantic period is over. In knowing acknowledgment of its belatedness, the song's clichéd Romantic images (e.g. solitary flowers, looming cliffs) are filtered through a digital, twenty-first-century lens: "A red rose grew up out of ice frozen ground / With no one around to tweet it."[60]

folklore represented something of a departure for Swift, whose previous songs had largely been interpreted as autobiographical first-person monologues. During the mandated isolation of the COVID-19 pandemic, however, as Swift explains in the album's liner notes, "I found myself not only writing my own stories, but also writing about or from the perspective of people I've never met, people I've known, or those I wish I hadn't."[61] Swift's notoriously

---

[57] Taylor Swift, "The Lakes," track 17 on *folklore* (Republic Records, 2020).
[58] Swift, "The Lakes."
[59] Wordsworth, *The Prelude*, 172.
[60] Swift, "The Lakes."
[61] Liner notes for Swift, *folklore*.

dedicated fans proved eager to speculate about the artist's relation to this cast of characters. Of all the tracks, "The Last Great American Dynasty" provoked the most discussion. Though modern in its setting, the song, based on the life of the American socialite Rebekah West Harkness, features many aspects of a traditional ballad, including a four-beat line, an *abab* rhyme scheme, and a narrative plot that hinges on a social taboo. Rebekah, we learn in the opening verse, having married beyond her station, has become the gossip of the town. When her husband Bill, an heir to the Standard Oil fortune, subsequently dies from a heart attack, the townspeople smugly interpret his death as confirmation of Rebekah's interloper status:

> "There goes the last great American dynasty
> Who knows if she never showed up, what could've been
> There goes the maddest woman this town has ever seen
> She had a marvelous time ruining everything"[62]

Spurned by the town, the widowed Rebekah embraces her role as local provocateur, filling her swimming pool with champagne, hosting high-stakes card games, and carousing with visiting celebrities. At once culture warrior ("in a feud with her neighbor / she stole his dog and dyed it key lime green") and lonely outsider ("seen on occasion / pacing the rocks, staring out at the midnight sea"), Rebekah functions much like the spurned and ostracized women of *Lyrical Ballads*. She is part Goody Blake, enacting revenge on a neighbor through the dark arts, and part Martha Ray, the distraught mother of "The Thorn" returning compulsively to her infant's grave "[at] all times of the day and night" (*LB* 54).

After two verses and choruses, the song's bridge turns unexpectedly to the first person:

> Fifty years is a long time
> Holiday House sat quietly on that beach
> Free of women with madness, their men and bad habits
> And then it was bought by me

In 2013, Swift indeed bought the mansion once owned by Harkness. She too hosted parties that drew the ire of local residents. And she too was the target of sexist judgments about her merits as an artist. Having told a story about an eccentric person, Swift reveals that she is, in a way, that person. She tells, in

---

[62] Swift, "The Last Great American Dynasty," track 3 on *folklore* (Republic Records, 2020).

short, a lyrical ballad—a tale set to music that troubles, in order to confirm, its teller's selfhood. "I had a marvelous time ruining everything," Swift sings near the end of the song, reiterating the first-person pronoun to underscore the parallel between herself and Harkness.[63] When she repeats the line, she sings it an octave higher, giving the impression that a second voice has entered the song, even as the notes remain chromatically identical.

As the study of poetry, both new and old, moves deeper into an age of media, it will grow less and less tenable to assume that the prosodic effects of poems are equivalent to the rhythmic features of visual texts read at a normal speaking pace.[64] After all, it was the sensation of overly boisterous, communal voice produced by Wordsworth's experiments in balladry that helped define the meditative lyric that modern criticism subsequently took as its norm. By reframing prosodic analysis as a form of media studies, whose object is neither a poem's language nor its printed text but rather the broader array of media that shape its sonic textures, we can begin to more fully account for the multimedial effects of poetry written before the twentieth century, along with the vibrant life of prosody after modernism in contexts like popular song. As we recover some of the acoustic punch of Wordsworth's ballads, so too will new lyric modes become visible in the present.

---

[63] Swift, "The Last Great American Dynasty."

[64] As Jerome McGann, *Radiant Textuality: Literary Studies after the World Wide Web* (New York: Palgrave, 2001), observes: "We have had many fine editions of ballads and songs since the late eighteenth century, but none has been able to accommodate, except in minimal ways, the auditional features of the texts" (61).

2

Ravens, Books, and Bells

Near the end of Edgar Allan Poe's 1838 fictional memoir *The Narrative of Arthur Gordon Pym*, the seafaring narrator Pym and his companion Peters, marooned at the South Pole and pursued by a tribe of islanders, escape into a series of linked subterranean chasms. In the final chasm, they discover "a range of singular-looking indentures" scored into the rock wall.[1]

> With a very slight exertion of the imagination, the left, or most northerly of these indentures might have been taken for the intentional, although rude, representation of a human figure standing erect, with outstretched arm. The rest of them bore also some little resemblance to alphabetical characters, and Peters was willing, at all events, to adopt the idle opinion that they were really such. I convinced him of his error, finally, by directing his attention to the floor of the fissure, where, among the powder, we picked up, piece by piece, several large flakes of the marl, which had evidently been broken off by some convulsion from the surface where the indentures were found, and which had projecting points exactly fitting the indentures; thus proving them to have been the work of nature. Figure 4. presents an accurate copy of the whole.[2]

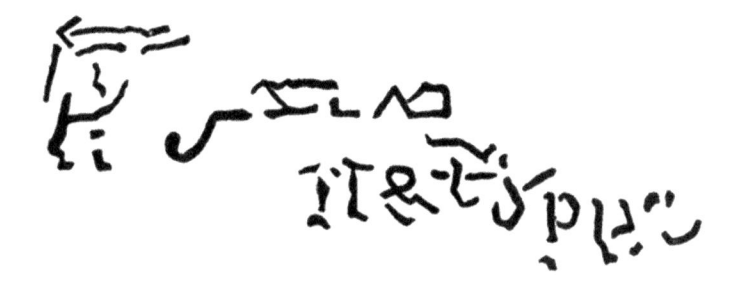

Though Pym determines the indentures to have been the result of natu-ral, rather than human, processes, a "Note" following the memoir, ostensibly written by an editor of Pym's manuscript, suggests that when not only the

[1] Edgar Allan Poe, *The Narrative of Arthur Gordon Pym* (London: Wiley & Putnam, 1838), 232.
[2] Poe, *The Narrative of Arthur Gordon Pym*, 232–33.

Poetry, Sound, and the Matter of Prosody 1800–2000. Peter Miller, Oxford University Press. © Peter Miller (2025).
DOI: 10.1093/9780198937210.003.0003

indentures but also the shapes of the chasms themselves are transcribed, the images "constitute an Ethiopian verbal root."[3] "It is not impossible," concludes the note's author, "that 'Tsalal,' the appellation of the island of the chasms, may be found, upon minute philological scrutiny, to betray either some alliance with the chasms themselves, or some reference to the Ethiopian characters so mysteriously written in their windings."[4]

Across the many genres he worked in, Poe relished puzzles of interpretation. Thus Pym and Peters debate the intentionality of the chasm markings in the South Pole—which slide from pictographs to phonetic script to meaningless marks—only for their debate to be further contextualized by an anonymous American editor (who informs readers of "the late sudden and distressing death of Mr. Pym").[5] As a poet, Poe narrowed this contextualizing project to matters of prosody. The thorny metrics of a poem like "The Bells," for instance, made it an irresistible Victorian showpiece but also, for the same reason, an accident waiting to happen. In "The Raven," whose human narrator is gradually driven mad by the talking bird's monotonous refrain, Poe illustrated how seemingly meaningless prosodic material could take on unsettling human significance. Yet while Poe's prose work has earned extensive critical attention, his poetic innovations have often been neglected, dismissed, or openly derided. There are two main reasons for this. First, Poe's poetry and criticism bring a severe level of irony to a cultural discourse—metrical and prosodic theory—that, as Meredith Martin has shown, was in the nineteenth century a quite serious matter.[6] Poe's chief entry into this discourse, his 1848 essay "The Rationale of Verse," despite opening with the tenable argument that the visual logics of print have obscured the acoustic core of poetry, concludes by offering a still more arcane system of visual scansion to support his argument. The second reason is that it remains difficult to reconcile the critical ambition of Poe's prosody with his image as a social outsider and literary charlatan, an image calcified during the literary and media revolutions of modernism.[7] Emerson's early putdown of Poe as "the jingle man" retains its sting and captures a broad academic sentiment rearticulated the following century, if in more nuanced

[3] Poe, *The Narrative of Arthur Gordon Pym*, 251.
[4] Poe, *The Narrative of Arthur Gordon Pym*, 252.
[5] Poe, *The Narrative of Arthur Gordon Pym*, 249.
[6] See Meredith Martin, *The Rise and Fall of Meter: Poetry and English National Culture, 1860–1930* (Princeton: Princeton University Press, 2012), and the essays collected in *Meter Matters: Verse Cultures of the Long Nineteenth Century*, ed. Jason David Hall (Athens: Ohio University Press, 2011).
[7] Recent scholarship has tempered this romanticized image of Poe by detailing his canny engagement with, and by, contemporary print culture. See Chs. 4 and 5 of Meredith McGill, *American Literature and the Culture of Reprinting, 1834–1853* (Philadelphia: University of Pennsylvania Press, 2003), Eliza Richards, *Gender and the Poetics of Reception in Poe's Circle* (Cambridge: Cambridge University Press, 2004), and the essay collection *Poe and the Remapping of Antebellum Print Culture*, ed. J. Gerald Kennedy and Jerome McGann (Baton Rouge: Louisiana State University Press, 2012).

terms, by T. S. Eliot.[8] Assessing Poe's significance for American and indeed world literature, Eliot concludes that "sound and sense must cooperate; in even the most purely incantatory poem, the dictionary meaning of words cannot be disregarded with impunity."[9] Nevertheless, Eliot concedes, "one cannot be sure that one's own writing has *not* been influenced by Poe," since certain of his poems "are as well remembered by everybody, as any poems ever written."[10] Poe's sonorous poetry, Eliot implies, hovers in the collective unconscious like a radio jingle, hollow if examined closely, but pervasive and, in its own way, profound.

This chapter recovers what Eliot could only half grasp: Poe's critique of Romantic lyricism, which by the 1830s had become poetry's de facto mode and whose ideal of unmediated voice Poe's work seeks to deconstruct.[11] Poe's work historicizes and delyricizes poetic voice by revealing its embeddedness in media, even as it reveals the multiplicity of prosodic options available when individual readers verbalize the same poetical text. In more concrete terms, Poe's poems and critical essays gather various sound media—phonetic script, meter, scansion, musical form, ravens, bells—and then show how these media produce different prosodic effects when engaged by different readers. Using the term "media" here helps offset the too easy assumption that these sound reproduction technologies, for that's what they are in Poe's work, are somehow rendered non-technological, homogenous, or obsolete by the arrival of modern sound reproduction technologies (e.g. the phonograph and its successors).[12] Poe's work shows that the prosodic structure of a poem is comprised of multiple overlapping sound media, which are not coextensive with that poem's

---

[8] Emerson's comment is quoted in Edwin Watts Chubb, *Stories of Authors British and American* (New York: The Macmillan Company, 1926), 285.

[9] T. S. Eliot, "From Poe to Valéry," *The Hudson Review*, 2/3 (Autumn 1949): 332. The anglophone modernist academy took a still more negative stance toward Poe. See, for instance, the opinions of Laura Riding, "The Facts in the Case of Monsieur Poe," in Laura Heffernan and Jane Malcolm, eds., *Contemporaries and Snobs* (Tuscaloosa: University of Alabama Press, 2014), 86–112, and Yvor Winters, "Edgar Allan Poe: A Crisis in the History of American Obscurantism," *American Literature*, 8/4 (January 1937): 379–402. Harold Bloom, *Edgar Allan Poe's "The Tell-Tale Heart" and Other Stories*, ed. Bloom (New York: Infobase, 2009), reasserts the consensus for our own time: "I can think of no American writer . . . at once so inevitable and so dubious" (3).

[10] Eliot, "From Poe to Valéry," 327. Eliot acknowledges that "we should be prepared to entertain the possibility that these Frenchmen have seen something in Poe that English-speaking readers have missed" (328). Yet he struggles to square this possibility with the fact that in Mallarmé's translations of Poe "the rhythms, in which we find so much of the originality of Poe, are lost" (336).

[11] Robert Browning's contemporaneous critique of lyric exceptionalism has been better documented. See Herbert Tucker, "Dramatic Monologue and the Overhearing of Lyric," in Virginia Jackson and Yopie Prins, eds., *The Lyric Theory Reader* (Baltimore: Johns Hopkins University Press, 2014), 144–58. For Tucker, Browning's dramatic monologue became a space in which "the charmed circle of lyric finds itself included by the kind of historical particularity that lyric genres exclude by design" (145).

[12] This claim extends from one of the major insights of recent work in sound studies, which emphasizes the intercompatibility of modern and pre-modern sound media. Seminal studies include Lisa Gitelman, *Scripts, Grooves, and Writing Machines: Representing Technology in the Edison Era* (Stanford: Stanford University Press, 1999), and Jonathan Sterne, *The Audible Past: Cultural Origins of Sound*

printed text. To the question of whether prosodic form can be said to have a historical character, then, Poe answers yes and no. Yes, all poetic verbalizations are historical acts linked to specific physical media. But no, we cannot historicize these acts at the level of readerly affect, since the psycholinguistic processes that bring prosodic form into palpable being are ultimately singular and inscrutable.[13] We can and should, Poe's work suggests, recover documentary evidence that speaks to how prosodic form was experienced, defined, and regulated in the past. But we should also acknowledge that this is not the same as knowing what readers in 1800 or 1900 or 2000 actually felt as they enunciated a poem's language and sensed its form take shape.

Eliot's assessment that Poe's poetry betrays an "irresponsibility towards the meaning of words" is in many respects a fair reading.[14] Prioritizing prosodic effects over semantic precision, poems like "The Raven," "Annabel Lee," and "The Bells" cultivate a logic of catchiness anticipating that of modern advertising.[15] Anticipating Jonathan Culler's more recent characterization of "the lyric event," Poe presents it as axiomatic that a poem should be experienced in real time, prioritize sound effects, and engage human affect.[16] "A poem deserves its title only inasmuch as it excites, by elevating the soul," Poe writes in "The Poetic Principle."[17] Because "all excitements are, through a psychal necessity, transient," poems are by definition brief. "After the lapse of half an hour, at the very utmost, it flags—fails—a revulsion ensues—and then the poem is, in effect, and in fact, no longer such."[18] *Paradise Lost*, Poe suggests, is best understood as "a series of minor [i.e. short] poems."[19] Poe therefore turns repeatedly to music as the art form poetry should strive toward, going as far as to define poetry simply as *"The Rhythmical Creation of Beauty."*[20]

Reproduction (Durham: Duke University Press, 2003). For an application of sound studies methods to poetry studies, see Marit MacArthur, "Monotony, the Churches of Poetry Reading, and Sound Studies," *PMLA*, 131/1 (January 2016): 38–63.

[13] A comparison might be drawn between the historicity of prosodic form and that of, say, the novel. Enunciating a novel's language activates a reader's prosodic protocols just as much as does poetry, but the acoustic-temporal contours of this enunciation are generally considered less generically determinant than such higher-order concerns as plot, theme, and character development.

[14] Eliot, "From Poe to Valéry," 333.

[15] "Annabel Lee," observes Neil Baldwin, *Edison: Inventing the Century* (Chicago: University of Chicago Press, 1995), was one of Edison's favorite poems to record and reproduce for phonographical demonstrations (90).

[16] Jonathan Culler, *Theory of the Lyric* (Cambridge: Harvard University Press, 2015), 353.

[17] Edgar Allan Poe, "The Poetic Principle," in Stuart Levine and Susan F. Levine, eds., *Edgar Allan Poe: Critical Theory, the Major Documents* (Springfield: University of Illinois Press, 2009), 178.

[18] Poe, "The Poetic Principle," 178.

[19] Poe, "The Poetic Principle," 179.

[20] Poe, "The Poetic Principle," 187.

Poe marshals his severe formalism against the legacy of English Romanticism, which he feels has cultivated an inaccurate picture of the nature of
poetic craft. "Most writers—poets in especial," Poe writes in 1846, "prefer having it understood that they compose by a species of fine frenzy—an ecstatic
intuition."[21] Coleridge indeed claimed to have composed "Kubla Khan" in a
drug-induced dream vision. Wordsworth famously described poetry as "the
spontaneous overflow of powerful feelings."[22] By 1836, John Stuart Mill provided a memorable definition of lyric poetry as "feeling confessing itself to
itself, in moments of solitude."[23] Seeking to unmask the Romantic fiction of
spontaneous lyricism, Poe suggests that the reading public would benefit from

> [taking] a peep behind the scenes, at the elaborate and vacillating crudities of
> thought—at the true purposes seized only at the last moment—at the innu-
> merable glimpses of idea that arrived not at the maturity of full view—at the
> fully matured fancies discarded in despair as unmanageable—at the cautious
> selections and rejections—at the painful erasures and interpolations—in a
> word, at the wheels and pinions—the tackle for scene-shifting—the step-
> ladders and demon-traps—the cock's feathers, the red paint and the black
> patches, which, in ninety-nine cases out of the hundred, constitute the
> properties of the literary *histrio*.[24]

The medium of poetry is not feeling, Poe suggests, but language, and language
as it is bound up in a shifting set of social conditions and material forms. Thus
Poe's own poetry, to extend the technical language above, seeks to glitch the
lyric, to dispel the illusion of solitary voice by focusing attention on the range
of media that sustain it.

One way Poe does so is by blurring the semantic and lexical divisions
between words, troubling the connection between signs and signifieds, as in
the opening lines of "Dream-Land":

> By a route obscure and lonely,
> Haunted by ill angels only[25]

---

[21] Poe, "The Philosophy of Composition," in *Edgar Allan Poe: Critical Theory, the Major Documents*, 61.

[22] William Wordsworth and Samuel Taylor Coleridge, *Lyrical Ballads: 1798 and 1802*, ed. Fiona
Stafford (Oxford: Oxford University Press, 2013), 98.

[23] John Stuart Mill, *Essays on Poetry*, ed. F. Parvin Sharpless (Columbia: University of South
Carolina Press, 1976), 12.

[24] Poe, "The Philosophy of Composition," 61.

[25] Edgar Allan Poe, *Poetry, Tales, and Selected Essays*, ed. Patrick F. Quinn and G. R. Thompson (New
York: The Library of America, 1984), 79. Subsequent references to this edition are cited parenthetically
and abbreviated *POE*.

If we commit to honoring the trochaic stress pattern established by line 1 ("**By** a | **route** ob | **scure** and | **lonely**"), we find ourselves enunciating the rather off-putting phrase "**bile ang**els" in line 2; alternately, if we choose a different "route" by privileging semantic units over metered phonetics, the end of line 2 yields a weird syncopation built on imperfectly alliterative vowel sounds ("**ill ang**els **only**"). Similar tactics inform "Ulalume—A Ballad," which undercuts its title's promise of musical, forward-moving narrative with a stanza structure that consistently denies readers the satisfaction of a fourth beat, creating an awkward start-and-stop effect:

> But Psyche, uplifting her finger,
>> Said—"Sadly this star I mistrust—
>> Her pallor I strangely mistrust—
> Ah, hasten!—ah, let us not linger!
>> Ah, fly!—let us fly!—for we must."
> In terror she spoke; letting sink her
>> Wings till they trailed in the dust—
> In agony sobbed; letting sink her
>> Plumes till they trailed in the dust—
>> Till they sorrowfully trailed in the dust. (*POE* 90)

It is not wrong to classify Poe's stanza as an instance of anapestic trimeter: three-foot lines in which each foot (for the most part) obeys an unstressed-unstressed-stressed syllable pattern ("at the **end** | of our **path**"). Nor is it wrong to observe that, in recitation, one tends naturally to add a silent fourth beat at the end of each line, which in effect preserves the ballad stanza's four-beat norm.

Yet precisely to the extent that we enforce such large-scale prosodic structures are we made aware of smaller-scale idiosyncrasies at the level of individual lines, phrases, and words. Note, for instance, the severe awkwardness caused when, as line 6 enjambs into line 7, the poem's trimeter-with-an-extra-beat format collides with norms of English pronunciation and syntax. Primed by a sequence of rhyming nouns and verbs (*finger, mistrust, linger, we must*) that conclude end-stopped phrases and therefore nicely accommodate each line's silent fourth beat, the reader would expect the pattern to continue into subsequent lines. It can indeed be made to do so, but at the cost of a comically long pause between the possessive adjective "her" and the noun "Wings," two words that in natural speech would follow in quick succession. Poe intensifies this sense of syntactical limbo by omitting from the beginning of line 7 the unstressed syllables that usually appear in this position, thereby adding still more dead air to the space between lines. And in case we missed the prosodic joke, Poe repeats it two lines later, "Plumes" replacing "Wings" in lines that are otherwise lexically identical. It is as if Poe, in devising "Ulalume," expanded a traditional four-line ballad stanza to anywhere between nine and thirteen lines, while retaining its two-rhyme limit (*abab*), in order to showcase the result-ing prosodic and narrative bagginess. Proper nouns appearing near the end of stanzas thus seem to derive not from any historical or geographic reality native to the poem but from mere phonetic coincidence, Poe's "dim lake of Auber" seeming all the more hazy for emerging from the words "sober" and "October," just as "the misty mid region of Weir" seems that much harder to find when one's only guide is the words "sere" and "year."

Wordsworth in "Tintern Abbey" is quite clear that "five years have passed" since he last occupied "these steep woods," which despite "long absence, have not been to me / As is a landscape to a blind man's eye."[26] But blindness toward a landscape is precisely the condition of Poe's speaker in "Ulalume," who realizes only in retrospect that, despite having been in exactly this place one year ago,

> We noted not the dim lake of Auber,
>   (Though once we had journeyed down here)
> We remembered not the dank tarn of Auber,
>   Nor the ghoul-haunted woodland of Weir. (*POE* 89)

Language and memory for Poe's speaker are not, as for Wordsworth, ramify-ing sources of self-knowledge, but human tools prone to error and ambiguity. Note, in the lines above, the cumbersome prosodic substitutions in lines 1 and 3, which require the reader to squeeze four syllables into the second foot in order to maintain the trimeter scheme:

> We **not** | ed not the **dim** | lake of **Aub**er
>
> . . .
>
> We re**mem** | bered not the **dank** | tarn of **Aub**er

Prosodic hiccups such as these thus trope the poem's larger thematic con-cern with its speaker's inability to integrate his experience one year ago with his experience today. What in "Tintern Abbey" prove to be self-affirming

---

[26] Wordsworth, *Lyrical Ballads*, 87.

differences—between Wordsworth and his past self, and between Wordsworth and his sister Dorothy—are in "Ulalume" offered as evidence of the speaking subject's inability to know himself. If Dorothy's belated appearance serves to bolster her brother's place in a collective humanity, Poe's third-person "we" refers to a traveling companion ("Psyche, my Soul") who was never really there.

We saw in the previous chapter that Wordsworth's early readers often considered blank verse compositions such as "Tintern Abbey," as weighed against ballad meter, to be the proper venue for philosophical thought. More recently, the critic Simon Jarvis has advanced a similar claim in arguing "that a different kind of thinking happens in verse," that "verse is itself a kind of cognition," basing his argument largely on Wordsworth's blank verse compositions.[27] Poe would seem to think otherwise, based on a blank verse passage he inscribed in the notebook of his friend Margaret Bassett:

Who hath seduced thee to this foul revolt	Milton Par. Lost. Bk. I
From the pure well of Beauty undefiled?	Somebody
So banish from true wisdom to prefer	Cowper's Task, Book I
Such squalid wit to honourable rhyme?	
To write? To scribble? Nonsense and no more?	Shakespeare
I will not write upon this argument do.	Troilus & Cressida
To write is human—not to write divine.	Pope Essay on Man

(POE 23)

Poe's poem is a cento, a patchwork of lines cribbed from other well-known works, which he cites in the right-hand column only to deliberately misquote in the left. Line 5, for instance, cobbles together material from multiple lines of Hamlet's famous soliloquy ("To be, or not to be"; "To die: to sleep; / No more"), while line 7 parodies an equally famous line from Pope ("To err is human, to forgive divine"), which in fact comes not from his *Essay on Man* but his *Essay on Criticism*. Poe's semi-plagiarized blank verse knowingly travesties the kind of self-knowledge that poets like Wordsworth or later critics like Jarvis take to be the object of poetry. Poe's lines suggest, moreover, that the private experience of powerful feeling had by 1830 becomes an all too familiar starting point for poetic composition, and so what Jarvis says blank verse should *not* be—a "thoughtless ornament or reliquary" into which a poet deposits the requisite ten syllables—Poe takes as his model.

---

[27] Simon Jarvis, *Wordsworth's Philosophic Song* (Cambridge: Cambridge University Press, 2006), 4.

In ways such as this, Poe presents prosody not as a measure of thought but as an effect of various linguistic, sonic, and textual media. Perhaps his most explicit acknowledgment of this philosophy appears in his discussion of the composition of "The Raven," a poem he claims "proceeded, step by step, to its completion with the precision and rigid consequence of a mathematical problem."[28] Having chosen his famous "Nevermore!" refrain based not on any narrative or thematic grounds but, as noted earlier, simply on the aptness of "the long *o* as the most sonorous vowel, in connection with *r* as the most producible consonant," Poe explains that

> The next *desideratum* was a pretext for the continuous use of the one word "nevermore." In observing the difficulty which I had at once found in invent-ing a sufficiently plausible reason for its continuous repetition, I did not fail to perceive that this difficulty arose solely from the pre-assumption that the word was to be so continuously or monotonously spoken by *a human* being—I did not fail to perceive, in short, that the difficulty lay in the reconciliation of this monotony with the exercise of reason on the part of the creature repeating the word. Here, then, immediately arose the idea of a *non*-reasoning creature capable of speech, and very naturally, a parrot, in the first instance, suggested itself, but was superseded forthwith by a Raven, as equally capable of speech, and infinitely more in keeping with the intended *tone*.[29]

Though Poe died before the invention of modern sound-recording technology, he describes his raven's sound reproduction capacities in recognizably ana-log terms. He chooses the bird, in other words, because it processes language as a function of continuous frequency vibrations rather than discrete seman-tic meanings. While the "*non*-reasoning" raven can accurately reproduce the sounds of speech, it lacks the psycholinguistic ability to break this sound into phonological units that can be meaningfully rearranged and re-voiced in the future.[30]

---

[28] Poe, "The Philosophy of Composition," 61–2.

[29] Poe, "The Philosophy of Composition," 64–5.

[30] Poe's interest in the biomechanics of human and non-human speech extends beyond "The Raven" to tales such as "The Black Cat," "The Man Who Was Used Up," and "The Murders in the Rue Morgue," the last of which, observes Jason David Hall, *Nineteenth-Century Verse and Technology: Machines of Meter* (London: Palgrave Macmillan, 2017), endeavors to "[distinguish] rational, educated speech from vocalizations that are 'absolutely alien from humanity' (foreign voices, the raving of madmen, animal cries)" (44). Poe would surely be intrigued by recent work by the cognitive scientist Irene Pepper-berg, "Grey Parrots Do Not Always 'Parrot': The Roles of Imitation and Phonological Awareness in the Creation of New Labels from Existing Vocalizations," *Language Sciences*, 29 (2007), that has recorded "evidence . . . for a form of imitation, vocal segmentation, by a Grey parrot," which suggests the bird "has phonological awareness" (1). Though Poe in "Philosophy" presents his parroting raven as devoid of phonological awareness, the poem generates its power by troubling the assumption that language facility categorically distinguishes human from non-human animals.

Having established the technical and philosophical stakes of the poem, Poe proceeds in "The Raven" by contrasting the linguistic orientations of bird and narrator. If language is to the bird a meaningless stream of acoustic matter, to the poem's human narrator, a scholar of "forgotten lore" (*POE* 81), language is a meaningful textual affair, a writeable and analyzable set of letters, syllables, and words. As readers, we know that the narrator should realize that the intrusive raven cannot comprehend the symbolic codes of the human world and so cannot speak truthfully to that world. Initially, the narrator does realize this: "Much I marveled this ungainly fowl to hear discourse so plainly, / Though its answer little meaning—little relevancy bore" (*POE* 83). But even as he discounts the raven's capacity for meaningful "discourse," the narrator, "linking / Fancy unto fancy" (*POE* 84), concocts an origin story for the bird's linguistic competence: "'Doubtless,' said I, 'what it utters is its only stock and store / Caught from some unhappy master whom unmerciful Disaster / Followed fast and followed faster till his songs one burden bore'" (*POE* 84). The narrator, we come to realize, cannot help translating the raven's meaningless soundings into the facticity of print. And once the "ebony" (*POE* 83) bird perches on the "pallid" (*POE* 86) bust of Pallas—a black character on a white surface—it begins to speak a maddening human message about the lost love Lenore. The narrator is the victim, as it were, of over-zealous prosodic analysis.

We are too. If the poem is about a scholar who over-interprets meaningless sounds and goes insane, the poem also *is* that. Poe could have written "The Raven" without its propulsive rhythm and interlocking rhymes. With these prosodic elements, we ourselves become the scholar in the poem the moment we make an interpretive decision about why he succumbs; we, too, take a series of monotonously repeated sounds and turn them into human meanings that they, in themselves, do not possess. Once we fall into Poe's trap, it can be hard to see the poem as anything but a cautionary tale about the dangers of fixing stable historical meaning to something as fleeting as poetic sound. Historical prosodists, beware, the poem seems to say, throwing a prescient smirk toward Eliot and other scholarly types hoping to make sound and sense cooperate. The poem's reception history would seem to underscore this warning. As scholars including Eliza Richards and Meredith McGill have demonstrated, one of the most attractive features of Poe's poetry for nineteenth-century readers was not its self-identical, historically stable character, but its openness to creative reproduction and repurposing. "The Raven" in particular, a poem openly cobbled together from past sources, during and after Poe's lifetime came to denote not a single text as much as "a discursive network that mediated a range of cultural conversations via proliferation."[31] "Poe casts the poem," writes Richards, "as a linguistic machine abandoned by its maker that invites readers to discover its mode of functioning and take over its operations."[32] So simultaneously derivative and generative were the sounds of Poe's poetry that, McGill observes, his work was frequently attributed to less well-known writers even as their work was attributed to him.[33]

The ongoing repurposing of Poe's poetry across the twentieth century and into our own, moreover, makes clear that this dimension of his work was not simply a nineteenth-century phenomenon. In 1990, when *The Simpsons* included a version of "The Raven" in its annual "Treehouse of Horror" Halloween special, the television series was extending this history of creative repurposing. Watching *The Simpsons*' "Raven" from start to finish, one is struck by how prosodically nuanced the sketch is and indeed how compatible it is with Poe's reflections on the poem. The sketch opens in the family's treehouse, where Lisa Simpson is reading from Poe's poem to her brother Bart and younger sister Maggie. "Once upon a midnight dreary," she begins, but at the midline caesura of Poe's long trochaic octameter lines, Lisa's girlish tenor voice is joined by the gravelly bass voice of James Earl Jones, best known to American audiences as the voice of Darth Vader. By the beginning of line 2, Jones is the sole narrator, and the scene has shifted to a somber, book-lined, though still cartoonish "chamber" recognizable as the setting of "The Raven." The poem's scholarly protagonist is played by the siblings' father Homer, who is initially seen slumbering in an armchair holding a book titled "Forgotten Lore: Vol. II."[34]

Equal parts high drama and grinning spoof, the sketch's campy mood is underscored when Bart's voice interjects after the first stanza to ask, sarcastically, "Are we scared yet?" To which Lisa responds, "Bart, he's establishing mood!" A similar exchange occurs when Homer's voice interrupts Jones's to speak the quoted parts of Poe's text (e.g. "'Sir,' said I, 'or Madam, truly

---

[31] Eliza Richards, "Poe's Lyrical Media: The Raven's Returns," in J. Gerald Kennedy and Jerome McGann, eds., *Poe and the Remapping of Antebellum Print Culture* (Baton Rouge: Louisiana State University Press, 2012), 209.

[32] Richards, "Poe's Lyrical Media," 206.

[33] See McGill, *American Literature and the Culture of Reprinting*, 141–44. Richards, "Poe's Lyrical Media," suggests that "Poe's 'Raven' trains readers in mass-media functions and encourages them to internalize that knowledge by rewriting the poem within their own media contexts. The poem's reproducibility, not its originality, underpins its exceptional longevity and vast, self-perpetuating, international literary presence" (201).

[34] David Silverman, "Treehouse of Horror," *The Simpsons*, Season 2, Episode 3, Fox, 30:00, October 25, 1990.

your forgiveness I implore'"), producing rapid shifts of vocal timber and pacing while nevertheless maintaining the lines' larger trochaic structure. These
interruptions come across as comic, but their very abruptness lets us see them
as what linguists call segments, "discrete unit[s] that can be identified, either
physically or auditorily, in the stream of speech."[35] In contrast to what I earlier called the raven's merely analog processing power, which can reproduce
speech but not segment it, the television spectacle of The Simpsons' "Raven"
puts on full display the wide range of tools that an audio-visual medium can
use to splice and organize verbal matter.[36] While many of these segmentation
tools are of a more technical nature than would typically concern a linguist, the
TV sketch explores the more properly linguistic level of consonants, vowels,
and phonemes as well. The first sounding of the "Nevermore!" refrain, which
concludes stanza 8 in Poe's original text, occurs differently in the Simpsons version. Instead of the refrain we all expect, a raven with Bart's head speaks his
character's trademark insult: "Eat my shorts!" Lisa is again annoyed: "Bart,
stop it! He says 'nevermore' and that's all he'll ever say." But Bart's cheeky
substitution is entirely consistent with Poe's conception of the poem and its
reception history, built as Bart's phrase is around the "o" and "r" phonemes Poe
claimed as the germs of "The Raven." That Bart creatively repurposes while
Lisa demands lockstep repetition is further ironic in that the series portrays
Lisa as the gifted and conscientious student while Bart, in each episode's opening credits, is seen rotely transcribing a sentence beginning "I will not . . . " at
the school blackboard as punishment for his most recent misdeed. Later in the
"Raven" sketch, Homer is struck in the head by the poem's "unseen censer" and
responds with his own trademark exclamation ("d'oh!")—yet another variant
of the germinal "o" sound that is at once semantically meaningless and unmis-
takably Homeric. "Stupid censer," Homer mopes, and the unlikelihood that
this endearingly slow-witted father would know what a censer is underscores
again the purely phonetic aptness of much of the poem's linguistic materials.

In consulting the Simpsons' "Raven" it may seem that I am opposing scholarly prosodic analysis to popular remediation. But popular repurposings of
Poe's poetry also entail prosodic judgments, whether called that or not. As
writers, producers, voice actors, and cartoonists perform and modify a poem
like "The Raven," they necessarily gain a deeper understanding of its verbal
structures, often precisely by modifying these structures. One reason this creative modification can be difficult to see as a form of prosodic analysis is

---

[35] David Crystal, A Dictionary of Linguistics & Phonetics, 5th Edition (New York: Blackwell, 2003),
408–9.
[36] As if in winking acknowledgment of this fact, a portrait of Marge (who plays the role of "lost
Lenore") splices her famously tall hairdo across two distinct canvases.

that academic criticism tends to think of literature in terms of printed texts; indeed our professional and pedagogical obligations depend, in a quite practical sense, on being on the same page as students and fellow scholars. Yet as Richards and McGill have shown, and as popular remediations of Poe continue to show, such a model does not capture the "complex forms of authorial agency" that characterize Poe's poetics.[37] Though printed editions are by definition meant to present functionally equivalent texts to readers, when it comes to something as intimate and idiosyncratic as prosodic form, no text is self-identical. "The Raven," its reception history, and Poe's commentary on the poem insist on this point by revealing how minute, seemingly neutral phonological features of a verbal text (e.g. "the long *o* ... in connection with *r*") can signify in drastically different ways when engaged by different people using different media platforms. Each prosodic rubric brought to bear on a poem, regardless of sophistication, will not simply measure verbal structure but will help determine it.

And yet "The Rationale of Verse" suggests the opposite. If Poe's poetry, as I have suggested, performatively exposes the gap between local prosodic effects and larger prosodic rubrics, his long treatise on prosody and versification seems intent on closing this gap. Claiming to have developed a one-size-fits-all theory of prosody that will reveal poetry's basically oral, acoustic nature, the essay proceeds as if the raft of developments in literary and media history from the origins of human vocalization to the present—chief among them, writing and print—could be seamlessly integrated into this oral poetics; as if, in other words, these developments did not themselves alter the nature of poetic composition and reception. The essay's logical contradictions and its bombastic, vituperative tone have led generations of critics to wonder if Poe is writing in jest or is simply off his rocker.[38] As Poe's editors Stuart Levine and Susan F. Levine admit, "Viewed in the terms in which we customarily think of English verse, 'The Rationale of Verse' seems perverse and not very sensible."[39] Yet in staging its brazenly transhistorical argument, Poe's essay effectively exposes the centuries-long sedimentation of media and literary practice that comprise the modern poetic voice, and which no strictly

---

[37] McGill, *American Literature and the Culture of Reprinting*, 149.

[38] See the opinions of Edmund C. Stedman and George Edward Woodberry, *The Works of Edgar Allan Poe*, ed. Stedman and Woodberry, vol. 6 (Chicago: Stone and Kimball, 1895), xiv, and Arthur H. Quinn and Edward H. O'Neill, *The Complete Poems and Stories of Edgar Allan Poe*, ed. Quinn and O'Neill, vol. 2 (New York: Knopf, 1946), 1087.

[39] Stuart Levine and Susan F. Levine, Introduction to "The Rationale of Verse," in *Edgar Allan Poe: Critical Theory, the Major Documents*, 77.

linguistic (i.e. non-media-informed) theory of prosody can adequately parse.[40] Given the many ironies and contradictions of "Rationale," I have found it most effective to present Poe's salient claims as genuine claims before critiquing or contextualizing them. This allows the essay's long ironic arc to become visible, though it is no substitute for reading the essay oneself. As in Poe's poetry, the critical content of "Rationale" emerges as a function of readerly performance. Indeed, it is precisely by leading his readers through forty pages of increasingly convoluted descriptions of acoustic phenomena that Poe is able to illustrate the media contingencies bearing on all verbal and poetical acts.

Poe begins "Rationale" by locating the origin of poetry in what he calls a universal human predilection for acoustic "equality," for affective experiences of sonic patterning that yield a sense of "similarity, proportion, identity, repetition, and adaptation or fitness."[41] With equality as a "natural principle," Poe suggests that "The rudiment of verse may, possibly, be found in the *spondee*. The very germ of a thought seeking satisfaction in equality of sound, would result in the construction of words of two syllables, equally accented" (*ROV* 88).[42] From the primordial spondee, Poe posits, poets would have proceeded to develop verse of greater rhythmic complexity until a need to "[curtail] . . . the length of a sequence" would have led them to establish the concept of the poetic line as such (*ROV* 90). "Lines being once introduced, the necessity of distinctly defining these lines *to the ear*, (as yet written verse does not exist,) would lead to a scrutiny of their capabilities *at their terminations*:—and now would spring up the idea of equality in sound between the final syllables—in other words, of *rhyme*" (*ROV* 90–91). Even as poets developed these layers of sonic complexity, Poe stresses, their verse would have maintained a regular temporal pulse: "The principle of *equality* in verse," Poe explains, "admits . . . of variation at certain points, for the relief of monotone . . . but the point of *time* is that point which, being the rudimental one, must never be tampered with at all" (*ROV* 96).

---

[40] Poe's penchant for critical hoaxing has been more thoroughly documented in relation to "The Philosophy of Composition." Stéphane Mallarmé, "Notes on the Poems of Poe," in Jean Alexander, *Affidavits of Genius: Edgar Allan Poe and the French Critics, 1847–1924* (Port Washington: Kennikat Press, 1971), calls the essay a "pure intellectual game" (217). Dennis Pahl, "De-Composing Poe's 'Philosophy,'" *Texas Studies in Literature and Language*, 38/1 (Spring 1996), suggests we read it as another one of Poe's tales, "just as highly wrought and complex" (2).

[41] Poe, "The Rationale of Verse," in *Edgar Allan Poe: Critical Theory, the Major Documents*, 87. Subsequent references to this essay are cited parenthetically and abbreviated *ROV*.

[42] Poe's arch claims about the primitive spondee find a dead-serious counterpart in Simon Jarvis, "Prosody as Cognition," *Critical Quarterly*, 40/4 (1998): "Could we really say what a stress is, we might have come to the end of our nihilism, because we might be able to understand a single affective duration not as the endless repetition of an instantaneous passage from being into nothing, but as a real experience, the foundation of any possible ontology" (13).

Yet how to represent and enforce these temporally equal intervals? That is, which medium, or which arrangement of media, is best equipped to sustain the desired "equality" effect? This is less of a problem in the pre-literate "night of Time" in which "Rationale" imaginatively begins, an age whose primary orality well suits a purely acoustic poetics (*ROV* 91). In a modern age, however, poetry's sounds are represented by alphabetic scripts whose discrete, approximate mode of capturing speech sounds—unlike the continuous mode of a phonographic raven—opens the door to prosodic variance when these visual texts spur future readings. Anticipating media theorists such as Walter Ong and Marshall McLuhan, Poe cautions readers to keep in mind the "oil and water of the eye and ear" when scanning lines of verse (*ROV* 106).[43] Ideally, he suggests, a reader confronted with a poem's printed text should not need to adjust her reading practices in order for the poem's prosodic features to be accurate and audible. "*That* rhythm is erroneous," Poe elaborates, "which *any* ordinary reader *can*, without design, read improperly. It is the business of the poet so to construct his line that the intention *must* be caught *at once*" (*ROV* 100).[44]

Poe cites the opening lines of Lord Byron's "Bride of Abydos" as an example of a poem whose text has been crafted to support this kind of democratic prosody. "The flow of these lines . . . is very sweet and musical," Poe observes (*ROV* 104). "Yet I have heard men, professing to be scholars, who made no scruple of abusing these lines of Byron's on the ground that they were musical in spite of *all law*" (*ROV* 105). Such bookish prosodies, according to Poe, transform poetry that "flows so smoothly to the ear" into "a mere jumble of catalecticism, acatalecticism, and hypermeter—not to say worse" (*ROV* 106). To cleanse his reader's audio-visual palate, Poe relineates Byron's poetry as prose, marking the divisions between audible poetic feet only to underscore that such visual markings are, in fact, superfluous:

> Know ye the | land where the | cypress and | myrtle Are | emblems of | deeds that are | done in their | clime— Where the | rage of the | vulture, the | love of the | turtle Now | melt into | softness, now | madden to | crime? (*ROV* 106)

---

[43] Marshall McLuhan, *The Gutenberg Galaxy: The Making of Typographic Man* (Toronto: University of Toronto Press, 2011), explores how "literary qualities" are also functions of specific media environments, discerning within a culture of "print technology . . . the diminution of oral qualities" and within "the electronic age . . . a great diminishing of the special qualities of print culture, and a revival of oral and auditory values in verbal organization" (108). See also Walter Ong, *Orality and Literacy* (New York: Routledge, 2002).

[44] At the risk of getting ahead of ourselves, we should note the irony of Poe's liberal usage of italics— printed prose's coarse prosody—to demand acoustically felicitous poetic rhythms.

Poe's point is that whether one calls these units *dactyls, triplets,* or *whatchamacallits,* nearly all anglophone readers will feel, in the act of enunciation, the regular musical beats this poetic text lays down.[45]

Yet not all verse employs rhythmically regular units, as Poe concedes. Many poems incorporate metrical substitutions or extra syllables that risk throwing off the "flow" of the prosody. Poe points to a line by Pope:

> or laugh | and shake | in Rab | elais ea | sy chair, | (*ROV* 96)

In this line of iambic pentameter the fragment "elais" poses a problem, Poe notes, because it contains two syllables instead of the single short or unstressed syllable. To fix this, Poe suggests that "each syllable must be pronounced as distinctly as possible . . . but with twice the rapidity in which the ordinary short syllable is enunciated" (*ROV* 97). Poe is, in effect, requesting a musical subdivision. He is asking that readers perform "elais ea" as two sixteenth notes followed by a quarter note, in order to fit an iambic schema that normally runs as one eighth note followed by a quarter note. A trickier prosodic case presents itself in lines Poe cites by the American poet Christopher Pearse Cranch:

> Many are the thoughts that come to me
> In my lonely musing;
> And they drift so strange and swift
> There's no time for choosing (*ROV* 100)

These lines eventually settle into a trochaic ballad meter, but the very first foot squeezes four syllables ("Many are the") into a space that would normally contain just two. To maintain the strict 2:1 temporal relationship Poe requires between a trochee's "long" and "short" syllables, the poet suggests that the final three syllables of the foot ("y are the") must be made to occupy precisely half as much time as the first syllable ("Man"). In other words, the final three syllables must each be performed six times as fast as the first syllable. This rhythm

---

[45] George Saintsbury, *A History of English Prosody: From the Twelfth Century to the Present Day,* vol. 1 (London: Macmillan and Co., 1910), makes the same point in the introduction to his three-volume study: "Therefore the battle of Accent v. Quantity, which seems to interest most writers on Prosody so much . . . When I speak of Prosody I mean: *The laws and variations observable in the rhythmical and metrical groupings of sets of the two values just referred to.* And I call these two values 'long' and 'short' just as I might call them 'Abracadabra' and 'Abraxas'—absolutely without prejudice or preference to any theory of the exact process by which the one becomes Abraxas or the other Abracadabra" (5).

could certainly be put toward satisfying ends in a piece of music, but as an unaccompanied poetic speech act it is highly unnatural. The final three syllables ("y are the") are simply too fast as Poe would have them. Slow them down to compensate, and the first syllable ("Man") becomes comically elongated.

We might pause here to note the irony that has developed around Poe's stated goal of theorizing a purely oral, acoustic poetics. Putting aside the question of whether individual rhythms are performable or not, we can't help noticing how thoroughly "Rationale" exploits the visual and spatial affordances of print—segmented words, textual citations, odd diacritical marks, sheer paginated length—to mount its argument. This irony reaches its apex when Poe unveils an elaborate system of visual scansion that he claims "will answer the real purpose . . . the purpose of expressing to the eye the exact relative value of every syllable employed in Verse" (ROV 109). Featuring a mix of whole numbers and fractions, some placed above the line, some below, the arcane visual language of Poe's scansion is anything but an aid to rhythmically accurate performance (Figure 2.1). Even if it were, we should recall the lesson of "The Raven," which builds its phonological parable around "o" and "r," to demonstrate that there is no such thing as "the exact relative value of every syllable employed in Verse." Different readers will respond to the same textual material in different ways. Poe accentuates these ironies by glossing his system's new and improved poetic feet with some of the essay's most comic terminology. "That the syllables *elais ea* do not compose an anapæst is evident, and the signs of their accentuation are erroneous. The foot might be written thus (ˇ ˉ), the inverted crescents expressing double quick time; and might be called a bastard iambus" (ROV 97). To the "bastard iambus" and "double quick time" Poe adds a "bastard trochee," "quick trochee," and a caesura that is "always *longer than 'long'*" (ROV 110). The caesura, Poe explains, "must be accented, above [the line], with 1½; for this is the relative value of the iambus . . . For the complex 1½, however, it would be advisable to substitute the simpler expression $^3/_2$ which amounts to the same thing" (ROV 110). Anticipating questions regarding the quick trochee's absent counterpart, Poe explains: "The quick iambus is not yet created, and most probably never will be; for it would be excessively useless, awkward, and liable to misconception—" (ROV 110).

It would be hard to find a better assessment of "Rationale" as a whole, which having opened with an affect-oriented acoustical poetics, ends very near the jumble of bookish jargon Poe first set out to overturn. Indeed, as Stuart and Susan Levine observe, "had [Poe's system] caught on . . . foundries

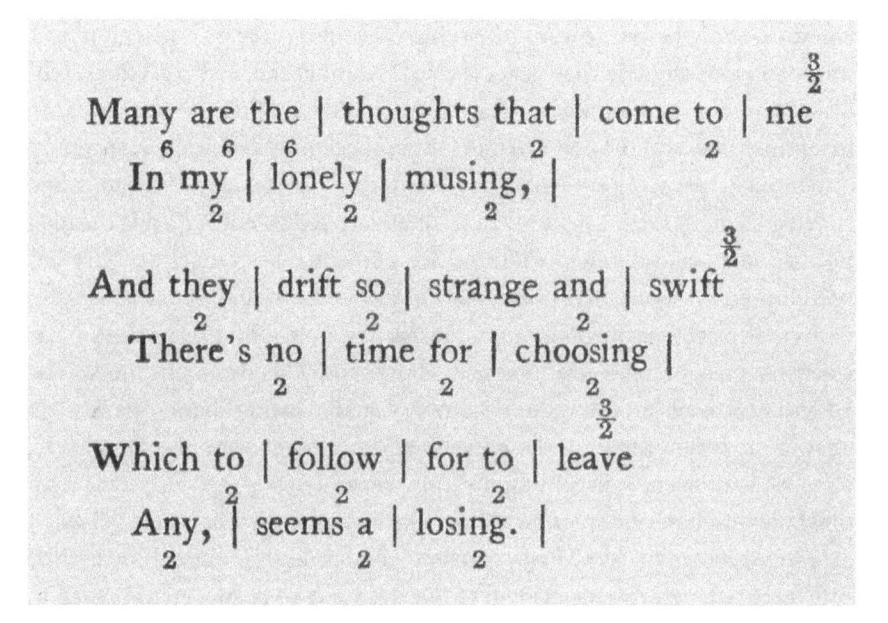

Figure 2.1   Edgar Allan Poe's system of scansion from "The Rationale of Verse,"
as reproduced in *The Complete Works of Edgar Allan Poe*, vol. 14, ed. James A.
Harrison (New York: Crowell & Co., 1902), 251. Bodleian Library, Oxford
University

would have cast special type to handle it. Since it did not, each reprinting
of 'The Rationale of Verse' has involved improvisation, errors, or both."[46]
Moving from primitive spondees, to acoustic "lines" of verse defined by end-
rhyme, to scripted poetical texts, to a paratextual system of scansion aimed at
print distribution, Poe's attempt to strong-arm the prosodic contours of verse
into a temporally homogenized, ahistorical grid exposes the range of developments in media and literary history that make such an effort so open to
critique. I take this irony to be deliberate, but the essay makes the same point
whether or not we think Poe is in on the joke. That point comes in the form
of a warning against taking prosodic theory as natural law.[47] Ingeniously, Poe

[46] Levine and Levine, Introduction to "The Rationale of Verse," 79. Indeed, even typing this chapter
in Microsoft Word required some digital legerdemain to render Poe's wonderful "3/2."
[47] The closest thing to a natural prosodic law may be what modern linguists term isochrony, the
division of speech into perceptibly equivalent temporal units. Christopher Aruffo, "Reconsidering Poe's
'Rationale of Verse,'" *Poe Studies*, 44/1 (2011): 69–88, argues that "Rationale" is a straight-faced attempt
to articulate a theory of isochrony *avant la lettre*. For examples of later nineteenth-century poets who
developed isochronous theories of prosody, see Coventry Patmore, *Essay on English Metrical Law*,
ed. Mary Augustine Roth (Washington: The Catholic University of America Press, 1961), and Sidney
Lanier, *The Science of English Verse* (New York: Charles Scribner's Sons, 1880).

administers this warning by enlisting us in a long-form performative exercise: in physically articulating his extreme rhythms or attempting to reproduce his scansion typographically, we are made to realize the basically ad hoc nature of all prosodic systems. What "Rationale" finally suggests, then, is not that scansion and prosodic analysis are useless, but that they are partial and, when administered on broad social scales, ideological. Products of culture, these analytic tools register and privilege certain classes of sonic features over others. They do not sit neutrally apart from what Poe calls "the poem per se" but, once evoked, themselves become mediating agents in the production of prosodic form.[48]

We might summarize the previous two sections by observing that, if "The Raven" underscores the gap between verbalization and prosodic analysis, "Rationale" ironically attempts to close it. The first instance alerts historicist approaches to the limits of assigning singular historical meaning to something as ephemeral and idiosyncratic as phonetic sound, while the second instance alerts formalist approaches to the limits of standardizing formal features in order to open them to transhistorical comparative analysis. Here I turn to a single poem, "The Bells," to illustrate further how Poe's double critique plays out in practice, which is to say in real-time performance interspersed with prosodic reflection. A perennial favorite for virtuoso recitation, "The Bells" has also enjoyed a particularly dubious reputation among academic readers. If the conceit of "Rationale" is that we are enlisted in judging Poe's misguided attempt to synthesize and supersede centuries of prosodic debate, the invitation of "The Bells" seems at first glance more simple: enunciate the poem's language as scripted, and you will hear the bells of the title.

Taking the poem from the top, a traditional prosodic analysis would likely scan the opening lines, and most of the poem, as a series of trochees:

> **Hear** the **sledg**es with the **bells**—
> **Silver bells!**
> ***What*** a **world** of **merri**ment their **melo**dy fore**tells**! (*POE* 92)

The trochaic reading gets the natural stress patterns of individual words correct, and from a certain perspective is quite acceptable.[49] But the overall result

---

[48] Poe, "The Philosophy of Composition," 62.

[49] For turn-of-the-century trochaic readings of "The Bells," see J. Scott Clark, *A Practical Rhetoric for Instruction in English Composition and Revision in Colleges and Intermediate Schools* (New York: Henry Holt, 1886), 349, and Margaret S. Mooney, *Composition-Rhetoric from Literature: For High Schools, Academies and Normal Schools* (New York: Brandow Printing Company, 1903), 291.

is pretty heavy-footed. How else might we perform these lines? A second option takes the poem in a more explicitly musical direction. For while its irregular lineation disguises the fact, other aspects of the poem's text—phrasal structure, syllabic rhythms, punctuation—map out a musical framework of regular beats and four-beat bars. The virtue of this reading is that it decreases the accentual-syllabic density of the trochaic model by introducing the fleeter sixteenth note as the smallest unit of prosodic measure. In this reading, the first two words of the poem ("Hear the") serve as sixteenth-note pick-ups to the downbeat arriving on "**sledge**s":

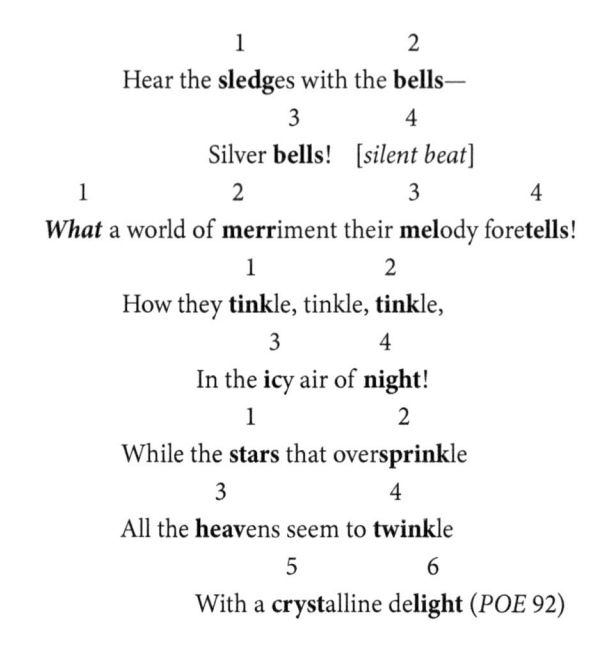

```
                    1              2
        Hear the sledges with the bells—
                         3         4
               Silver bells!  [silent beat]
        1            2             3         4
   What a world of merriment their melody foretells!
                      1            2
           How they tinkle, tinkle, tinkle,
                    3          4
           In the icy air of night!
                    1            2
        While the stars that oversprinkle
           3                 4
       All the heavens seem to twinkle
                    5            6
           With a crystalline delight (POE 92)
```

Note how Poe arranges his text to vary what might otherwise be a pretty incessant and uniform string of sixteenth notes, while still maintaining the beat. Some lines (1, 3, 5) end with words that receive the temporal value of an eighth note; others (4, 6, and 7) enjamb propulsively into the next in a flurry of unbroken sixteenths; and one line (2) ends with a word ("bells!") that insists we wait two full beats before proceeding to the following downbeat, which Poe cues—precisely, in italics—on "*What*."[50]

---

[50] If this musical reading of "The Bells" seems willful, try performing the poem with my posited musical beats shifted either left or right by half and see how unnatural it feels: "What a **world** of merri**ment** their melody foretells!"

Yet if the musical reading addresses the poem's initial trochaic sluggishness, it is not a long-term fix. In fact, it is by accepting the musical structure as normative that, in a turn befitting Poe's self-defeating ironies, our performance is subsequently sabotaged. That anomalous six-beat phrase in section 1, it turns out, is merely a foretaste of the challenges to come. Try performing aloud the opening of section 2 according to the musical structure:

> Hear the mellow wedding bells
>   Golden bells!
> *What* a world of happiness their harmony foretells!
>   Through the balmy air of night
>   How they ring out their delight!—
>   From the molten-golden notes,
>   And all in tune,
>   What a liquid ditty floats
> To the turtle-dove that listens while she gloats
>   On the moon! (*POE* 92–93)

The prosodic shape of the first three lines echoes fairly exactly that which opens section 1 and thus reaffirms the poem's larger four-beat musical structure. After this, however, the syntax and phrase lengths, rhymes and rhythms, and even typography so conspire to syncopate the line that the music is fled. Things are perhaps salvageable through line 6, but the pretty baldly iambic line 7 causes problems. Treating the words "And all in" as unaccented pick-up notes buys some time, but at the cost of making "tune" the end of a musical phrase even as it is, syntactically, very much in the middle of things. The poem's keyword "What" in line 8 may seem to promise a fresh start, but here it lacks italics, suggesting that it may not indicate a downbeat this time around. Later in the poem, lines like "By the **side** of the **pale-faced moon**" (*POE* 93) do not add or syncopate beats as much as scuttle the tempo entirely. Such lines can with practice be accommodated to the poem's four-beat musical bar, but it requires an anticipatory phonemic jiu-jitsu that is virtually impossible to pull off on a first or even second reading.

"The Bells," in an extreme but characteristic demonstration of Poe's prosody, presents itself as a palimpsestic layering of incongruous sound reproduction technologies: trochees that dissolve into sixteenth notes, rhymes that strengthen and then distort grammar, musical form dispelled by intransigent phonetic script. These mediating forces are gathered by the stable printed object we call a poem, yet the poem's prosodic structure is not self-identical.

This is the case not only because each reader engages the poem differently, but because each of the poem's constituent sound media has a different way of "Keeping, time, time, time" (*POE* 92). As Jason Camlot observes, "Poe's poem . . . seems to offer itself up as an empty bell jar whose pitch, shade of force, and tempo are wholly dependent on how the poem is sounded by its reader."[51] When these media are engaged by readers, they may well constellate into certain larger prosodic structures (e.g. a "trochaic" or a "musical" structure), but these structures are a matter of consensus rather than a feature of the poem's language as such. We can probably all agree that the poem's most notorious lines ("Of the bells, bells, bells, bells— / Bells, bells, bells—" [*POE* 93]) all but mandate a single prosodic option: namely the primitive, lockstep spondee Poe claims in "Rationale" to be the rudiment of verse. But this is the conformist exception that Poe uses to prove the rule of prosodic multiplicity. The utter temporal regularity of "bells, bells, bells, bells" casts in relief the enunciative indecision the poem induces at so many other points. This indecision, to reiterate a key point, is a function of the poem's language as a mediated substance. And all mediating elements are potentially significant. At 113 lines, "The Bells" takes up at least three pages in nearly any printed edition. Anyone performing the poem from a book must therefore contend with that most basic challenge to continuous sounded reading: the page turn. Such considerations tend to disappear in theory; in practice they cannot. This is what Jacques Derrida is getting at when he singles out "The Bells" as a cardinal instance not of language, but writing, and applauds Poe for throwing "semantic and thematic [meanings] . . . into indecision by the swinging or the suspended beat, the oscillation of the tongue."[52]

One way to respond to these performative gambits is to do what popular renditions of "The Bells" have often done to the poem: edit it. Such editing, I suggested earlier, is not non-prosodic. Rather, it registers and engages prosodically thorny spots in Poe's text by revising them or editing them out, modifying the text to better conform to an alternative, internally consistent prosodic logic, such as that offered by music.[53] Consider, for instance, the 1964 recording of "The Bells" by the folk singer Phil Ochs.[54] Like nineteenth-century readers who approached Poe's poetry not as self-identical visual texts

[51] Jason Camlot, *Phonopoetics: The Making of Early Literary Recordings* (Stanford: Stanford University Press, 2019), 56.

[52] Jacques Derrida, *Glas*, trans. John P. Leavey, Jr. and Richard Rand (Lincoln: University of Nebraska Press, 1986), 157.

[53] Poe, "The Poetic Principle," suggests that "There can be little doubt that in the union of Poetry with Music in its popular sense, we shall find the widest field for the Poetic development. The old Bards and Minnesingers had advantages which we do not possess—and Thomas More, singing his own songs, was, in the most legitimate manner, perfecting them as poems" (184–85).

[54] Phil Ochs, "The Bells," track 7 on *All the News That's Fit to Sing*, Elektra, 1964.

but as "discursive networks[s] that mediated a range of cultural conversations," Ochs edits the poem to meet his needs.[55]

The song opens with four unadorned, metronomic C# guitar tones that set the tempo at about 50 beats per minute. After one measure, Ochs adds a finger-picked guitar riff that accelerates, over the next two measures, until reaching a new tempo of 65 beats per minute. The accelerando effect is precipitous, producing the sensation, not inappropriate for "The Bells," that the wheels may be coming off. But Ochs has it under control and when his vocal part enters at the pick-up to measure 4, the edits he has made to Poe's poem ensure that syllabic and musical prosodies are mutually reinforcing. In the text below, which reproduces the first three sections of "The Bells," I have relineated Poe's original text so that it corresponds with Ochs' four-beat bar. Words that Ochs deletes from Poe's text are indicated with a strikethrough; words he adds are indicated with italics; and bolded syllables indicate the location of beats in each four-beat line. When Ochs drops entire lines from Poe's text, as he does increasingly as the poem progresses, the cancelled lines are indented to make clear that the leftmost lines are the ones he retains.

I.

Hear the **sledg**es with the **bells**, Silver **bells**   [*silent beat*]
What a world of **merr**iment their **mel**ody fore**tells**
How they **tink**le, tinkle, **tink**le, in the icy air of **night**
~~While the stars that oversprinkle~~
All the **heav**ens seem to **twink**le with a **cryst**alline de**light**

Keeping **time**, time, **time**, ~~in~~ *with* a **sort** of Runic **rhyme**
~~To~~ *From* the **tint**inabulation that so **mus**ically **wells**
From the **bells**, bells, **bells**, bells, **bells**, bells, **bells**
From the **jing**ling and the **tink**ling of the **bells**   [*silent beat*]

II.

Hear the **mell**ow wedding **bells**, Golden **bells**   [*silent beat*]
What a world of **happ**iness their **harm**ony fore**tells**
Through the **balm**y air of **night**, how they **ring** out their de**light**
~~From the molten-golden notes,~~
~~And all in tune,~~
~~What a liquid ditty floats~~
~~To the turtle-dove that listens, while she gloats~~

---

[55] Richards, "Poe's Lyrical Media," 209.

~~On the moon!~~
~~Oh, from out the sounding cells,~~
~~What a gush of euphony voluminously wells!~~
*Through the**dances** and the**yells**and the**rapt**ure that impels*

How it **swells**, how it **dwells**, on the **Fut**ure, how it **tells**
     ~~Of the rapture that impels~~
~~To~~ *From* the **swing**ing and the **ring**ing *of the **molten** golden **bells***
     ~~Of the bells, bells, bells,~~
Of the **bells**, bells, **bells**, bells, **bells**, bells, **bells**
~~To~~ *Of* the **rhym**ing and the **chim**ing of the **bells**   [*silent beat*]

                    III.
Hear the **loud** alarum **bells**—Brazen **bells**   [*silent beat*]
What tale of **terr**or, now, their **turb**ulency **tells**
          ~~In the startled ear of night~~
          ~~How they scream out their affright!~~
~~Too much~~ *Much too* **horr**ified to **speak**, *oh*, **they** can only **shriek**, ~~shriek,~~
          ~~Out of tune,~~
          ~~In a clamorous appealing to the mercy of the fire,~~
          ~~In a mad expostulation with the deaf and frantic fire,~~
*For **all** the ears to **know** how the **dang**er ebbs and **flows***

Leaping **high**er, higher, **high**er, with a **des**perate des**ire**
*In a **clam**orous ap**pea**ling to the **mercy** of the **fire***
          ~~And a resolute endeavor~~
          ~~Now—now to sit or never,~~
          ~~By the side of the pale-faced moon.~~
          ~~Oh, the bells, bells, bells!~~
          ~~What a tale their terror tells~~
          ~~Of Despair!~~
          ~~How they clang, and clash, and roar!~~
          ~~What a horror they outpour~~
          ~~On the bosom of the palpitating air!~~
          ~~Yet the ear it fully knows,~~
          ~~By the twanging,~~
          ~~And the clanging,~~
          ~~How the danger ebbs and flows;~~
          ~~Yet the ear distinctly tells,~~

~~In the jangling,~~
~~And the wrangling.~~
~~How the danger sinks and swells,~~
~~By the sinking or the swelling in the anger of the bells—~~
~~Of the bells—~~
Of the **bells**, bells, **bells**, bells, **bells**, bells, **bells**
In the **clam**or and the **clang**or of the **bells**   [*silent beat*]

Beginning at the largest prosodic level and borrowing from the vocabulary of song-writing, we can observe that Ochs repackages each stanza of Poe's poem into a four-line verse and a four-line chorus. Ochs therefore retains less and less of the poem's latter, longer sections because he needs only eight lines from each. To make his lines run smoothly, Ochs drops text that, in my earlier analysis, caused the most prosodic challenges. What I called the "anomalous six-beat phrase" in section 1, for instance, Ochs resolves by cutting two beats' worth of words ("While the **stars** that over**sprink**le"). Similarly, Ochs retains verbatim the three lines opening section 2 and then cuts the seven prosodically problematic lines that follow, replacing them with a single line of his own devising that is nevertheless cobbled together from bits of text taken from elsewhere in Poe's poem.[56] Whether or not one follows Ochs in consciously editing the linguistic content of the text, each voicing of "The Bells" entails a score of split-second editorial decisions, verbal shapings of, and in response to, the sound media the text assembles. This voice is an aspect of history, not autonomous lyricism. But the very multiplicity of prosodic options enabled by the poem is also a reminder that this voice's historical character is multiple, contingent, and open to revision.

In a passage near the end of "The Rationale of Verse," Poe invites us to join him in imagining a scene of poetic interpretation.

Now let us suppose that, a thousand years hence, when the "American language" is dead, a learned prosodist should be deducing from "careful observation" of our best poets, a system of scansion for our poetry. And let us suppose that this prosodist had so little dependence in the generality and

---

[56] The earliest textual material composed for "The Bells" was written not by Poe but by his friend Marie Louise Shew. See Arthur Hobson Quinn, *Edgar Allan Poe: A Critical Biography* (Baltimore: The Johns Hopkins University Press, 1998), 563–64. Poe reworked Shew's text over eighteen months into three distinct versions of the poem, two of which were published following Poe's death in 1849. Ochs' most significant revision to "The Bells" a century later is arguably its D major key signature, which resists or ironizes the descent into "moaning and groaning" that Poe's original text pursues.

immutability of the laws of Nature, as to assume in the outset, that, because we
lived a thousand years before his time, and made use of steam-engines instead
of mesmeric balloons, we must therefore have had a *very* singular fashion of
mouthing our vowels[.] (*ROV* 114)

This prosodist of the far distant future will not be merely gathering data, Poe
implies, but entering into an aesthetic experience shaped by the cultural and
technological differences between America in 1848 and his own interpretive
community in 2848. The "system of scansion" this prosodist produces, we are
to infer, will say as much about his own culture as about the "dead" world
of antebellum America. Poe exaggerates his timescale to make his point, but
he means it to apply at any scale. No prosodist, no matter how learned or
historically proximate to a given poetic composition, can ever close the gap
between real-time verbalization and second-order analysis, perceived form
and received discourse. This is what poems like "The Raven" and "The Bells"
so cleverly show and tell us. As scholars, we must therefore tease out the material, historical basis of poetry's media while also acknowledging the finally
idiosyncratic and ephemeral aspects of prosodic form as experienced from
one reader to the next. We can and should follow Poe's learned prosodist in
recovering evidence that speaks to how poetry was sounded in the past. But
Poe's fable is also a reminder that the value of this recovery can only ever manifest itself from the vantage of the present—the only place, after all, that we can
form a poem's language and feel it forming ours in return.

3

Syllable from Sound

In a poem composed in 1863, Emily Dickinson marvels at the power of the human brain:

> The Brain - is wider than the Sky -
> For - put them side by side -
> The one the other will contain
> With ease - and you - beside -[1]

A half century earlier, Wordsworth concluded *The Prelude* by praising "the mind of man."[2] Here Dickinson offers a more distinctly physiological take on human cognition, celebrating the biological organ rather than the philosophical abstraction. Romantic-era symbols of mental boundlessness—the sky in stanza 1, the sea in stanza 2—she presents as the results *of* brain function rather than adequate proxies for it. The very notion of a stable, expressive self (the first stanza's "you"), a notion on which the lyric tradition would seem to depend, Dickinson presents as the by-product of neurobiology. Only "God," she concedes in the poem's final stanza, might be considered equal to the brain's "weight." And yet the equivalence of Brain and God is not exact:

> For - Heft them - Pound for Pound -
> And they will differ - if they do -
> As Syllable from Sound -

Human beings partake of godliness but also swerve away from it, Dickinson's analogy proposes, in the same manner that a "Syllable" partakes of but also swerves away from "Sound." We are at once most divine and most ourselves when we contemplate the mysterious space between sound and sense, phonetics and phonology—when we practice prosody.

---

[1] Emily Dickinson, *The Poems of Emily Dickinson: Reading Edition*, ed. Ralph Franklin (Cambridge: Harvard University Press, 1998), 269. Subsequent references to this edition are cited parenthetically as *F* and refer to the poem number assigned by Franklin.
[2] William Wordsworth, *The Prelude: 1799, 1805, 1850*, ed. Jonathan Wordsworth, M. H. Abrams, and Stephen Gill (New York: Norton, 1979), 482.

Poetry, Sound, and the Matter of Prosody 1800–2000. Peter Miller, Oxford University Press. © Peter Miller (2025).
DOI: 10.1093/9780198937210.003.0004

Dickinson's own prosody may not on a first reading seem all that innovative. "The Brain - is wider than the Sky," like the majority of her poems, is written in ballad stanzas, a verse form often seen as simple or unsophisticated when compared to iambic pentameter or free verse. As we saw in Chapter 1, early readers of *Lyrical Ballads* made exactly this judgment when they distinguished between the collection's "barbarous" ballads and its "higher species" of blank verse. Academic readers of Poe's clamorous poetry dismissed it on similar grounds. Yet Dickinson's prosody grows more complex when we consider her poems not as self-identical linguistic texts but as media objects prone to historical change. As recent scholarship has highlighted, the manuscripts Dickinson produced in her Amherst bedroom in the latter half of the nineteenth century are quite different from the printed poems readers encountered in the century that followed.[3] Consider the manuscript of "The Brain - is wider than the Sky" (Figure 3.1), which boasts so many striking visual features that it can be difficult to know where to begin. Perhaps we first notice the ample space Dickinson leaves between words, which makes them appear almost to float independently of one another, weakening our sense of the poem's syntactical and prosodic form while strengthening our sense of its visual characteristics. Dickinson's short dashes, which resemble full stops, reinforce this effect, ambiguous in their rhetorical import yet unmissable as a feature of the manuscript. Another feature we are sure to notice is Dickinson's line breaks, which do not match those given in print editions. In the manuscript, the words "Sky," "Sea," "of God," and "do" each receive their own line. We might assume that these are simply runovers, instances where Dickinson ran out of page space and was forced onto a new line. Yet the manuscript of "The Brain - is wider than the Sky" is part of one of Dickinson's so-called fascicles, hand-bound booklets of poems that served as the poet's form of (private) self-publication, leaving open the possibility that the poem's lineation and layout may in fact be in the form the author intended.

Since the first printed edition of Dickinson's poetry appeared in 1890, successive generations of editors and critics have often seen their job as one of stripping away layers of prior editorial intervention, returning the poems to something like what Dickinson actually wrote. If Dickinson's first editors, Mabel Loomis Todd and Thomas Wentworth Higginson, altered the poet's work to make it more palatable to late nineteenth-century tastes—adding titles where there were none, standardizing odd spellings and punctuation,

---

[3] Broader interest in Dickinson's manuscript conventions dates to Thomas Johnson's 1955 scholarly edition of the poems, *The Poems of Emily Dickinson: Including Variant Readings Critically Compared with All Known Manuscripts* (Cambridge: Harvard University Press, 1955).

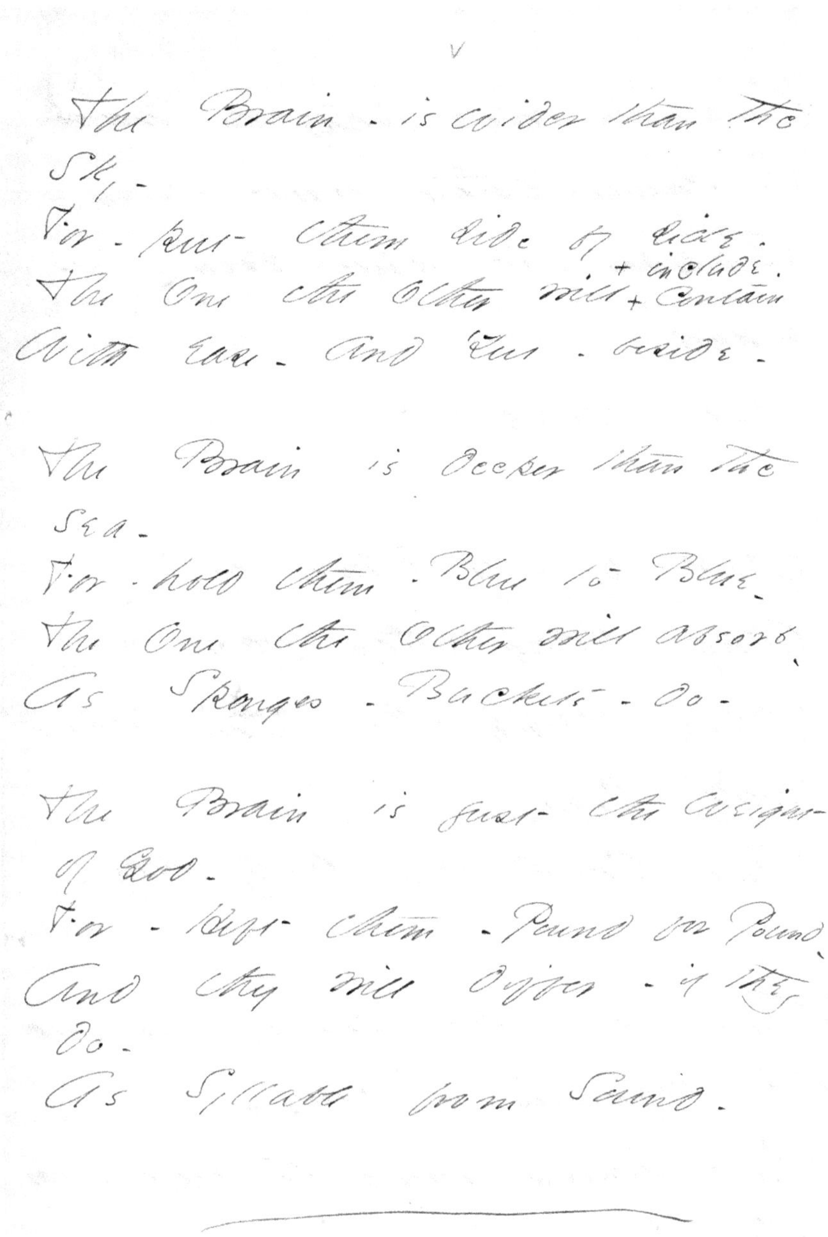

Figure 3.1 Manuscript of Emily Dickinson's 1863 poem "The Brain - is wider than the Sky." Emily Dickinson Collection, manuscript number A 84–6, Archives and Special Collections, Amherst College

smoothing out rhythms and rhymes, grouping poems in thematic clusters—
the most recent scholarly edition of the poems, Ralph Franklin's 1998 edition,
promises to restore "the text of each manuscript . . . including, within the capacity of standard type, Dickinson's spelling, capitalization, and punctuation."[4] A
facsimile edition of Dickinson's "Manuscript Books," also edited by Franklin,
allows readers to study "the bosses on the stationery, the sewing holes and
tears, the poet's alternate readings and penciled revisions, ink spots and other
stains offset onto adjacent leaves, and later markings by Susan Gilbert Dickinson, Mabel Todd, and others."[5] Meanwhile, the online Emily Dickinson
Archive makes high-resolution color images of Dickinson's manuscripts available to a still wider swath of readers, seeming to make good on Jerome
McGann's 1991 prediction that "the full significance of Dickinson's writing
will begin to appear when we explicate in detail the importance of the different papers she used, her famous 'fascicles,' her scripts and their conventions
of punctuation and layout."[6] As interest in the manuscripts has increased,
however, another camp of readers has wondered whether this "scriptural"
strand of Dickinson criticism has, in the poet John Shoptaw's words, "forfeit[ed] the aural experience of her poems for the graphic delights of her
manuscripts."[7] The longer we gaze at the curious visual features of Dickinson's
poems, Shoptaw suggests, the harder it is to appreciate their real-time prosodic
effects. Just because Dickinson's ballad meter is a well-worn form does not
mean it can be ignored.

Dickinson does not provide an answer as to whether readers are to prioritize her prosodies or her manuscripts, her verbal contours or her visual
forms. But her poems do contemplate a version of this choice at the level
of image and trope, routinely juxtaposing images of fluidity and gradience
with those of discrete particularity: "tint - and spot" (F 367), "Thread & Needle" (F 681), "Sound" and "Syllable" (F 598). Such pairings, instances of what
Mary Loeffelholz calls Dickinson's "wave-particle duality," trope an expan-
sive, supple lyricism as the obverse of a physical or conceptual singularity
(e.g. a stream of sound from which a single syllable is carved).[8] In doing so,

[4] Emily Dickinson, *The Poems of Emily Dickinson: Variorum Edition*, ed. Ralph Franklin, vol. 1
(Cambridge: Harvard University Press, 1998), 36. Margaret Dickie, "Dickinson in Context," *American
Literary History*, 7/2 (Summer 1995), surveys the editorial dilemma: "The issue is, then, how to allow
Dickinson her proper space and voice without trapping her in someone else's idea of her space and
voice, a problem without solution because if she is to be printed, she will have to be trapped" (323).
    [5] Emily Dickinson, *The Manuscript Books of Emily Dickinson*, ed. Ralph Franklin, vol. 1 (Cam-
bridge: Harvard University Press, 1981), xvi.
    [6] Jerome McGann, *The Textual Condition* (Princeton: Princeton University Press), 87. The Emily
Dickinson Archive, a collaboration of multiple New England archives holding Dickinson manuscripts,
is available at edickinson.org.
    [7] John Shoptaw, "Listening to Dickinson," *Representations*, 86/1 (Spring 2004): 21.
    [8] Mary Loeffelholz, "'We send the Wave to find the Wave': Dickinson's Wave-Particle Duality," *Dick-
inson Electronic Archives*, https://www.emilydickinson.org/emily-dickinson-lyrical-ecologies-forays-

they suggest that poetic form is not a feature of text as much as an effect produced at the intersection point of vocal performance and textual media. "Did
you ever read one of her Poems backward, because the plunge from the front
overturned you?" Dickinson wrote on an undated piece of stationary, apparently in reference to her own work. "I sometimes (often have, many times)
have – A something overtakes the Mind."[9] In this act of unconventional reading, Dickinson reads her own poetry backwards in order to dispel the illusion
of lyric presence, thrilling at the gap between the sounds she enunciates and
the words scripted on the page. Reading in the same spirit of creative remediation, this chapter approaches prosodic analysis of Dickinson's work not in
terms of scanning the sounds of a given text, nor of restoring a certain document to its original discourse network, but in terms of foregrounding certain
aspects of a poem's media system (e.g. syntactic structure, metrical convention,
manuscript and/or print layout, punctuation) within a given performance.
Remediating rather than reconstructing Dickinson's work, I examine the shifting historical character of her prosody as evidenced by her use of ballad
meter and punctuation, by contemporaneous developments in sound recording technology, and by the recent Apple TV series *Dickinson*, perhaps the most
overtly multimediated version of Dickinson to date.

In his ground-breaking 1955 edition of Dickinson, Thomas Johnson transcribes poem 910 as follows:

> Experience is the Angled Road
> Preferred against the Mind
> By – Paradox – the Mind itself –
> Presuming it to lead
>
> Quite Opposite – How Complicate
> The Discipline of Man –
> Compelling Him to Choose Himself
> His Preappointed Pain –[10]

Dickinson's poem explores the metaphor of "Experience" (i.e. collective wis-
dom or authority) as an "Angled Road," a route forward that we accept despite
not knowing where it will lead and "against" our own intuitive sense of

---

into-the-field/we-send-the-wave-to-find-the-wave-dickinson-s-wave-particle-duality. As Loeffelholz
puts it: "Is a lasting poem more like the obdurate, unique, indivisible atom, or like the endlessly
propagating form of the wave?"

[9] Emily Dickinson, qtd. in Susan Howe, *My Emily Dickinson* (New York: New Directions, 1985),
23. Some readers have suggested that Dickinson's "her" refers to either Elizabeth Barrett Browning or
George Eliot.

[10] Dickinson, *Poems*, ed. Johnson, 668.

direction. The "Paradox" is therefore the mind's ability to perceive its own limits, to defer agency to an outside authority even though, or perhaps precisely because, one cannot fathom the grounds of that authority. "Discipline," by contrast, names a position of agential or hermeneutic confidence. When we operate by discipline, any resulting "Pain" is "Preappointed" because the choice was our own. Asserting individual agency, we produce the context for subsequent affective and intellectual sensations.

In Johnson's transcription, the poem presents a straightforward case of ballad meter, alternating regularly between iambic tetrameter and iambic trimeter lines, with line endings reinforced by the slant rhymes of *Mind/lead* and *Man/Pain*. Interpreted against the poem's theme, Johnson's text appears content to side with "Experience," with the aural, collective, mutually reinforcing prosodic elements that make up ballad meter. Yet Dickinson's manuscript is lineated differently and contains other visual elements (e.g. word spacing, size and position of dashes) that Johnson's text regularizes. Believing that these elements are important to Dickinson's poem, the poet Susan Howe offered her own transcription in her 1993 book *The Birth-mark*:

> Experience is the Angled
> Road
> Preferred   against   the
> Mind
> By - Paradox - The
> Mind   itself -
> Presuming it to lead[11]

Howe's transcription gains its power by disrupting what she calls the "hymn-like stanzas" of Johnson's version. Extra white space between words slows recitation, while line breaks in the middle of iambic feet (e.g. "the **Ang** | led / **Road**") seem to both pause and rush the transition into the next line. "These lines traced by pencil or in ink on paper," writes Howe, "were formed by an innovator." "This visible handwritten sequence establishes an enunciative clearing outside intention while obeying intuition's agonistic necessity."[12] The poem as Howe presents it now sides with "Discipline," with intuition, innovation, and singularity of intellectual purpose as evidenced by the singularity of Dickinson's handwriting. Bringing her theory to Ralph Franklin, then currently at work at a new edition of the

[11] Susan Howe, *The Birth-mark: Unsettling the Wilderness in American Literary History* (Middleton: Wesleyan University Press, 1993), 136. Howe's transcription features hand-drawn dashes that seek to more accurately reproduce the shape, length, orientation, and placement in Dickinson's manuscripts.
[12] Howe, *The Birth-mark*, 136.

poems, Howe was disappointed when he wrote back saying that her "suggestion about line breaks depended on an 'assumption' that one reads in lines; he asked, 'what happens if the form lurking in the mind is the *stanza*?'"[13]

Without attempting to adjudicate between as formidable of Dickinson scholars as Johnson, Howe, and Franklin, we can nevertheless note that while each of their versions of "Experience is the Angled Road" contains the same words in the same order, their texts' prosody differs depending on which mediating elements the editor chooses to foreground. Franklin sides with Johnson in accepting the acoustically defined ballad stanza as the poem's decisive prosodic unit, whereas Howe places more importance on the visible, scriptural elements of Dickinson's manuscripts. Still more permutations appear when we consult the earliest printed version of the poem, in Martha Dickinson Bianchi and Alfred Leete Hampson's 1929 edition. This version accepts a ballad meter lineation while also normalizing capitalization, eliminating dashes, and adding periods and commas in an attempt to clarify Dickinson's syntax. Yet these changes ironically produce a text that obscures the poem's highest-level, quatrain-based prosodic architecture:

> Experience is the angled road
> Preferred against the mind
> By paradox, the mind itself
> Presuming it to lead
> Quite opposite. How complicate
> The discipline of man,
> Compelling him to choose himself
> His pre-appointed pain.[14]

Instead of two visually discrete ballad stanzas, whose prosodic symmetry echoes the poem's thematic balancing of Experience and Discipline, the dominant structure of Bianchi and Hampson's single-stanza version is syntactical: two grammatically complete statements followed by modifying dependent clauses:

> 1a. Experience is the angled road preferred against the mind by paradox,
> 1b. the mind itself presuming it to lead [//] quite opposite.

[13] Howe, *The Birth-mark*, 134.
[14] Emily Dickinson, *Further Poems of Emily Dickinson*, ed. Martha Dickinson Bianchi and Alfred Leete Hampson (Boston: Little Brown & Co., 1929), 18.

2a.   How complicate the discipline of man,
2b.   compelling him to choose himself his pre-appointed pain.

I indicate the stanza break above [//] to underscore just how odd it feels, after having read Johnson, Franklin, or Howe's version, for the poem's syntax to continue across this threshold. Likely Bianchi and Hampson combined the poem's two quatrains precisely to make their innovative lineation appear less so. Push one stylistic element in a more conservative direction and another appears to gain new transgressive energies.[15]

If the conservative-experimental binary blurs when tested against the many possible arrangements of Dickinson's poetic media, so too does the aural-visual binary. John Shoptaw's illuminating analysis of Dickinson's prosody distinguishes between "*speech beats* (emphases we give to words in speech—usually nouns, main verbs, and polysyllabic words) and *song beats* (where we expect the beat: in Dickinson it's generally on alternating syllables, or where the sound patterning—long vowels, alliterating or clustered consonants—calls for it)."[16] To indicate moments where these two categories overlap, Shoptaw explains, he "use[s] a grave accent to distinguish syllables that are unstressed or lightly stressed in ordinary speech but carry a song beat in her verse."[17] Even as he critiques the visualist bias in Dickinson studies, then, Shoptaw employs paratextual notation features to mount his auralist argument. This is not a criticism of Shoptaw's central claim—that the attention to Dickinson's manuscripts can distract from her poetry's aural characteristics—but simply an observation of how difficult it is to theorize and discuss poetic sound without recourse to the visual affordances of writing and print.

In part this is because poets themselves incorporate para-linguistic visual elements into their work, as Dickinson does with her famous dashes. Do these punctuation marks contain prosodic information? Readers have often assumed so. Yet so ubiquitous are the dashes, and so unconventionally placed in terms of syntax, that they tend if anything to disrupt rather than guide pronunciation, particularly for first-time readers. Anyone who has taught

---

[15] A similar conclusion might be drawn from the range of opinions on Dickinson's ballad stanzas more generally. Victoria Morgan, *Emily Dickinson and Hymn Culture: Tradition and Experience* (London: Routledge, 2016), suggests that Dickinson's ballad meter evokes Christian hymns "only to rupture and radically reconfigure them" (45), whereas Michael Manson, "'The Thews of Hymn': Dickinson's Metrical Grammar," in Martha Nell Smith and Mary Loeffelholz, eds., *A Companion to Emily Dickinson* (Oxford: Wiley Blackwell, 2014), 368–90, suggests that Dickinson's ballad meter is inherently conservative and that her poetry's radicalness emerges not from its prosody but its diction and syntax.

[16] Shoptaw, "Listening to Dickinson," 30.

[17] Shoptaw, "Listening to Dickinson," 30.

Dickinson can vouch for the palpable awkwardness the dashes induce in students asked to read in front of their peers. Consider this stanza from a poem composed in 1862:

> Geraniums - tint - and spot -
> Low Daisies - dot -
> My Cactus - splits her Beard
> To show her throat - (*F* 367)

Because only one dash interrupts the syntax of lines 3 and 4 (splitting the subject "Cactus" from the verb "splits"), their iambic rhythm comes through largely intact. Retroactively, we can apply this iambic norm to lines 1 and 2 and make the syllabic bookkeeping work: "Ge**ran** | iums **tint** | and **spot**." But the iambic rhythm just detected comes at the expense of the dashes, whose prosodic meaning remains unclear. If we instead privilege the dashes, taking them to indicate rests or pauses, as some readers have proposed, we weaken the stanza's larger metrical structure—alternating trimeter and dimeter lines—while drawing attention to individual words. Each of these options, exemplifying a trope that recurs throughout Dickinson's poetry, asks us to query the relation of a "tint" to a "spot," to think of something characterized by fluidity and gradience (i.e. speech sound) in terms of a conceptual unit premised on discreteness and iterability (i.e. iambs, dashes). As Mary Loeffelholz observes, "in the vernacular physics of Dickinson's poetry . . . atomistic and undulatory descriptions of the world co-exist in creative tension."[18]

We have been considering the Dickinson dash as a feature whose meaning is obscure. But here again spots shade to tints, posited singularities into swerves of action. Print typographies make individual punctuation marks appear self-identical, but the dashes in Dickinson's manuscripts vary widely in length, size, angle, curvature, and position.[19] As early as 1960, Charles Anderson suggested that the variable dashes were not grammatical or even strictly rhetorical marks but were part of Dickinson's "attempt to create a new system of musical notation for reading her verse."[20] Edith Wylder developed the suggestion into a working theory of Dickinson's graphical notation system, arguing

---

[18] Loeffelholz, "Dickinson's Wave-Particle Duality."
[19] Johnson adopts a medium-length endash for his edition. Franklin adopts a narrower hyphen.
[20] Charles Anderson, *Emily Dickinson's Poetry: Stairway of Surprise* (New York: Holt, Rinehart and Winston, 1960), 305.

that her punctuation habits were drawn directly from nineteenth-century elocution primers and indicated specific performance instructions.[21] Concurrently, however, other scholars pushed back against musical or elocutionary interpretations of Dickinson's visual elements. In *The Editing of Emily Dickinson*, Ralph Franklin concluded that, "To an editor seeking authority, not inconsistency, [Dickinson's punctuation marks] appear to have none. To the biographer or the curious, they would be, if properly dated, merely the historical record of a passing performance."[22] Franklin's remark is itself rather curious, since it both discounts the marks' authority and then, in the next sentence, suggests that "if properly dated" they may in fact reveal specific performance decisions made by Dickinson. Indeed, that Franklin himself proceeded over the next three decades to date with admirable precision the vast majority of Dickinson's poems would seem to open still further, rather than put to rest, the question of the poet's intended prosodic cues.

It seems unlikely that there will ever be a scholarly consensus about the prosodic import of Dickinson's manuscript notations. But perhaps this is as it should be, considering how often Dickinson takes the contingencies of verbal mediation as the explicit theme of her work. F 681, for instance, juxtaposes the iterative, punctual act of needlework with the continuous whistling of birdsong to ask which textual form best supports the project of self-knowledge:

> Dont put up my Thread & Needle -
> I'll begin to Sow
> When the Birds begin to whistle -
> Better stitches - so -
>
> These were bent - my sight got crooked -
> When my mind - is plain
> I'll do seams - a Queen's endeavor
> Would not blush to own -
>
> Hems - too fine for Lady's tracing
> To the sightless knot -
> Tucks - of dainty interspersion -
> Like a dotted Dot -

---

[21] Edith Perry Wylder, *The Last Face: Emily Dickinson's Manuscripts* (Albuquerque: University of New Mexico Press, 1971).

[22] Ralph Franklin, *The Editing of Emily Dickinson: A Reconsideration* (Madison: The University of Wisconsin Press, 1967), 119. By 1975, Robert Weisbuch, *Emily Dickinson's Poetry* (Chicago: The University of Chicago Press, 1975), felt it safe to dismiss the "wild theories" scholars had attached to "these simple little marks" (73).

> Leave my Needle in the furrow -
> Where I put it down -
> I can make the zigzag stitches
> Straight - when I am strong -
>
> Till then - dreaming I am sowing
> Fetch the seam I missed -
> Closer - so I - at my sleeping -
> Still surmise I stitch -

Dickinson's poem proposes that "Better stitches" are produced when the physical, durable aspects of art (poetry as "Thread & Needle") are held in balance with art's evanescent, immaterial manifestations (poetry as birdsong). And the poem seems to achieve this: Dickinson has literally hand-stitched the sheets of her poem's fascicle together, and she writes in musical lines of trochaic ballad meter whose syllabically clipped, or catalectic, trimeter lines produce a satisfying breath or pause every two lines. Yet the speaker of the poem, a seamstress or artisan, is out of balance. "These were bent," she explains, describing an aesthetic contortion that she links to a failing of vision or mental health ("my sight got crooked"). Once restored to her full powers, the speaker will be able to produce "Hems - too fine for Lady's tracing," crafts that belie their craftedness. Like "a dotted dot," a sequence of marks that produces the illusion of continuity, the restored speaker's artwork will fuse physical and lyrical textualities, just as does the "Needle in the furrow," which embeds its punctual force within the sinuous curves of fabric. (This latter image strikingly anticipates the mechanics of a technology that did not exist in 1863, Thomas Edison's phonograph, which by placing a needle in furrows in wax or vinyl could draw living voices from inanimate matter.) In the final stanza, Dickinson restates the *sew/so* pun that we realize, in hindsight, has governed the whole poem: "I am sowing . . . so I" (i.e. "I produce texts, therefore I am"). But because the poem's speaker is not yet at her full powers, she can only "dream" of this future condition of perfect signification, of lossless semiotic transfer. Until then, she must depend on other people to "Fetch the seam [she] missed," despite not knowing precisely what they will make of her texts. Indeed, some of the earliest people to encounter this particular text, Todd and Higginson, did not fetch Dickinson's seams but opened them, unbinding the hand-sewn fascicles as they embarked on their effort to see the poet into print. Needle marks are still visible in the inner margins.

Reflecting near the end of her career on the manuscript debates, Edith Wylder observes, somewhat wistfully, "[how] much simpler it would be for

scholars to accept the fact that, for several sound reasons, Dickinson preferred the spoken over the written word, and, accordingly, devised a simple
but ingenious system of accentual punctuation, borrowed from the elocu-
tionists but based in the original Greek accent marks, to allow her written words to be heard as if they were actually being spoken. With this
acceptance, reflected in a simple, more exact transcription of the notations
in the next variorum edition, we could be rid of the distracting and dis-
turbingly ungrammatical commas that mar the present text and finally be
allowed to hear more clearly the finer, defining tones of the voice speaking
in the poems."[23] If scholars could agree that each of the elements Wylder
considers are related in the way she describes, things would indeed be
simpler. But the host of media she surveys—spoken and written English,
nineteenth-century elocution practices, Greek accent marks, pseudo-facsimile
print editions—inevitably remediate, rather than simply deliver, "the voice
speaking in the poems." The fascicles may indeed come closest to embody-
ing the poet's commitment to "choosing not choosing," in Sharon Cameron's
phrasing, to a "transgressive indifference to all those distinctions on which
speech that has limits manifestly depends."[24] But as readers, even as we
can admire the transgressive openness of Dickinson's texts, verbalizing them
requires us to choose—to accept certain prosodic and formal options over
others.

We have no audio recordings of Dickinson reading her work, as we do for
her contemporaries Alfred Tennyson, Robert Browning, and, perhaps, Walt
Whitman. Though Dickinson was still living in 1877 when Thomas Edison
unveiled his phonograph, it is unlikely that she encountered the device, tantalizing as the prospect of a long-lost Dickinson recording is. Dickinson's
reclusiveness and her ambivalence about publication may well have predis-
posed her against the gadgetry that would launch a modern culture industry
in the following century. Nevertheless, Dickinson's career overlaps with early
experiments in modern sound recording, and her poetry, as we have seen,
poses questions about the material basis of speech and sound, and of cognition
and memory, that were concurrently being explored by early users of sound-
recording technology. Dickinson's juxtaposition of fluid and concrete imagery
(e.g. fabric enveloping a needle), moreover, anticipates the mechanism of

---

[23] Edith Wylder, "Emily Dickinson's Punctuation: The Controversy Revisited," *American Literary
Realism*, 36/3 (Spring 2004): 222.
[24] Sharon Cameron, *Choosing Not Choosing: Dickinson's Fascicles* (Chicago: The University of
Chicago Press, 1993), 192.

modern sound-recording technology, which preserved speech as a function of continuous frequency vibrations while producing physical records that were themselves static, singular, and durable.[25] Early versions of the phonograph captured sound waves with a vibrating diaphragm, transferred them to a stylus, and then inscribed acoustically analogous grooves into tin foil wrapped around a cylinder. By reversing this process—turning the cylinder to vibrate the stylus—the recorded sounds were played back. By the twentieth century, grooved records became so associated with musical experience that the term "groove" took on a new meaning as "an unspecifiable but ordered sense of something that is sustained in a distinctive, regular and attractive way, working to draw the listener in."[26]

One of the remarkable things about a poem Dickinson composed in 1863 is how nearly it anticipates this modern sense of groove:

> The Brain, within it's Groove
> Runs evenly - and true -
> But let a Splinter swerve -
> 'Twere easier for You -
>
> To put a Current back -
> When Floods have slit
> the Hills -
> And scooped a Turnpike
> for Themselves -
> And trodden out the Mills -

Dickinson's poem imagines the human brain as a spinning or rotating object that must stay true to its "Groove" in order to maintain a coherent sense of selfhood. And her prosody acts out what her words say: the iambic trimeter groove of the opening lines runs evenly and true through the first stanza, but at stanza's end the current of her syntax overflows the meter's bounds, flooding into stanza 2 and leaving its lineation in disarray. The cognitive dissonance the poem performs at the levels of theme and prosody, moreover, is borne out by the poem's textual history as well. Her 1863 manuscript is lineated

---

[25] Sabine Kim, *Acoustic Entanglements: Sound and Aesthetic Practice* (Heidelberg: Universitatsverlag Winter, 2017), traces a "phonographic logic" through Dickinson's work, noting that in many poems about death and dying, "voice becomes detached from its body not only in space but also in time" (185).

[26] Steven Feld, "Aesthetics as Iconicity of Style, or 'Lift-up-over Sounding': Getting into the Kaluli Groove," *Yearbook for Traditional Music*, 20 (1988): 76.

as transcribed above.[27] Todd and Higginson's 1890 edition relineates the text according to its perceived ballad meter but presents it as a single eight-line stanza, obscuring Dickinson's stark inter-stanza enjambment and her sly linking of overflowing water with overflowing syntax. Johnson's 1955 edition, like Franklin's 1998 edition after it, restores Dickinson's original stanza division but retains the ballad meter lineation. And the online Dickinson Archive provides a digital facsimile of the manuscript while allowing users to examine, in a column to the right, the different texts of each of the poem's print editions. Toggling between these texts lets us see how the poem's shifting material form illustrates quite beautifully what its language describes. Just as a river shapes, and is shaped by, the land it inhabits, so too is Dickinson's voice shaped by the readers and editors, books and websites, that see it on its way. Dickinson's poem is about the process whereby a speaking consciousness grows estranged from itself. And in a startling, uncanny move, the poem also enacts that process, for as Dickinson's prosody carries us across the text(s) of her poem, at some point we realize that we're the ones carrying it. How and where Dickinson's voice becomes ours is impossible to say, since the effect depends on both our sense of ontological separation from her (we "Splinter") and verbal continuity with her (the poem's voice "swerve[s]" but remains continuous). Dickinson's poem is both a grooved and a groove-inducing object.

Nearly two decades after Dickinson wrote her poem, the philosopher Jean-Marie Guyau covered similar ground when he speculated that the brain processed language, and perhaps even produced subjectivity, in the same manner that the newly unveiled phonograph processed sound:

> Upon speaking into a phonograph the vibrations of one's voice are transferred to a point which engraves lines onto a metal plate that correspond to the uttered sounds—uneven furrows, more or less deep, depending on the nature of the sounds. It is quite probable that, in analogous ways, invisible lines are incessantly carved into the brain cells which provide a channel for nerve streams. If after some time the stream encounters a channel it has already passed through, it will once again proceed along the same path. The cells vibrate in the same way they vibrated the first time; psychologically, these similar vibrations correspond to an emotion or a thought analogous to the forgotten emotion or thought.

---

[27] The manuscript itself presents multiple possible texts in that it retains, as do other fascicle poems, alternate readings for individual words, which Dickinson indicates with a plus sign. Thus instead of "a Current" we may read "the Waters," and instead of "trodden out" we may read "blotted out" or "shoved away."

This is precisely the phenomenon which occurs when the phonograph's small copper disk, held against the point which runs through the grooves it has etched, starts to reproduce the vibrations: to our ears, these vibrations turn back into a voice, into words, sounds and melodies.

If the phonographic disk had self-consciousness, it could while replaying a song point out that it remembers this particular song; and what, to us, appears as the effect of a rather simple mechanism would, quite probably, strike the disk as a miraculous ability: memory.[28]

Guyau's 1880 essay describes the process of healthy brain function that Dickinson's poem describes in terms of estrangement. Both writers turn to water imagery to capture the fluid plasticity of brain function; both locate "grooves" and "furrows" as the friction points where liquid forces take on durable material form; and both attribute a miraculous, god-like power to the brain's language processing ability. But whereas Guyau's account concludes optimistically with the notion of an artificially intelligent phonograph, Dickinson's poem draws out the nightmarish implication of this possibility: that the human mind itself may be no more than a high-functioning machine, and so no less glitch-prone than a phonograph.

Though the phonograph has attracted the most attention from literary scholars and cultural historians, a still earlier sound-recording device provides an equally compelling lens onto Dickinson's work. The phonautograph, invented in 1857 by a French typesetter named Édouard-Léon Scott de Martinville, operated similarly to the phonograph, but Scott's device inscribed its sound recordings not into tinfoil or wax but onto sheets of soot-blackened paper. These sound recordings, somewhat counterintuitively, were not intended to be replayed acoustically but functioned simply as visual representations of sound. As Jonathan Sterne observes, "Scott sought to produce a 'natural stenography' that would smash the distinction between orality and literacy because sound could literally write itself—hearing and speaking would become equivalent to reading and writing."[29] Surprisingly, Scott's pathbreaking work was largely unknown until fairly recently. His recorded phonautograms, as he called them, sat in the French Academy of Sciences until the mid-2000s, when they were rediscovered by Patrick Feaster, a media historian at Indiana University. Feaster arranged for scans to be made of the

---

[28] Jean-Marie Guyau, qtd. in Friedrich Kittler, *Gramophone, Film, Typewriter*, trans. Geoffrey Winthrop-Young and Michael Wutz (Stanford: Stanford University Press, 1999), 30–31.
[29] Jonathan Sterne, *The Audible Past: Cultural Origins of Sound Reproduction* (Durham: Duke University Press, 2003), 45.

phonautograms, which were then sent to Carl Haber, an experimental physicist at the Lawrence Berkeley Laboratory in Berkeley, California. Haber and his team, using a technique called optical metrology developed in experiments at the CERN particle collider in Switzerland, created super-precise three-dimensional measurements of Scott's soot-on-paper phonautograms. From these digitized physical measurements they were able to evoke sounds of a human voice that had been encoded in them nearly 150 years earlier. This 1860 recording, later identified as Scott himself singing the French folk song "Au Claire de la Lune," is today the oldest human sound on record.

The fate of Scott's phonautograms—inscribed documents whose lyrical content is made public through a specialized act of reading—parallels nicely the fate of Dickinson's manuscripts, whose posthumous publication and interpretation evokes, in Virginia Jackson's phrasing, a "pathos of transmission," a pained knowledge that "[her] poems can speak for all of us because they do not speak *to* any of us."[30] Like Scott's phonautograms, Dickinson's manuscripts orient us toward a single, originary scene of writing. Their marks capture the idiosyncrasies of Dickinson's hand and perhaps, as scholars such as Wylder have suggested, attempt to close the gap between enunciation and writing through a new system of graphical notation. These characteristics, moreover, stand in contrast to those of Dickinson's print editions, just as Scott's phonautograph stands in contrast to Edison's phonograph records, since books and phonograph records alike aim at popular consumption and thus, by necessity, standardization. Resisting such standardization, the autographic thrust of Dickinson's manuscripts and Scott's phonautograms promises singularity, authenticity, and historical groundedness.

Yet even as it is illuminating to contrast the two devices, and to map their differences onto aspects of Dickinson's work, it is also valuable to consider ways that all three textual practices participate in the same long process whereby, in Sterne's words, "sound itself became an object and a domain of thought and practice."[31] The acoustic principles that underwrite Edison and Scott's devices underwrite human aurality in general, and neither inventor could quite predict the fate of his device. Edison initially assumed his phonograph would be used to create and share linguistic texts: automatic letter-writing, dictation, and

---

[30] Virginia Jackson, *Dickinson's Misery: A Theory of Lyric Reading* (Princeton: Princeton University Press, 2005), 208, 204. As Jason Camlot, *Phonopoetics: The Making of Early Literary Recordings* (Stanford: Stanford University Press, 2019), observes, the acoustic reproduction of Scott's phonautograms "represents an audible rendering, through new media, of a visual script of voice that was never intended to be heard and is, in effect, a digital reversal of Scott de Martinville's intentions" (179).

[31] Sterne, *The Audible Past*, 2.

audiobook creation were among the three applications he envisioned.[32] But it soon became clear that music would be the most popular and lucrative application for his device. Scott's phonautograph, meanwhile, though it produced visual texts, was conceived as a tool for examining linguistic sound *as* sound, as frequency vibrations that might be studied in all their minute acoustic details. Perched between the philological paradigm of the nineteenth century, which had erected a humanist science around tracing language's shifting historical meanings as preserved in written texts, and the nascent structuralist paradigm of the twentieth century, which was turning an ear for the first time to the acoustic and phonetic properties of speech, Scott, Edison, and Dickinson's work illuminates the permeability of newer and older ways of thinking about linguistic media.

John Guillory has argued that the arrival of new technical media like the phonograph "seemed to reposition the traditional arts [e.g. poetry and music] as ambiguously both media and precursors to the media."[33] The work of someone like Dickinson can therefore seem both non- and pre-medial when viewed through the lens of the media revolutions of modernism, in need of no mediating context or, conversely, in need of careful reconstruction within her own historical moment. Yet the choice is false. The Dickinson manuscripts held in archives throughout New England may be largely the same as the ones the poet produced in her Amherst bedroom, just as the phonautograms held in the French Academy are largely the same as the ones Scott recorded in Paris. But we bring to Dickinson's manuscripts today a historical perspective that separates us irrevocably from their scene of creation. Writing about Scott's recordings, Jason Camlot makes a similar point: "While originating from a material visual object, the audio artifacts generated from this technique [optical metrology] are born digital and thus represent a digital realization of the abstract idea of the phonautogram as an audible artifact."[34] Even if we were lucky enough to gain access to the Dickinson manuscripts in the Houghton Library at Harvard and examine them with our own eyes, we would know both too much (e.g. of the coming of free verse, of Harvard's modern prestige, of the institutional fate of the humanities) and too little (e.g. of a time before electric lights, of the identity of Dickinson's mysterious "Master") to fully inhabit Dickinson's world. But neither is it the case that Dickinson's first readers, her sister-in-law Susan ("Sue") Gilbert Dickinson for instance,

---

[32] See Thomas Edison, "The Phonograph and Its Future," *The North American Review*, 126/262 (May–June 1878): 527–36.
[33] John Guillory, "Genesis of the Media Concept," *Critical Inquiry*, 36/2 (Winter 2010): 322.
[34] Camlot, *Phonopoetics*, 180.

enjoyed unmediated access to her poems via the manuscripts. A poem in 1860 was not equivalent to its manuscript, just as it is not today. Then as now poems existed as complex assemblies of language, physical media, and readerly convention. When Dickinson enclosed a leaf or a cricket along with the scripted text of a poem and sent it next door to Sue or Austin, she was underscoring poetry's assembled, multimedial, and affective basis. And just as song settings of Dickinson's verse can bring out prosodic textures invisible in a printed text, so can digital facsimiles of her work, though dependent on computer technology often seen as threatening earlier book and manuscript cultures, make us feel paradoxically closer to Dickinson. Because past and present cannot be as cleanly severed as both historicist or formalist approaches sometimes imply, we might instead think in terms of foregrounding different aspects of the evolving media cluster that comprises Dickinson's poetry.

One of the most ambitious remediations of Dickinson's work in recent years is the television series *Dickinson*, created by Alena Smith, which aired on Apple TV in 2019. Set in Amherst in the late 1850s, the show follows Emily, played by Hailee Steinfeld, as she embarks on a quest to "become the world's greatest poet."[35] In the series' opening scene, Emily wakes before dawn, lights an oil lamp, pulls a scrap of paper from her desk, and writes animatedly while mouthing words to herself. We cannot hear or see what she is writing, and after a few moments she is interrupted by a knock at the door. "You have to go fetch water," Emily's sister Lavinia tells her:

EMILY: "It is four o'clock in the morning. I'm writing."
LAVINIA: "Mother says you have to. I did it yesterday."
EMILY: "Why doesn't Austin do it?"
LAVINIA: "Austin is a boy."
EMILY: [Pauses] "This is such bullshit."[36]

The exchange introduces the conceit that will structure the series as a whole: while Emily's success as a poet is at all turns curtailed by the gender conventions of nineteenth-century New England, her indignant response to these conventions comes in a decidedly contemporary idiom. *Dickinson*'s younger characters in particular—Emily, her siblings, and their friends—speak and think in ways that locate the show in recent American cultural history. In

---

[35] *Dickinson* home page, Apple TV+, accessed December 7, 2022.
[36] David Gordon Green, "Because I could not stop," Season 1, Episode 1 of *Dickinson*, Apple TV+, 34:00, November 1, 2019, tv.apple.com/us/show/Dickinson.

one episode, Lavinia rebuffs her fiancé's desire for a "traditional, normal wife" with a burst of feminist angst that feels more at home on Instagram than in the Dickinson homestead: "I'm not normal, okay? I am a twisted, witchy, creative, horny woman, and you can't accept that—you can't accept me."[37] In another episode, Emily enters a baking contest that is being judged by her aunt. When Emily is declared the winner, one of her Asian-American peers mutters "Amherst baking contest so white," an allusion to the 2015 Twitter campaign #OscarsSoWhite that protested the lack of racial diversity among nominees for Best Actor and Best Actress.[38] At various points throughout the series, Emily slips away from social gatherings to rendezvous with a personification of Death, played by the rapper Wiz Khalifa, who chauffeurs her around Amherst in a ghostly carriage in a literal rendition of "Because I could not stop for Death" (F 479).

At first blush, the pseudo-historical mode seems like a ploy to make the canonical Dickinson appealing to a millennial and Gen Z audience. Yet the show's blatant anachronisms are of a piece with its larger narrative and conceptual project, which is to present Dickinson not as an historical person, but as a poet—that is, a figure whose voice is produced and reimagined by each successive generation of readers. As the show creator Smith explains, "Everything you see in the show had to be precisely perfect for the period, so the music and the language could perform their act of rebellion against that perfection."[39] The show's heavy-handed anti-patriarchalism thus comes to function less as a truth about Dickinson, her family, or Amherst and more as a truth about the anxieties of influence that make up literary and cultural history in general. *Dickinson* is at its best when creatively misreading canonical figures of American literature to carve out a new vision of its protagonist's significance. Midway through Season 1, Emily and her friend George make a pilgrimage to Walden Pond hoping to enlist Thoreau in an effort to stop construction of a railroad through Amherst. To Emily's dismay, Walden is far from the secluded haven Thoreau presents in his 1854 memoir. People are picnicking. Musicians are playing folk tunes. A hipster atmosphere prevails. As Emily and George approach Thoreau's cabin, they bump into his mother, who is returning her son's freshly laundered clothes. "You must be fans of his," she

---

[37] Stacie Passon, "I'm Nobody! Who are you?" Season 2, Episode 8 of *Dickinson*, Apple TV+, 32:00, February 12, 2021, tv.apple.com/us/show/Dickinson.
[38] Christopher Storer, "Fame is a fickle food," Season 2, Episode 2 of *Dickinson*, Apple TV+, 25:00, January 8, 2021, tv.apple.com/us/show/Dickinson.
[39] Jennifer Schuessler, "A 21st-Century Emily Dickinson Finds a Home in the Archives," *New York Times*, December 10, 2021.

says, "and I imagine you want to get that book signed." Dickinson almost certainly never met Thoreau, but the show fudges this detail to make its larger point: Thoreau's program of solitude, introspection, and self-reliance was itself a selective representation of biographical facts justified in the name of art. Thoreau did in fact receive laundry services from his mother and financial support from his father's pencil-making business. "Never meet your heroes," Thoreau smirks at the disillusioned Emily, who leaves the encounter that much more ambivalent about whether or not to publish her own work.[40]

The realities of publication and the nature of literary fame are taken up again in Season 2 during a conversation between Emily and the ghost of Edgar Allan Poe, whom she meets in Death's carriage.

DEATH: "May I introduce to you the great, and recently late, Mr. Edgar Allan Poe."

POE: [To Dickinson] "Yeah, that's me. Want an autograph?"

EMILY: "Wow, I can't believe you're here."

DEATH: "He just died a few years ago."

POE: "That's right, I'm a ghost—the ghost of Edgar Allan Poe. Died of mysterious circumstances. Very on brand."

DEATH: "No, you drank yourself to death, bro."

POE: [Grinning, in a slow drawl] "All right . . . "[41]

Unlike Thoreau, Poe readily acknowledges that his popular image as a solitary, troubled genius is a "brand," a set of compelling associations related to, but distinct from, historical fact. In offering Emily an autograph, Poe is trading on this brand, idealizing a singular, hand-written document whose value emerges, ironically, from the networks of mass print that Poe so cannily exploited during his lifetime. Poe's offer also underscores the fact that Emily's work, at the moment of their fictional meeting in 1859, exists almost entirely in (autograph) manuscripts. "Who's your publisher?" Poe asks. "Wiley & Putnam?"

EMILY: "I just published a poem in the *Springfield Republican.*"

POE: [Sarcastically] "I'm sorry, did you say the *New York Tribune?*"

EMILY: "No, the, uh, *Springfield Republican.*"

DEATH: "He heard what you said. He's just being rude."

---

[40] Lynn Shelton, "Alone, I cannot be," Season 1, Episode 1 of *Dickinson,* Apple TV+, 28:00, November 1, 2019, tv.apple.com/us/show/Dickinson.

[41] Stacie Passon, "I'm Nobody! Who are you?" Season 2, Episode 8 of *Dickinson,* Apple TV+.

POE: "One poem in a newspaper and you think you're hot shit. I mean this
with all due respect, I have no idea who you are and it's too late for me to
learn. My dear young lady, you do not even know what fame is . . . Fame is
an addiction. Get one little taste and look at you, you're hooked. And you'll
keep searching for that next high. Rich or poor. Known or obscure. But it'll
never be enough. I mean, look at me. I'm famous as shit and I'm dead as
shit."

Dickinson presents Emily as both enthralled by the idea of literary fame and
mortified by the prospect of having her voice mediated by other people. As we
watch her agonize over whether to let the newspaper editor Samuel Bowles
publish one of her poems in the *Springfield Republican*, we savor the dramatic irony at the heart of the series: Emily in 1859 cannot know the fame
her work will achieve, but we do, indeed the very act of watching the series
on Apple TV confirms that Dickinson will achieve a global fame incon-
ceivable to the historical Dickinson. As Poe finishes his gloomy monologue,
Emily speaks aloud the first line of a poem her editors have been unable to
date—

> Fame is a bee.
> It has a song—
> It has a sting—
> Ah, too, it has a wing. (*F* 1788)

—and despite Poe's warning, she leaves Death's carriage committed to sharing
her poetry with the world. "I want to be seen by people," Emily declares as,
back at the Evergreens, she looks for her sister-in-law Sue: "I want to be seen
by you."

The equivocal difference between these two desires—writing for "you"
(Sue) versus writing for "people" (anonymous readers of published books of
poetry)—maps the terms of what is arguably the central question in Dickinson studies: for whom did the poet write? Ultimately, the TV show succeeds
not because it provides an answer but because it illustrates the complex-
ities of the question. As creator Alena Smith explains in a discussion of
Season 2:

> This season of *Dickinson* takes places in the fall of 1859, and by this time
> the Dickinsons themselves subscribe to several newspapers. The invention
> of the telegraph has made it possible to communicate almost instantaneously.

It's almost like a Victorian internet. It feels like time is speeding up, with the whirring of the printing press and this constant stream of news and information. And so Emily's very quiet insular world starts to be punctured and intruded upon by this, and even more so by Sam Bowles, who is the young, progressive editor of the *Springfield Republican*, which is one of the places that Emily Dickinson was published during her life.[42]

Smith makes the question of verbal mediation the entry point to the series and to Dickinson's poetics. The voice we see Emily develop over the course of the series is, accordingly, distributed and intertwined among multiple media forms: not just the actor Hailee Steinfeld's actual voice, but also envelopes and scraps on which Emily writes verses, letters to Sue, bound fascicles, printed newspapers, conversations with other writers, and even the modern pop songs that feature prominently in the show's soundtrack.

Television is particularly suited to represent this multimedial texture, given its ability to juxtapose multiple visual and acoustic texts in real time. In one particularly striking scene, Emily and Sue are in bed together. (The series presents the women as romantic partners, as has some Dickinson scholarship.) Earlier that day, the two women had dressed as men to gain entrance to a lecture on volcanoes at Amherst College. As the two women embrace, the opening strums of Mitski's 2015 song "Your Best American Girl" echo in the background.[43] As the song's first verse ends, we hear Emily recite, in voiceover, the opening lines of "I have never seen volcanoes" (*F* 165). In time with Emily's recitation, lines of manuscript text are superimposed on the screen, creating a kind of verbal-visual palimpsest that could be transcribed something like this:

You're the sun, you've never seen the night but you
Hear its song from the morning birds
I have never seen volcanoes
Well, I'm not the moon, I'm not even a star but
But, when travelers tell   How those old phlegmatic mountains
Awake at night I'll be singing to the birds
Usually so still   Bear within appalling Ordnance

[42] Alena Smith, "Alena Smith on the Media," Apple TV+, 2:00, January 8, 2021, tv.apple.com/us/show/Dickinson.

[43] David Gordon Green, "I have never seen 'Volcanoes,'" Season 1, Episode 2 of *Dickinson*, Apple TV+, 27:00, November 1, 2019, tv.apple.com/us/show/Dickinson.

Don't	wait	for	me
Fire, and smoke, and gun		***Taking villages for breakfast***	
I	can't	come	
And appalling men			

The scene is stirring, and the comparatively underwhelming experience of reading it in transcription underscores that Dickinson's prosody is a feature of her media, not simply her language. Only by watching and listening to the scene can we confirm that both Dickinson's poem and Mitski's song obey the four-beat norm of ballads and pop songs, even as each text organizes its language differently around the beats.[44] Certain phrases parallel one another syllabically—

Well, | I'm not | the moon,
But, | when trave | lers tell

—while others diverge, as when Mitski's spacious "Don't wait for me" spreads across two full measures to overlap with thirteen of Dickinson's syllables. This sense of rhythmic consonance and divergence makes it all the more satisfying when the two texts arrive together for Mistki's heavy metal chorus.

There are of course possible objections to interpreting this material as part of Dickinson's textuality. Mitski's words are not Dickinson's. The show's superimposed manuscript text is only a pseudo-facsimile, similar in style to Dickinson's handwriting but not the real thing. Moreover, the convention of placing snippets of text on screen in synch with a character's mental processing of that text smacks of the smartphone era, when TV shows like *House of Cards* pioneered the technique as a means of subtly sharing the content of text messages with audiences. Perhaps most significantly, the chief agent of rhythmic form in the TV scene is the sheer acoustic force of Mitski's song, the bodily, rock 'n' roll kick it lends to Dickinson's poem. Yet each of these objections itself invites qualification. Some of Mitski's words are indeed Dickinson's: the title "Your Best American Girl" echoes a phrase from one of Dickinson's enigmatic Master Letters, where she refers to herself as "your best little girl."[45] The word "Forevermore" is likewise apt, given its explicit association with Sue, as in the closing lines of one of the earliest poems Dickinson ever wrote (*F* 5):

---

[44] On other occasions, Emily recites her verse in time with the beat of the show's soundtrack. Her rendition of "Fame is a bee" in Death's carriage, for instance, is synchronized fairly closely with Leonard Cohen's 2016 song "You Want It Darker."

[45] Emily Dickinson, *The Master Letters of Emily Dickinson*, ed. R. W. Franklin (Amherst: Amherst University Press, 1986), 29.

> I spilt the dew,
> But took the morn -
> I chose this single star
> From out the wide night's numbers -
> Sue - forevermore!

This poem, like many of Dickinson's, shares with Mitski's song the age-old imagery of day and night, sun and stars, and the birdsong that weaves together the lovers' lives. *Dickinson's* superimposed text may not be a perfect facsimile of the manuscripts, but by sitting somewhere between the singularity of script and the standardization of print, the pseudo-facsimile is perhaps a more forthright rendering of the layers of mediation through which we always engage Dickinson's work.[46] In a similar vein, while the superimposed text is indeed a smartphone era convention, the poems Dickinson sent to Sue and others arguably functioned like nineteenth-century text messages: brief communications, often witty or elliptical, and meant for immediate consumption by a specific person. Lastly, regarding the incongruity of Dickinson's quiet poem and Mitski's loud song, we might consult Dickinson's oft-cited definition of poetry, which surely evokes something nearer a rock concert than a modern poetry reading: "If I read a book and it makes my whole body so cold no fire can warm me, I know that is poetry. If I feel physically as if the top of my head were taken off, I know that is poetry. These are the only ways I know it. Is there any other way?"[47]

As scholars, our impulse may be to critique or pare back the overextensions of a show like *Dickinson*. But these overextensions, in their very starkness, can help illustrate that no attempt to return Dickinson's poems to their earliest mediating conditions can ever be complete. We cannot return to a moment before Dickinson's work was printed, set to music, digitized, or turned into a television series. *Dickinson* itself has fun with this fact: after Emily publishes her first poem in the *Springfield Republican*, she becomes literally invisible and inaudible to her family and friends, as if to suggest that, once the discourses of print have confirmed Emily as a poet, she no longer exists as an historical person. If we see our job in predominantly historical terms, then the voice we hear coming from Dickinson's poems, or Scott's phonautograms, or the *Dickinson* TV series, will arrive as the production of later sound reproduction techniques:

---

[46] A student of mine was disappointed that the show's facsimile wasn't quite right, something she could have discovered only after consulting the actual facsimiles on the Dickinson Archive.

[47] Thomas Wentworth Higginson, letter to his wife, August 16, 1870, *The Letters of Emily Dickinson*, ed. Thomas Johnson, vol. 1 (Cambridge: Harvard University Press, 1958), 473–74.

close reading, optical metrology, streaming-era television. Conversely, if we see our job in predominantly formalist terms, then we will experience Dickinson's sounds—whether abstractions like voice or particularities like iambs—in conjunction with the poet herself, having posited a continuity of genre that bridges her time and ours. By allowing these approaches to blend into each other, we engage Dickinson's prosody neither as an artifact of its earliest context, nor as a set of sounds scanned from a printed text, but as the product of remediation, a swerving and splintering of her language into our own.

4

Modernist Grooves

No figure was more vocally skeptical of the value of traditional prosodic categories than Ezra Pound. "You don't ask an art instructor to give you a recipe for making a Leonardo da Vinci drawing. Hence the extreme boredom caused by the usual professorial documentation or the aspiring thesis on prosody. The answer is: LISTEN to the sound that it makes."[1] Pound's pronouncement, which appears in his 1936 *ABC of Reading*, echoes other of his strictures on prosodic form: "As regarding rhythm . . . compose in the sequence of the musical phrase, not in sequence of a metronome," Pound writes in "A Few Don'ts by an Imagiste."[2] Or as he puts it in a famous line from the *Cantos*, "To break the pentameter, that was the first heave."[3] Pound rejects Victorian metrics for being overly mechanical, so it comes as no surprise that he also rejects actual mechanical sound recording technologies, which had proliferated in the early decades of the twentieth century. "Our ears are passive before the onslaught of gramophones," Pound writes in the *Egoist* in 1917. "By persuading ourselves that we do not hear two-thirds of their abominable grind, we persuade ourselves that we take pleasure in the remainder of what they narrate."[4] As producers are transformed into consumers, Pound continues, those who still create their own aesthetic experiences do so with increasing "rigidity." "The old way of music," he observes, "teaching a man that a piece of music was a structure, certain main forms filled in with certain decorations, stimulated his intelligence, spurred on his constructive faculty. You might play the same lute-piece as many others, but you thought about playing it differently (i.e. with different notes), of playing it better. In a sense this is true of any performer, but the contemporary way of approach lays stress on having a memory like a phonograph."[5]

---

[1] Ezra Pound, *ABC of Reading* (New York: New Directions, 2010), 201.

[2] Ezra Pound, *Literary Essays of Ezra Pound* (New York: New Directions, 1935), 3.

[3] Ezra Pound, *The Cantos* (New York: New Directions, 1996), 538. Subsequent references to this edition are cited parenthetically and abbreviated C.

[4] Ezra Pound, *Ezra Pound and Music: The Complete Criticism*, ed. R. Murray Schafer (New York: New Directions, 1977), 49.

[5] Pound, *Music*, 47, 48.

Poetry, Sound, and the Matter of Prosody 1800–2000. Peter Miller, Oxford University Press. © Peter Miller (2025).
DOI: 10.1093/9780198937210.003.0005

Pound's distaste for the phonograph would appear to find its positive counterpart in his affection for the printed book. The poet's founding role in Imagism and his close collaboration with printers and bookmakers lends credence to the notion that poetic modernism came into its own by embracing literature's visual and bibliographical elements.[6] Yet too narrow a focus on Pound's bibliographical commitments risks masking the ways that his work in fact betrays an ambivalent fascination with analog sound recording. Just a few months before bashing the phonograph for offering listeners a touristic hodgepodge of "Arabic and Japanese and Zulu and Malay music," Pound had published in *Poetry* magazine early drafts of his epic *Cantos* project whose admittedly "rag-bag" organizing principles would ultimately generate the most ambitiously and controversially multicultural poem of the twentieth century.[7] Given the importance to Pound of such bardic figures as Homer and the Provençal troubadours, moreover, the phonograph might have offered—as it did early century linguists, folklorists, and anthropologists—a tool for exploring the nature of orality and literacy in a modern age.[8] Perhaps most to the point, many of Pound's arguments about sonic and rhythmic form invoke technical language and acoustic principles associated with forms of mechanical sound recording. "Rhythm is a form cut into TIME," Pound writes in his *ABC of Reading*, evoking the process of phonographic inscription that translated sounded events into physical texts.[9] Here and elsewhere, Pound's twinned commitment to acoustic and bibliographical forms appears as a *groove*, a troping of real-time verbal performance as the obverse of physical inscription. From the replacement of Imagism with Vorticism, to handprinted editions of the *Cantos* whose title nevertheless evokes song, to the bizarre time signatures of his original opera *Le Testament de Villon*, Pound's work labors to capture what he provocatively terms "time-space."[10] Far from rejecting prosody,

---

[6] The entry on "Modernism" in the *Princeton Encyclopedia of Poetry & Poetics*, ed. Roland Greene, Stephen Cushman, Clare Cavanagh, Jahan Ramazani, and Paul Rouzer (Princeton: Princeton University Press, 2012), notes that, "For many of its protagonists, the opening phase of literary modernism signaled a decisive shift from music to painting as the privileged model for a new poetry" (P. Nicholls, 889). Influential studies of modernist poetry's visual and bibliographical turn include Marjorie Perloff, *The Futurist Moment: Avant-Garde, Avant Guerre, and the Language of Rupture* (Chicago: The University of Chicago Press, 1986), Charles Altieri, *Painterly Abstraction in Modernist American Poetry* (University Park: The Pennsylvania State University Press, 1989), and Jerome McGann, *Black Riders: The Visible Language of Modernism* (Princeton: Princeton University Press, 1993).

[7] Pound, *Music*, 49; Ezra Pound, "Three Cantos," *Poetry*, 10/4 (July 1917): 180–88.

[8] See Erika Brady, *A Spiral Way: How the Phonograph Changed Ethnography* (Jackson: University Press of Mississippi, 1999), and Peter H. Kylstra, "The Use of the Early Phonograph in Phonetic Research," *Phonographic Bulletin*, 17 (1977): 3–12.

[9] Pound, *ABC of Reading*, 198.

[10] Ezra Pound, "Dissertation on Rhythm," 8. Ezra Pound Papers (YCAL MSS 43). Box 96, folder 4068. American Literature Collection, Beinecke Rare Book and Manuscript Library, Yale University.

Pound's work transforms it for an age of modern media, grounding prosody's tenets in the discourses of mechanical sound recording.

This transformation is visible across the broad range of artistic genres and media about which Pound wrote. "The performing musician cuts his form in the air and in the time flow," Pound writes in his *Guide to Kulchur*: "He writes it as in less stable water."[11] In this and other instances, Pound's imagery casts what is typically considered a temporal phenomenon—sounded poetic or musical rhythm—as a function of space. Rhythm is not simply a fleeting acoustic effect but a physical structure that could theoretically be measured. As such, the equation can be run in the other direction: when Pound praises sculpture, it tends to be for its ability to produce in static objects a sense of living, restive energy.[12] Modern sound recording technology operates on similar principles, spatializing sound and temporalizing space via the grooves of the phonograph records Theodor Adorno would dub "acoustic photographs."[13] Though musical scores had for centuries served a similar purpose, the phonograph's analog form of sonic reproduction was something new, for it encoded sound not as a series of theoretically posited intervals (e.g. musical pitches, metrical feet) but as a temporally continuous function of frequency vibrations.

The distinctly analog character of Pound's prosodic thinking comes into view in his 1924 *Treatise on Harmony*, which opens by observing that, "The element most grossly omitted from treatises on harmony up to the present is the element of TIME."[14] "The former treatises on harmony dealt with static harmony . . . they did not consider that the lateral motion, the horizontal motion, and the time interval between succeeding sounds MUST affect the human ear, and not only the ear but the absolute physics of the matter. The question of where one wave-node meets another . . . must be considered."[15] "To make my simple statement even simpler; let us consider the nature of the ear, and of sound. Sound, we are told, consists of vibrations of from 16 to 36,000 per second. The ear is an organ for the detection of frequency."[16] Though Pound is writing about music, he believes the same acoustic principles should

[11] Ezra Pound, *Guide to Kulchur* (New York: New Directions, 1970), 170.
[12] Michael Golston, *Rhythm and Race in Modernist Poetry and Science: Pound, Yeats, Williams, and Modern Sciences of Rhythm* (New York: Columbia University Press, 2007), suggests that Pound "vacillates in his writing on rhythm between analogies drawn from sculpture (rhythm is a 'shape,' it cuts) and analogies drawn from music" (62).
[13] Theodor Adorno, "The Form of the Phonograph Record," trans. Thomas Levin, *October*, 55 (1990): 57.
[14] Ezra Pound, *Antheil and the Treatise on Harmony* (Chicago: Pascal Covici, 1927), 9.
[15] Pound, *Treatise*, 17.
[16] Pound, *Treatise*, 23.

underwrite poetic rhythm. "I believe in an absolute rhythm," he explains, restating an idea first put forth in his 1910 translation of Cavalcanti.[17] This absolute rhythm, as Pound elaborates across his career, is not something that can be standardized or described in primers on versification or musical composition. Rather, it names the very ground of rhythmic experience, necessarily singular and idiosyncratic, but at the same time universally vouchsafed by the jointly analog character of both sound ("the absolute physics of the matter") and human aurality.

Pound received what he considered empirical proof of his ideas about rhythm sometime around 1912 in the laboratory of the French phonetician Jean-Pierre Rousselot. Rousselot had invented a device he called the phonoscope ("sound seer"), which by measuring the vibrations of a speaker's vocal apparatus could inscribe on soot-blackened paper the durational value of individual vowels and consonants comprising the words of a given speech act.[18] Pound read his poem "The Return" into Rousselot's device and would later reflect on its usefulness for holding poets and scholars accountable to the sounds of spoken verse. The phonoscope provided "the scientific justification of *vers libre*," Pound writes in 1920, and with it "the scientific proofs that a lot of 'rules' and 'laws' of prosody as taught in the text-books, have no sort of relation to spoken reality."[19] Pound elaborates by pointing to textual material from his poem "The Return": "Given the phonoscope one finds definitely a reason why one cannot *hear* the *in the* in a phrase like *in the wind*, as a 'long.' It isn't long. Whatever the Greeks may have done, one does not *hear* the beginning consonants of a word as musically part of the syllable of the last vowel in the word preceding; neither does the phonoscope so record them. All of which with many other finer distinctions can now be examined with great saving of breath and paper, whenever the questions are considered of sufficient interest, either by professors, or by neophytes in the arts of versification."[20] Pound's specific complaint is somewhat opaque, but he seems broadly to be objecting to prosodic conventions, whether Greek or English, that force poets to distort the natural cadences and intonation patterns of speech in order to fit a metrical schema. Individual words and phrases, Pound suggests, possess an acoustic integrity that it is the modern poet's duty to preserve. Rather than "[chopping] your stuff into separate *iambs*" or "[making] each line stop dead at the end," he

---

[17] Pound, *Treatise*, 13.

[18] See Golston, *Rhythm and Race*, 64–73, for an extended discussion of Pound's encounter with the phonoscope.

[19] Ezra Pound, "The Island of Paris: A Letter," *Dial*, 69/5 (October 1920): 639.

[20] Pound, "The Island of Paris," 639.

suggests in "A Few Don'ts," "Let the beginning of the next line catch the rise of the rhythm wave."[21] Anticipating his language of "waves" and "vibrations" in the *Treatise on Harmony*, Pound praises Rousselot's phonoscope for its ability to honor the analog contours of what he calls "spoken reality."

A comparison can be drawn between the sound-pictures the phonoscope produced and the painterly Chinese ideograms that Pound, via the American sinologist Ernest Fenollosa, would incorporate into his poetic thinking. If Rousselot's device produced visible writing that bore a direct, proportional, and continuous relation to the phonetic sounds it registered, the Chinese ideogram, in Pound's and Fenollosa's eyes, offered a form of writing that more accurately captured the innate temporal energy of objects in the world.

"A true noun, an isolated thing," Fenollosa explains, "does not exist in nature. Things are only the terminal points, or rather the meeting points of actions, cross-sections cut through actions, snap-shots." A person viewing an ideogram, Fenollosa writes, "sees noun and verb as one: things in motion, motion in things."[22] Fenollosa was only partially correct about the degree to which classical Chinese was a pictographic as opposed to a phonetic script. Yet we might nevertheless observe that the enticingly analog phonoscopic pictures Pound saw in Rousselot's laboratory were "ideogrammic" in precisely the sense Fenollosa wishfully believed Chinese was, since by following the "natural suggestion" of a thing in nature (i.e. sonic frequency vibrations) these drawings arguably did "[get] back to the fundamental reality of *time*."[23]

If Fenollosa's ideograms appealed to the poet in part for their seemingly analog rendering of the spatial world, so too did the "Vortex" Pound claimed as an icon not only for his own poetic project but for modernism as a whole. Tired of the Imagist movement he helped launch, Pound turned to the Vortex to underscore the temporal dynamism he understood all well-crafted artwork to possess. Insofar as Pound's poetry remained after 1913 a poetry of the "image," this revamped image was not static but was "a radiant node or cluster . . . a

---

[21] Pound, *Literary Essays*, 6.
[22] Ezra Pound, *Instigations of Ezra Pound* (New York: Boni and Liveright, 1920), 364.
[23] Pound, *Instigations*, 363.

VORTEX, from which, and through which, and into which, ideas are constantly rushing."[24] In the first issue of the little magazine *Blast*, Pound's friend Wyndham Lewis drew the Vortex like this:

Like Fenollosa's ideograms and Rousselot's phonoscopic tracings, the Vortex, even as it focused attention on points of relative intensity, rendered these points as functions of a larger network of constituent force vectors.[25] The Vortex, that is, was spatio-temporally proportionate: the movement at its central axis also happened at its edges, but at a different scale and speed. In appearance and structural conception, then, the Vortex resembled something like a gramophone record merged with an original Edison cylinder, both of which revolved around a central axis in order to encode, and then decode, sonic data whose material instantiation bore a temporally continuous relation to all other sounds cut into it.

Analog forms of inscription, in other words, whether technically so (e.g. Rousselot's phonoscope) or figuratively so (e.g. ideograms, the Vortex), captured the poet's imagination because they produced durable material texts while still registering language the way human ears do: as continuous frequency vibrations rather than discrete semantic or prosodic units. It is this double capacity that allows Pound to, on the one hand, bemoan overly bookish approaches to prosodic analysis and, on the other, write poetry that draws its energy from charting the semantic and ontological integrity of texts over time. Pound reflects on this double agenda in the "Envoi" at the center of his 1920 poem *Hugh Selwyn Mauberley*. Recalling a woman "that sang me once that song of Lawes," Pound's speaker wistfully imagines a "magic amber" that, unlike print, could preserve human voices without stripping them of their acoustic vitality.[26] This substance would allow the woman's graceful singing to live

> As roses might, in magic amber laid,
> Red overwrought with orange and all made

[24] Ezra Pound, *Gaudier-Brzeska: A Memoir* (New York: John Lane, 1916), 106.
[25] Lewis's sketch appears in the first issue of *Blast*, June 20, 1914.
[26] Ezra Pound, *Selected Poems of Ezra Pound* (New York: New Directions, 1957), 557.

One substance and one colour
Braving time.[27]

Appearing in a work fixated on verbal mediation and published at the dawn
of the Jazz Age, Pound's "magic amber" would surely have conjured for some
readers the resinous shellac of the gramophone records presently taking the
world by storm, which likewise allowed voices to "[brave] time."[28] *Mauberley's* speaker dictates the lines above to his "dumb-born book," which in turn is
meant to admonish "her that sheds/Such treasure in the air" for not knowing
the history behind the song she sings—that, for instance, its text was composed by the seventeenth-century English poet and statesman Edmund Waller
and only later set to music by Henry Lawes.[29] Yet even while chastising the
singer for lacking such historical information, Pound's speaker remains equally
convinced that her song's beauty depends on its status *as* song, as something acoustically singular and evanescent. Whether or not Pound thought
of commercial phonography when writing these lines, their equivocal ambition to have language both seen and heard, durable and fleeting, evokes the
textual condition the phonograph record's sinuous grooves appeared to have
achieved.

So, what's in a groove? By definition, nothing. But a spatially significant nothing. Among the word's oldest meanings the *OED* lists: "a mining shaft; a mine,
pit" (c. 1400); "a channel or hollow, cut by artificial means, in metal, wood,
etc." (c. 1660).[30] Already in these two early definitions we can detect a move
from semi-natural to decidedly "artificial" sources of the groove: a "mine" in
the earth becomes the more conspicuously crafted "channel or hollow . . . in
metal, wood, etc."[31] Following this, craft becomes industry, grooves in furniture
become grooves in rifles, and around 1900 the word takes its distinctly modern turn, as "The spiral cut in a gramophone record (earlier, in a phonograph
cylinder) which forms the path for the needle."[32] Not long after, the verbal
action latent in each of the groove's spatial definitions becomes active in its
phonographic context, yielding: "to play jazz or similar music with 'swing'; to

[27] Pound, *Selected Poems*, 557.
[28] We might further note that the most popular brand of the day, "His Master's Voice," sported a red
label "overwrought" with orange lettering, a presumably coincidental parallel to the red and orange
substance in *Mauberley* given Pound's stance toward commercial phonography.
[29] Pound, *Selected Poems*, 557.
[30] "groove, n.1a," *OED Online*, January 2023, Oxford University Press, https://www.oed.com/view/
Entry/81,733.
[31] "groove, n.2a," *OED Online*.
[32] "groove, n.2c," *OED Online*.

be 'in the groove'; to dance or listen *to* such music with great pleasure; hence, to make good progress or co-operate; to get on well *with* someone; to make love."[33] And then this verbal definition is fed back into its nominal one and comes to denote a sense of rhythmic "pulse," "an unspecifiable but ordered sense of something that is sustained in a distinctive, regular and attractive way, working to draw the listener in."[34] It is this active and reciprocal blurring of space and time, object and action, noun and verb that becomes the cardinal feature of what we might term the modern groove. For a groove in space suggests the manner of its "cutting," while a groove in time posits a structuring spatial logic that is "ordered" even if opaque.

In an 1888 article titled "The Perfected Phonograph," Thomas Edison characterizes the modern groove when he compares the operation of his device to the interaction of water and sand on a beach:

> To make the general idea of the recording of sound more clear, let me remark one or two points. We have all been struck by the precision with which even the faintest sea-waves impress upon the surface of a beach the fine, sinuous line which is formed by the rippling edge of their advance. Almost as familiar is the fact that grains of sand sprinkled on a smooth surface of glass or wood, on or near a piano, sift themselves into various lines and curves according to the vibrations of the melody played on the piano-keys. These things indicate how easily the particles of solid matter may receive an imparted motion, or take an impression, from delicate liquid waves, air waves, or waves of sound. Yet, well known though these phenomena are, they apparently never suggested until within a few years that the sound-waves set going by a human voice might be so directed as to trace an impression upon some solid substance, with a nicety equal to that of the tide in recording its flow upon a sand beach.[35]

Here the American inventor discusses spoken language not in terms of its written meanings, as he had when first unveiling his phonograph a decade earlier, but in terms of physical properties made newly evident by his device.[36] Semantics dissolve into acoustics, words into frequency vibrations, and he figures these shifts using the image of lines etched into a sand beach.

---

[33] "groove, v.5," *OED Online*.

[34] Steven Feld, "Aesthetics as Iconicity of Style, or 'Lift-up-over Sounding': Getting into the Kaluli Groove," *Yearbook for Traditional Music*, 20 (1988): 76.

[35] Thomas Edison, "The Perfected Phonograph," *The North American Review*, 146/379 (January 1888): 642.

[36] See Edison, "The Phonograph and Its Future" (1878), *The North American Review*, 126/262 (May–June 1878): 527–36.

Edison's account makes clear the phonograph's potential value to synchronic, structuralist approaches to language that would gain prominence in the twentieth century. But the device proved valuable for historical projects as well. Of particular relevance here is the case presented by the classical scholar Milman Parry, whose 1930s fieldwork among illiterate Slavic *guslars* coalesced what we today call the oral-formulaic theory of Homer. Less often remarked in discussions of Parry's scholarship is the fact that his research depended in no small part on a pair of modified disc recorders, referred to simply as "phonographs," that he hauled to Yugoslavia and used to record hundreds of hours of live performance. It was by applying philological methods developed across centuries of printed scholarship to an aggregated non-alphabetic audio archive that Parry was able to demonstrate the mnemonic, improvisatory, and communal basis of works that had at times been considered the crowning textual achievements of Western culture.[37] While we tend to think of Parry's work as opening a portal backward in time to the performance practices of ancient Greece, we might also consider the sense in which his work augments and hybridizes the material basis of Homer in the present. After Parry, Homer can be said to exist in the phonograph records housed in the Milman Parry Collection of Oral Literature at Harvard for the same reason Homer exists in the Venetus A manuscript in the Biblioteca Marciana in Venice, each document having proven decisive in shaping our conception of Homer's textuality. This is true even though the words Parry recorded were not Homer's words, indeed were not even Greek.

Many other examples could be gathered to illustrate the impact of modern sound recording on a host of academic and cultural fields. I offer the examples above for the light they shed on Pound. How does what I have termed the modern groove manifest in the *Cantos*? While Pound did produce audio recordings of portions of his epic poem, the *Cantos* is by and large a printed work. Reading for the groove, then, means reading for figures and tropes of analog sound recording, points at which Pound holds in tension ideals of continuous voicing with contingencies of physical medium. We can observe this dynamic in the first line of Canto 1, which opens, famously, in mid-stream:

[37] As Parry's student Albert Lord, *The Singer of Tales*, ed. Stephen Mitchell and Gregory Nagy (Cambridge: Harvard University Press, 2000), observes, "in spite of the number of books about Homer and his poems . . . the student of epic still lacks a precise idea of the actual technique of *poiesis* in its literal meaning. Thanks to Parry, however, we have the material for the research necessary to determine what this technique is. He has left us his collection of South Slavic texts, which is the record on phonograph discs and in manuscripts of experiments in the laboratory of the living epic tradition of the Yugoslavs" (3).

And then went down to the ship, (*C* 3)

Tantalizing us with narrative action that came before while removing it from view, Pound's opening underscores that this is a poem occurring in time, in the singular moment of its telling. Pound produces the same effect, in reverse, in the very last line of the Canto:

Bearing the golden bough of Argicida. So that: (*C* 5)

Here, instead of wondering what came before, we wonder what is coming next. Together, the opening and closing lines reinforce a sense that the text presented in Canto 1 is an incomplete record of continuous verbal matter. The poem was happening before Pound started transcribing it and continues after he stops. We might read Canto 1 as an extension into narrative space of Pound's notion of rhythm as "a form cut into TIME." It is a spatial structure that captures, but by the same token interrupts, the real-time unfolding of language.

The curtailed narrative shape of Canto 1 echoes another "cut form" hidden in plain sight, namely the woodcut capital A opening the first line, a feature typically omitted out of typographical expediency when the poem is quoted in critical works or included in anthologies. Decorated capitals open each of the *Cantos*. Here's how the capital in Canto 1 looks in the 1996 printing by New Directions:

Like the visibly broken syntax opening and closing the Canto ("And then"/"So that"), the woodcut A spatializes verbal time, rendering into visual form the phonemic matter contained in a single vowel. While this transcriptive process occurs anytime a phonetic script is used to represent spoken language, Pound's visually arresting capital reminds us of the fact, slowing down and denaturalizing the process whereby a reader's eye turns sight into sound, space into time. This effect occurs even more dramatically when we read Canto 1 not in the 1996 New Directions edition but in the earliest, 1925 printing of the *Cantos*, produced by Henry Strater in collaboration with Pound at the Three Mountain Press in Paris (Figure 4.1). Sprawled across the first page of the poem, so large that it can be inhabited by miniature illustrations of the action to come, the deep red 1925 capital A makes its later equivalents appear comparatively drab.

Noting that such visually ornate features are often simplified or omitted in later printings, George Bornstein argues that the more spartan design of the New Directions *Cantos* jettisons "whole levels of meaning ... levels particularly pertinent to the project of a poem that begins with an entire canto on cultural transmission."[38] Working from Jerome McGann's distinction between "bibliographical code" and "linguistic code" (i.e. the physical features of a text as distinguished from its words), Bornstein argues that later reprintings of modernist works that "emphasize only the linguistic code . . . correspond to the withering of the aura. They tend to set the text free from its original time and place, locating it in our own principally as an esthetic rather than historicized object."[39] Applying Walter Benjamin's notion of "aura" to printed materials as opposed to photography, film, and other new media, Bornstein details how intellectual and political valences of works can be tacitly suppressed when texts are adopted without critically evaluating their provenance.[40] To guard against such omissions, Bornstein proposes, scholars should "[examine] modernism in its original sites of production and in the continually shifting physicality of its texts and transmissions."[41] Bornstein's notion of "shifting physicality" pinpoints the challenge at hand. How can a printed work capture the sense of verbal flux that Pound is after? And which documents best represent the "original sites of production" in the case of the *Cantos*? Bornstein means the early printed editions, but we might also think in terms of Pound's manuscripts, or even the "odd inarticulate chant" with which Pound shaped the sound of his lines before settling on specific words.[42] While it is true that manuscripts and chants are not typically intended as public documents whereas printed books are, a mere ninety copies of *A Draft of XVI Cantos* were printed in the 1925 edition. Moreover, the word "Draft," which persists through the first three *Cantos* printings (1925, 1928, 1930) and then reappears in the final printing (1968), suggests the constantly evolving nature of Pound's epic.

---

[38] George Bornstein, *Material Modernism: The Politics of the Page* (Cambridge: Cambridge University Press, 2001), 37.

[39] Bornstein, *Material Modernism*, 7. Jerome McGann discusses this distinction in *The Textual Condition* (Princeton: Princeton University Press, 1991), 13.

[40] Though Pound's woodcuts are indeed a source of aura in the early *Cantos* printings, Walter Benjamin, *The Work of Art in the Age of Its Technological Reproducibility, and Other Writings on Media* (Cambridge: Harvard University Press, 2008), singles out "the woodcut" (20) as an early instance of mechanical reproducibility.

[41] Bornstein, *Material Modernism*, 1.

[42] Hugh Kenner, "Notes on Amateur Emendations," in Lawrence Rainey, ed., *A Poem Containing History* (Ann Arbor: University of Michigan Press, 1997), 21.

ᚦᚻᛖ
ᚠIᚱᛋᚦ
CᚨᚾᚦO

ND then went down to the ship,
Set keel to breakers, forth on the godly sea, and
We set up mast and sail on that swart ship,
Bore sheep aboard her, and our bodies also
Heavy with weeping, and winds from sternward
Bore us out onward with bellying canvas,
Circe's this craft, the trim-coifed goddess.
Then sat we amidships, wind-jamming the tiller,
Thus with stretched sail, we went over sea till day's end.
Sun to his slumber, shadows o'er all the ocean,
Came we then to the bounds of deepest water,
To the Kimmerian lands, and peopled cities
Covered with close-webbed mist, unpierced ever
With glitter of sun-rays;
Nor with stars stretched, nor looking back from heaven,
Swartest night stretched over wretched men there.
The ocean flowing backward, came we then to the place
Aforesaid by Circe.
Here did they rites, Perimedes and Eurylochus,
And drawing sword from my hip
I dug the ell-square pitkin;
Poured we libations unto each the dead,
First mead and then sweet wine, water mixed with white flour.
Then prayed I many a prayer to the sickly death's-heads;
As set in Ithaca, sterile bulls of the best
For sacrifice, heaping the pyre with goods,
A sheep to Tiresias only, black and a bell-sheep.
Dark blood flowed in the fosse,
Souls out of Erebus, cadaverous dead, of brides
Of youths and of the old who had borne much;
Souls stained with recent tears, girls tender,
       Aï

Νεκυομαντεία

Figure 4.1 First page of Ezra Pound's Canto 1, from *A Draft of XVI Cantos* (Paris: Three Mountain Press, 1925), 5. Beinecke Rare Book and Manuscript Library, Yale University

Another source of dynamism in the *Cantos* comes from its frequent allusions to other texts, which weave the work into a network of reference that exceeds the bounds of a single book. At the beginning of Canto 1, Pound produces this effect by presenting a passage from the *Odyssey* in language inflected by the prosodic conventions not of Homer's Greek but of the *Seafarer* poet's Old English:

> We set up mast and sail on that swart ship.
> Bore sheep aboard her, and our bodies also
> Heavy with weeping, and winds from sternward
> Bore us out onward with bellying canvas,
> Circe's this craft, the trim-coifed goddess. (*C* 3)

Rather than the quantitative meter of ancient Greek or the accentual-syllabic meter of the English Renaissance or indeed the *vers libre* of European modernism, Pound's lines are structured by the strongly stressed alliterative syllables and midline caesurae characteristic of Old English poetry:

> **Bore** sheep a**board** her, | and our **bod**ies also
> Heavy **with weep**ing, | and **winds** from stern**ward**

In these lines, "Homer's words" reveal themselves to be inhabited by the verbal traits of a later poetic tradition, just as the phonographically preserved voices of Parry's Slavic *guslars* are now inextricably woven into the voice we call Homer's. Later in Canto 1, Pound layers still more voices into his text. Odysseus, having dug and poured libations into an "ell-square pitkin" (*C* 3), confronts the ghost of his mother Anticlea, only for two more voices to emerge from seemingly outside the narrative space the Canto has established:

> And then Anticlea came.
> Lie quiet Divus. I mean, that is Andreas Divus,
> In officina Wecheli, 1538, out of Homer. (*C* 5)

The "I" in these lines is no longer Odysseus, but the modernist poet-translator Pound, who outs himself in conceding that he has been working not from the original Greek but from a 1538 Latin edition of Homer by the Renaissance scholar Andreas Divus, which Pound had picked up at a Paris bookstall "[in] the year of grace 1906, 1908, or 1910."[43] Divus's interruption is both one of

---

[43] Pound, *Literary Essays*, 259.

the great moments of modernist intertextuality and, within the diegetic space of the Canto, something the poet-translator would rather have avoided. His grudging, fumbling acknowledgment of his source ("I mean, that is . . . "), while establishing an intertext, is also at face value an assertion that he would have preferred to keep his cribbed voices hidden, where they could shape his prosody without showing up on his Works Cited page. There is a measure of irony, then, when critics point to the Divus episode to lament the fact that later editions of the *Cantos* fail to preserve Pound's original bibliographical codes. For Canto 1 is less about honoring bibliographical codes than about the happy ease with which linguistic codes—the text of a Latin *Odyssey*, say, or *The Seafarer*—can be stripped from books and braided into a poet's verbal imagination.

If the groove of the *Cantos* tropes voice as the obverse of inscription—grooves in time as the counterparts to grooves in space—then Pound's little-studied 1959 audio recording of Canto 1 might be understood as an almost literal instantiation of what is for the most part a figurative effect. Pound made the recording at Brunnenburg Castle during a visit from the radio producer D. G. Bridson, not long after the poet's release from St. Elizabeths Psychiatric Hospital. The recording of Canto 1 augments a purely visual, book-based understanding of the *Cantos* by adding to the poem's textual field an audio-text performed in Pound's own voice. Listening to this recording, one gains an appreciation of how important tonal effects are to Pound's poems. The most dramatic of these comes, as we might expect, in the phrase "Lie quiet Divus," or more precisely in the subsequent reiteration of this phrase ("I mean, that is Andreas Divus"). Here Pound breaks from the bardic, vibrato-laden chant he uses throughout the rest of the Canto, raising the pitch of his voice in a way that accentuates his bashfulness at having had his source discovered.[44] Someone experiencing Canto 1 for the first time via this recording would likely sense that something significant happens in the Divus line, even if they do not know precisely what. Someone working from the printed text, by contrast, receives no visual indication, aside from a line break, that Divus's arrival is the key to the Canto. Yet this distinction between acoustic and visual texts itself invites qualification. For while it is true that the New Directions editions offer no para-textual clues to Divus's importance, the 1925 *Draft of XVI Cantos* marks his arrival and signals his importance with a conspicuous marginal gloss, which reads, simply, "Divus of Capo d'Istria." What Canto 1 loses bibliographically after 1925, in other words, Pound restores phonographically in 1959 through

---

[44] Ezra Pound, "Ezra Pound: Readings and Recollections," with D. G. Bridson, recorded April 1959.

the tonal contours of his Brunnenburg recording. Precisely what he restores is harder to say, since the linguistic material that disappears is not the acoustic material Pound adds, yet these two things perform comparable functions within the poem.

As this reading suggests, the groove of the *Cantos* is not a feature of the text as much as a presumption that the text's materiality is tangled up with the prosodic and physiological mechanisms that bring it into verbal being. Thus Michael Golston's claim that "Pound develops a prosody of 'hidden' rhythms, that is, rhythms that must be *inaudible* and *invisible*."[45] This kind of rhythm, Golston explains, "is at once present and absent, a ghostly glimmer on the periphery of the writing."[46] There are also moments in the *Cantos* where grooves appear in more literal, localized forms. One of these is the "pitkin" that Pound-as-Odysseus digs in Canto 1: "I dug the ell-square pitkin." What exactly is a pitkin? From context we might infer that it is a hole or trench created by a downward cutting motion, another "cut form." But the word's origin remains obscure, and for good reason, since if we turn to the *OED* we find a single entry: "*nonce-wd*. A small pit. 1917 E. Pound. *Lustra* 199."[47] If "pitkin" is technically unprecedented, its meaning nevertheless remains legible ("pit" is an old word), as Pound suggests a few lines later when he offers another archaic word as a synonym: *fosse*, "a deep, wide-mouthed hollow or excavation." This definition fits nicely with the two early definitions of "groove" cited above: "a mining shaft" (c. 1400); "a channel or hollow, cut by artificial means" (c. 1660). Pound's inscriptive coinage "pitkin," in other words, is another attempt to merge utterance with inscription, time with space, much like Fenollosa's ideograms or Rousselot's phonoscope drawings appeared to do.

A still more obvious groove goes by that name, appearing ten lines into Canto 2. This "beach-groove" joins "pitkin" and "fosse" from Canto 1 as a site where liquid and solid forces combine to summon the voices of the dead:

> Hang it all, Robert Browning,
> there can be but the one "Sordello."
> But Sordello, and my Sordello?
> Lo Sordels si fo di Montovana.
> So-Shu churned in the sea.

[45] Golston, *Rhythm and Race*, 63.
[46] Golston, *Rhythm and Race*, 154.
[47] "pitkin, n.," *OED* Online, January 2023, Oxford University Press, https://www.oed.com/view/Entry/144,768.

> Seal sports in the spray-whited circles of cliff-wash,
> Sleek head, daughter of Lir,
>   eyes of Picasso
> Under black fur-hood, lithe daughter of Ocean;
> And the wave runs in the beach-groove:
> "Eleanor, ἑλέναυς and ἑλέπτολις!"
>   And poor old Homer blind, blind, as a bat,
> Ear, ear for the sea-surge, murmur of old men's voices   (C 6)

In contrast to Canto 1, the opening of Canto 2 flaunts its many interlocutors. Where to begin? We might start from the bottom and work up, since the play of audible and visible language Pound associates with Homer ("blind," but with an "ear for the sea-surge") emerges from a literal "beach-groove" in sand. Beginning with "old men's voices," we might glance ahead a couple of lines to note how these syllables shift into "Grecian faces" and seven lines later into "Grecian voices," phonetic modulations which translate vocal to facial data and back again.[48] Though contained within the scant space of a dozen lines of verse, these effects trope themselves as a kind of Great Vowel Shift in miniature, a gradual phonemic drift that in turn shifts the ground of semantic meaning. Conversely, the Greek alphabet a few lines above ("ἑλέναυς and ἑλέπτολις!"), inscrutable to many anglophone readers, reminds us that pronunciation can also be visually cued, scripted by fixed material forms.

What of the "beach-groove" itself? It's a curious kenning, which on a first pass invites misreading as the more poetically legible "beech grove": a cluster of trees, Dante's *selva oscura* perhaps. Twenty years after publishing *A Draft of XVI Cantos*, writing without access to his books in a Pisa prison camp, Pound will himself misremember (knowingly transform?) the phrase in just this way:

>   the tangent formed in the hand's cup
>   live wind in the beech grove
>   as strong air amid cypress (C 477)

Slipping phonemically toward "grove" while denoting material inscription, Pound's "beach-groove" is pure groove indeed, all the more so since "the wave

[48] Pound's phonemic displacements are similar to the mode of "phonemic reading" Garrett Stewart develops in *Reading Voices: Literature and the Phonotext* (Berkeley: The University of California Press, 1990), which attends to the ways consecutive printed words can blend their phonemic matter to allow new meanings to emerge. Stewart suggests that "cross-lexical slippages" in the act of silent reading can "generate an aural ambiguity that does indeed return writing to the condition of orality without the predetermined inflections of public oratory or private vocalization" (20).

[running] in the beach-groove" works much like a stylus tracing the grooves of a phonograph record, both of which motions elicit sound from matter. That "groove" and "grove" are allied in Pound's thought is suggested as well by a 1934 comment about James Joyce: "Joyce's mind has been deprived of Joyce's eyesight for too long . . . He has sat within the grove of his thought, he has mumbled things to himself, he has heard his voice on the phonograph and thought of sound, sound, mumble, murmur."[49] As it happens, Pound's location of Homer's voice in the "beach-groove" came not long after he helped see into print the story of a fictional Irishman named Stephen Dedalus that readers were to imagine as a modern Telemachus, who plods along a Dublin beach reading the language of the sea. "These heavy sands are language tide and wind have silted here," muses Joyce's wayward esthete in an episode titled "Proteus" whose corresponding "art" is Philology.[50] Earlier in the day, Stephen had traced his own phono-graphic line in the sand with his signature ashplant: "Steeeeeeeeeeeephen!" Now he stands still, eyes closed, listening: "fourworded wavespeech: seesoo, hrss, rsseeiss, ooos."[51]

The subtly displaced phonemic modulations of Pound's Canto 2 are in Joyce's rendition a condensed and continuous "wavespeech" of pure signification, a figurative melding of sign and signified under the banner of acoustic inscription. It is likely coincidental, but nonetheless significant, that both Pound and Joyce in their respective beachside scenes retrace fairly exactly the ground Edison covered in his own beachside essay of 1888, when he observed that "sound-waves set going by a human voice might be so directed as to trace an impression upon some solid substance, with a nicety equal to that of the tide in recording its flow upon a sand beach."[52] What each of these accounts registers is the fact that, in an age of analog sound recording, spoken language can be broken down and analyzed according to smaller conceptual units than alphabetic book-based methods had so far allowed. The word "phoneme" first appears in English in 1879, two years after the word "phonograph." In the opening of Canto 2, it might initially seem that Pound's quicksilver allusions partake of the logic of the book more than the logic of the phonograph. What but a library could contain and interlink the wide-ranging subjects he rattles off, beginning with the obscure thirteenth-century Italian poet Sordello? While a bibliographical logic is undoubtedly in play, so too is an acoustic, phonetic logic, which reveals itself in just two letters: *so*. Or more accurately, in

[49] Ezra Pound, "E. E. Cummings Alive," *New English Weekly*, 6/10 (1934): 210–11.
[50] James Joyce, *Ulysses* (New York: Vintage Books, 1986), 37.
[51] Joyce, *Ulysses*, 17, 41.
[52] Edison, "The Perfected Phonograph," 642.

two phonemes, /s/ and /oʊ/, which link such keywords as **So**rdello, **So**-Shu, **S**eal **sp**orts, Pica**sso**, and (in inverted position) **Oce**an, and do so phonetically as much as conceptually. Like Edison's phonograph, these phonemes process sounded frequencies rather than written meanings, and so are sonic equivalents to the woodcut capitals opening each Canto, phonemic forms cut in time echoing graphemic forms cut in space. They are, like Homer, blind, but with an ear for the sea-surge.

How do tropes of analog inscription, of the modern groove, shape a work Pound intended for audible performance rather than print publication? Between 1920 and 1924, while writing and revising the early *Cantos*, Pound began collaborating with the American composer George Antheil on an original opera titled *Le Testament de Villon*. The opera's language, Old French, combined with Antheil's musical notation, offered Pound a means of exploring what he provocatively terms "time-space":

> In 1923, that is to say two years after the completion of the original total manuscript of [*Le Testament*], arrived Mr. George Antheil; not until then particularly interested in the twelfth century, or the fifteenth, and ignorant of the language of my libretto (French of Villon); but exceedingly interested in "time-space."
>
> To my considerable surprise he was also very much interested in observing the difference between what I did in the division of time; to what I did differently from Mssrs. Stravinsky, Debussy, etc. In fact he proceeded to spend several months of his time finding out. He observed that I was exceedingly sensitive to duration, and he produced from my repeated dictation a new *graph* of the opera. Which, apart from any possible merit as music, ought to have a value as psychological experiment. Probably no two people have ever spent as much energy on producing so careful a record of durations in sequence.[53]

Antheil's musical score, which Pound calls its "graph," honors the poet's purported hypersensitivity to duration by employing a series of highly unusual time signatures: $^{11}/_{16}$, $^{25}/_{32}$, and $^{7}/_{8}$ are some of the more idiosyncratic examples. A note at the top left of the first page instructs musicians to perform "mechanically . . . ♩=♩ always." Designed to more accurately scan the speech sounds of Old French, Antheil's time signatures attempt a kind of manual

---

[53] Pound, "Dissertation on Rhythm," 8–9.

phonography, employing the binaristic tools of music notation to produce a temporally accurate record of continuous verbal data. Pound makes the project's analog ambition explicit when he suggests that one could assess the notation's accuracy by "[recording the opera] on Monsieur L'abbé Rousselot's phonoscope," recalling his visit to the French phonetician's lab a decade earlier.[54] It is worth emphasizing just how difficult it is to accurately perform Antheil's time signatures, which ask musicians to recalibrate their sense of pulse so rapidly and according to such subtle gradations as to render full temporal accuracy virtually impossible. As the composer Russell Pratt wryly observes, "The rhythmic notation is of a complexity that would have made Stravinsky blush."[55]

What the "pitkin" and "beach-groove" represent in the early *Cantos*, then— figurative attempts to collapse the dialectic of voice and inscription—become in *Le Testament* an actual attempt to "graph" syllables in a way that allows lossless transfer between audible and visible registers. It is a modernist version of the telephone game: Pound claims a hypersensitivity to durational elements of Old French, Antheil translates these durations into boutique time signatures, musicians perform sounded rhythms in response to this music notation, and no one is that surprised when the final product diverges from Pound's initial vision. Pound's and Antheil's ideas for mitigating these performance contingencies, however, are comically opposed. "I doubt if the instrumentalist will get much help from 'counting measures,'" suggests Pound. "Let him learn the *words* and make his noises when the singer reaches the *syllable* the instrument is to emphasize."[56] Antheil, meanwhile, begs that singers "not let the least bit of temperament affect in the least the correct singing of this opera, which is written as it sounds! Please do not embarrass us by suddenly developing intelligence."[57] We should pause to note the irony. As we saw at the outset of this chapter, Pound believes that the cardinal sin of modern musical practice is fetishizing accurate reproduction, what he calls "having a memory like a phonograph." Yet such a memory is exactly what Antheil demands when he asks singers to avoid developing intelligence. He wants them to perform the opera exactly as written. In a note scribbled by Pound near the bottom of the *Le Testament* score, he acknowledges that the goal of creating a score that would collapse "time-space" was never really feasible. Referring to a smaller arrangement of the opera performed in Paris in 1926, Pound writes, "In the

---

[54] Pound, "Dissertation on Rhythm," 11.
[55] Russell Pratt, "There Is Nothing Quite Like Ezra Pound's Opera," *The New Yorker* (April 29, 2017).
[56] Pound's and Antheil's comments are included on the title page of the score to *Le Testament*. Ezra Pound Papers (YCAL MSS 43). Box 238, folder 13. American Literature Collection, Beinecke Rare Book and Manuscript Library, Yale University.
[57] Pound, *Le Testament*.

case of the simpler notation used for the Paris concert, the performer is asked to understand that the music was not supposed to be changed. The difference in the *graph* is due merely to [the] question *which* graph was most likely to convey the idea of the music." Antheil's score may finally have less "merit as music," as we have seen Pound concede, than as "psychological experiment." These comments make clear the poet's more genuine belief in music as an activity that stimulates "intelligence" and "constructive faculty" instead of simply demanding rote reproduction. The opera's "graph," as Pound redefines it here, is not an attempt at perfect temporal capture, which is indeed the purview of the phonograph or phonoscope, but simply a spur toward aesthetic experience. The proof of this lies in what Pound calls "the confession that will damn me once and for all." Namely: "I did not do the damn thing exactly the same every time."[58]

Though the word "graph" in the twentieth century takes on certain flat, mathematical connotations, Pound's experiments in opera make clear that the word appeals to him primarily for its association with writing and inscription, the same association that led Edison to adopt the Greek termination when naming his own inscriptive device.[59] "Graph" gives us the modern English word "carve," and when Pound calls the *Le Testament* score its graph he is drawing once again on the notion of acoustic forms "cut into TIME," sounds carved into a physical medium for the purpose of later reactivation. Perhaps the most explicit merging of Pound's musical and poetic *graphs* occurs in Canto 75, composed while the poet was incarcerated in a Pisa prison camp, which aside from a few lines of introductory text is comprised entirely of a musical score (Figure 4.2). The score is an arrangement for violin of the choral work "Les Chants des Oiseaux" ("The Songs of the Birds") by the French composer Clément Janequin. In contrast to the score of *Le Testament*, the score in Canto 75 attempts to capture not continuous vocal data but the continuous movement of birds, which perch on barbed wire around the Disciplinary Training Center like quarter notes and half notes perched on the staves of a musical staff. The implication is that the score presented in Canto 75 is but one snapshot among many that Pound could have reproduced. For as the birds flit in and out of his visual field, the notes on the barbed wire staff change positions—"8 birds on a wire / or rather on 3 wires" (*C* 505); "5 of 'em now on

---

[58] Pound, "Dissertation on Rhythm," 11.

[59] Lawrence Rainey, *Ezra Pound and the Monument of Culture: Text, History, and the Malatesta Cantos* (Chicago: The University of Chicago Press, 1991), further contextualizes Pound's use of the word "graph": "Since [Pound] could not take his typewriter with him when he was traveling, he was forced to write letters and other works by hand, and for this purpose he preferred to use graph paper, perhaps because the close, fixed pattern of lines helped to anchor his unsteady pen" (231).

2; / on 3; 7 on 4" (*C* 506)—and the score rewrites itself in front of the poet's eyes:

> f f
>   d
>   g
>   write the birds in their treble scale (*C* 545)

What precisely are we looking at? Numerous competing answers present themselves, for Pound has rendered the birds as a function of multiple overlapping sound systems. Most obviously, the birds are inked letters, single graphemes taken from the Roman alphabet. In this, they double the woodcuts opening each Canto, also single letters, if more ornate, capitalized versions of the humble lowercase letters. Like the woodcuts, Pound's birds are also units of sound, not only because of their association with poetic lyricism but because single alphabetic letters customarily correspond to a language's smallest units of spoken sound. As if this were not enough, Pound further implicates his larks in a system of non-linguistic sound writing, that of musical notation, which borrows letters—or in the case of solfège, syllables (e.g. *do, re, me, fa*)—from the Roman alphabet to indicate individual pitches of the diatonic scale.

But of course the tonal values of letters as phonemes, letters as pitches, and letters as both syllables and pitches do not perfectly correspond.[60] Instead of straightforwardly cuing a single reading or performance, then, Pound's graphing of birds draws attention to the variety of notation systems—some complementary, others not—with which one might record verbal and acoustic data. More than anywhere in the *Cantos*, it is in Pisa that Pound, stripped of his books, produces a poetry that oscillates between phonetics and semantics, sounds in time and patterns in space. Often these phonetic-semantic effects are distributed across multiple pages, sometimes even across the entire *Cantos* corpus. In Canto 76 for instance, the phonemic murmur of "olives grey over grey" (*C* 473) suggests other resonant possibilities—*live, grave, grove*—but we have to wait four pages for these sounds to coalesce into "live wind in the beech grove" (*C* 477), which itself echoes back twenty years and 450 pages

---

[60] Pound makes exactly this observation in a humorous passage from his "Dissertation on Rhythm": "My stupidity about the Greek alphabet, and in fact about any alphabet save the Roman, has often amused me. Pitch I might have discovered thirty years since, but for early instruction. That is to say I was as an infant interested in words; and to be presented with DO (pronounced 'dough' and spelled like the verb 'to do'), RE (ray), MI (me), FA (not quite 'far'), SOL, LA, SI (see or sea), DOUGH; instead of with variations in a *sound*; all of which different noises were easily differentiable by their combinations of vowel and consonant; and to have the matter further bungled by a CHART with stripes of COLOUR on it! Plus the dullness of being asked about DOUGH! In a life full of other interest" (5).

LXXV

Out of Phlegethon!
    out of Phlegethon,
       Gerhart
           art thou come forth out of Phlegethon?
with Buxtehude and Klages in your satchel, with the
Ständebuch of Sachs in yr/ luggage
           —not of one bird but of many

Figure 4.2 First page of Ezra Pound's Canto 75, including the score to "Les Chants des Oiseaux" ("The Songs of the Birds"), from *The Cantos of Ezra Pound* (New York: New Directions, 1996), 470. Hauser Memorial Library, Reed College

to the "beach-groove" of Canto 2. What matters, Pound writes in some of the most famous lines of the *Pisan Cantos*, is not accurate sonic reproduction,

but the quality

of the affection—
in the end—that has carved the trace in the mind
dove sta memoria (*C* 477)

After three lines in English, and without any typographical heads up, we may read "dove" as another English monosyllable. But the word is Italian ("doh-vay"), part of a phrase borrowed from Cavalcanti meaning something like "where memory liveth." Memory lives, Pound suggests, in the dynamic inter-change of material texts and human minds, both of which are "carved" in relation to the other. And as language shuttles between sound and writing, data is inevitably mistranscribed and misremembered. A case in point, the sirens (sometimes referred to as "mermaids") in the church of Santa Maria dei Miracoli, a carving of such importance to Pound that his early promoter Hugh Kenner claims to have traveled to the Venetian church "at the behest of three words" in Canto 83 ("mermaids, that carving" [*C* 549]).[61] In fact, the sirens were carved not by father and son "Romano"—as Pound writes in Canto 76—but "Lombardo," that is, from Lombardy. Pound, lacking a library in Pisa, misremembered. Yet the error is felicitous, emerging as it does from an encounter with those "fabulous monsters, part woman, part bird, who were supposed to lure sailors to destruction by their enchanting singing" (*OED*). To carve a siren is to transcribe its enchantment, to graph its song, so to speak, knowing full well that the song's charm lies in its airy evanescence.

In the summer of 1911, twenty-five-year-old Pound journeyed to Freiberg to visit Emil Lévy, a German philologist then working on an eight-volume Provençal dictionary. Pound brought with him, Canto 20 recalls, "two strips of copy," transcriptions of musical settings of the troubadour Arnaut Daniel that he had made while at the Ambrosiana library in Milan. Lévy perused Pound's transcriptions with interest, and then asked, "Now is there anything I can tell you?" (*C* 89):

"Yes, Doctor, what do they mean by *noigandres?*"
And he said: Noigandres? NOIgandres!
"You know for seex mon's of my life

---

[61] Hugh Kenner, *The Pound Era* (Berkeley: The University of California Press, 1971), xi.

"Effery night when I go to bett, I say to myself:
"Noigandres, eh, *noi*gandres,
"Now what the DEFFIL can that mean!" (*C*89–90)

The mysterious "noigandres" appears in just one text, an 1883 edition of Daniel's poems edited by U. A. Canello.[62] Unable to cross-reference the word, Pound was lost, as had been Lévy "for seex mon's of my life." But the Canto gives clues as to how the riddle was solved: "Sound: as of the nightingale too far off to be heard" (*C* 90). Attending to sound, one loosens lexical boundaries normalized by print. Thus Lévy's searching prosodic contortions ("NOIgandres," "*noi*gandres"), which, the Canto divulges, dissolved the Provençal non-word into multiple words: "*d'enoi ganres*," meaning something like "wards off boredom." Pound renders this triumph of phonetics typographically even as his own phonetic transcriptions of Lévy's audibly accented English ("Effrey," "bett," "DEFFIL") generate words that, like "noigrandes," will never appear in a dictionary. The distance between sound and writing can be pronounced. When that distance is made the subject of poetry, "the cliff folds in like a curtain . . . Square groove in the cliff's face" (*C* 95). Cliffs like curtains, square grooves: forms cut in time like the sinuous woodcut S opening Canto 20 in its first printing (Figure 4.3). This particular woodcut puts the S in "SOUND," but as its ink drips down the text's left margin it suggests another word, too.

---

[62] Kenner meditates at greater length on the "noigandres" incident in *The Pound Era*, 113–18.

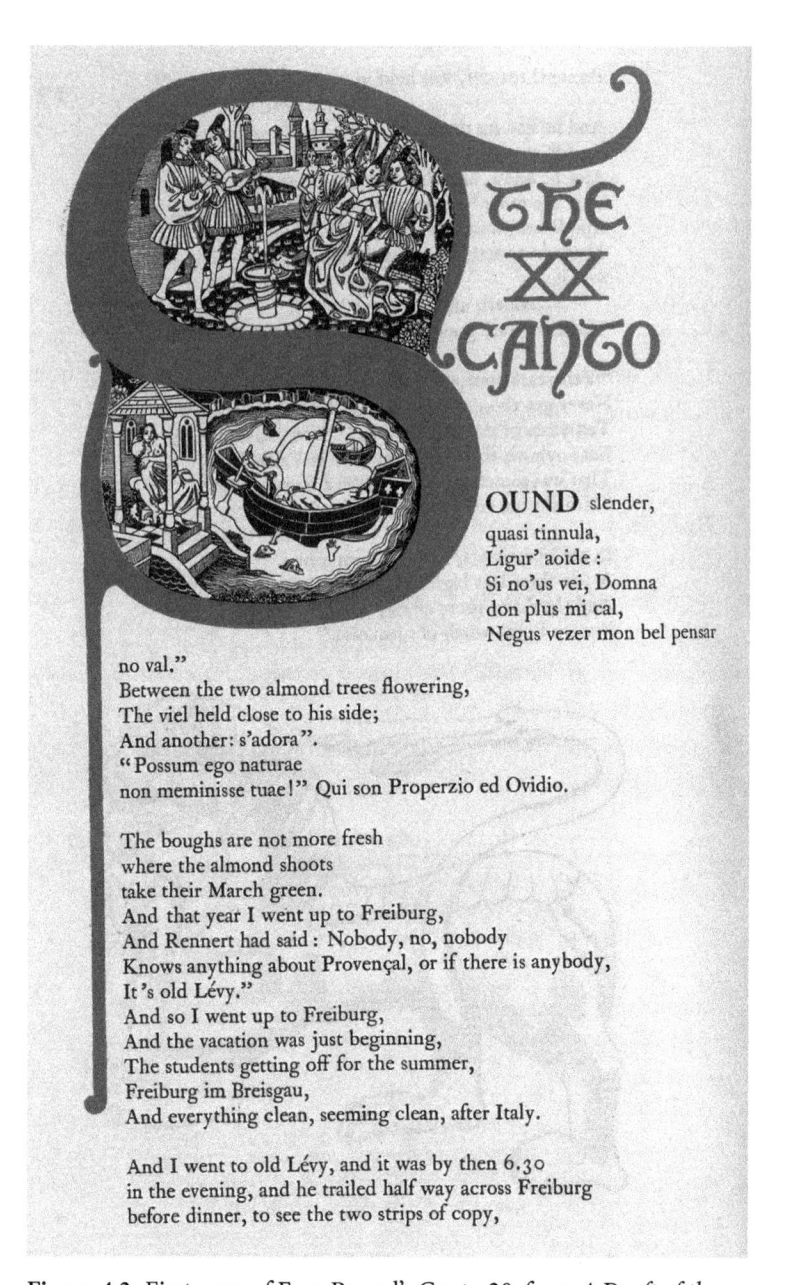

OUND slender,
quasi tinnula,
Ligur' aoide :
Si no'us vei, Domna
don plus mi cal,
Negus vezer mon bel pensar

no val."
Between the two almond trees flowering,
The viel held close to his side;
And another: s'adora".
"Possum ego naturae
non meminisse tuae!" Qui son Properzio ed Ovidio.

The boughs are not more fresh
where the almond shoots
take their March green.
And that year I went up to Freiburg,
And Rennert had said : Nobody, no, nobody
Knows anything about Provençal, or if there is anybody,
It's old Lévy."
And so I went up to Freiburg,
And the vacation was just beginning,
The students getting off for the summer,
Freiburg im Breisgau,
And everything clean, seeming clean, after Italy.

And I went to old Lévy, and it was by then 6.30
in the evening, and he trailed half way across Freiburg
before dinner, to see the two strips of copy,

Figure 4.3 First page of Ezra Pound's Canto 20, from *A Draft of the Cantos 17–27* (London: John Rodker, 1928), 18. Albert and Shirley Small Special Collections Library, University of Virginia

5

Paper Records

Langston Hughes's poem "Theme for English B" opens with a homework assignment:

> Go home and write
> a page tonight.
> And let that page come out of you—
> Then, it will be true.[1]

The instructor that assigns a college-aged Hughes the assignment presents poetry as a spontaneous outpouring of authentic selfhood, an idealized definition framed in the lines above by another idealized feature of English-language poetry: iambic rhythms. But the particular way Hughes packages the instructor's iambs—in a rhyming dimeter couplet, followed by a longer tetrameter line—makes them feel singsong, with the effect that the verse marks itself as self-consciously, rather than unknowingly, poetic. So in the following lines Hughes entertains a more critical theory of poetry:

> I wonder if it's that simple?
> I am twenty-two, colored, born in Winston-Salem.
> I went to school there, then Durham, then here
> to this college on the hill above Harlem.[2]

After two lines comprised of end-stopped sentences, Hughes's verse grows increasingly colloquial and enjambed, until autobiography morphs into a present tense, stream-of-consciousness transcript of the poet's real-time activities:

> then I cross St. Nicholas,
> Eighth Avenue, Seventh, and I come to the Y,

---

[1] Langston Hughes, *The Collected Works of Langston Hughes: The Poems, 1951–1967, Vol. 3*, ed. Arnold Rampersad (Columbia: The University of Missouri Press, 2002), 52.
[2] Hughes, *Poems, 1951–1967*, 52.

Poetry, Sound, and the Matter of Prosody 1800–2000. Peter Miller, Oxford University Press. © Peter Miller (2025).
DOI: 10.1093/9780198937210.003.0006

> the Harlem Branch Y, where I take the elevator
> up to my room, sit down, and write this page:[3]

In one sense, Hughes has fulfilled the instructor's assignment to the letter, penning a lyric passage that speaks truthfully to his lived experiences rather than attempting to conform to other people's demands or expectations. And yet Hughes also suggests that his brand of lyric may fail to register as such within the predominantly white social space of the college classroom and, by extension, the English tradition in poetry. Even as the instructor demands authentic individuality, the poem implies, he represents Anglo-American institutions and traditions that have historically sought to curtail Black expression. Organized around this contradiction, "Theme for English B" places the Romantic ideal of unfettered poetic speech in a fruitful tension with the social and material conditions of specific poetic acts.

The tension is one Hughes navigated across his career. By incorporating into his poetry Black vernacular speech and musical tropes borrowed from blues and jazz, Hughes produced a body of work often characterized as verbally authentic and sonically immediate. Hughes himself often characterized his work in these terms. Writing to Countee Cullen in 1923, he describes some lines of enclosed verse as "the poetry of sound, pure sound," claiming that it "[marked] the beginning of a new era, an era of revolt against the trite and outworn language of the understandable."[4] In his autobiography *The Big Sea*, Hughes downplays the role of craft and revision in his artistic process, recalling writing "The Negro Speaks of Rivers" on the back of an envelope while traveling by train from St. Louis to Mexico. "No doubt I changed a few words the next day," Hughes writes, "or maybe crossed out a line or two. But there are seldom many changes in my poems, once they're down."[5] Passages like this present Hughes's poetry as aural, transcriptive, and immediate, and one of the dominant strains of Hughes criticism has emphasized what Herman Beavers calls the poet's "aural aesthetic."[6] Hughes's biographer Arnold Rampersad names Hughes's 1927 collection *Fine Clothes to the Jew* his "greatest collection of verse" because it presents a "barely mediated recording of the sounds and sights of black life."[7]

---

[3] Hughes, *Poems, 1951–1967*, 52.

[4] Langston Hughes, *Selected Letters of Langston Hughes*, ed. Arnold Rampersad and David Roessel (New York: Knopf, 2015), 19.

[5] Langston Hughes, *The Big Sea: An Autobiography* (New York: Hill and Wang, 1993), 56.

[6] Herman Beavers, "Dead Rocks and Sleeping Men: Aurality in the Aesthetic of Langston Hughes," *The Langston Hughes Review*, 11/1 (Spring 1992): 2.

[7] Arnold Rampersad, "Langston Hughes's Fine Clothes to the Jew," *Callaloo*, 26 (Winter 1986): 144, 146. See also Steven Tracy, *Langston Hughes and the Blues* (Urbana: The University of Illinois Press, 1988), who focuses on musical immediacy and authenticity in observing that blues "is the very essence of the souls of the black folk who were so important to Hughes's artistic expression" (2).

From another perspective, of course, Hughes's poetry is highly mediated. The cover of his first collection, *The Weary Blues*, features an African-American blues musician in silhouette, which presents to the reader certain notions of Black expressiveness even before the poems do. As Lesley Wheeler observes, "From the beginning of his career, Langston Hughes sought ways to deliver voice and music into the visual medium of print. Even his famous musically based ventures—the development of poetic correlatives to blues and jazz—form part of his visual poetics, since in them he attempts to make sound visible."[8] Another significant medium was the commercial phonograph record, which by the 1920s was powering a surge of interest in jazz and blues music. "[In] Chicago in my teens," Hughes reflects in 1964, "all up and down State Street there were blues, indoors and out, at the Grand and the old Monogram theaters where Ma Rainey sang, in the night clubs, in the dance halls, on phonographs."[9] Hughes's timeline is not entirely accurate, since in the years he refers to no commercial blues records yet existed.[10] Yet the mistake fruitfully illustrates the way in which an ostensibly oral form like the blues is nevertheless enmeshed in the visual conventions of print and the acoustic conventions of modern phonography.[11]

This chapter presents Hughes as a key theorist and practitioner of a media-oriented prosody. As the poet quips in "Theme for English B," "So will my page be colored that I write?" (53), pointing out the difference between the production of race and the printing of books, while also asking us to contemplate how the elements of a visual text can indeed evoke certain racial concepts.[12] Few studies exist of African-American prosodic innovation. As Meta Jones observes, "Too often, studies of black poetics reveal a dearth of serious criticism of the craft that exacerbates a divide between craft and politics," a state of affairs that could be improved, Jones suggests, through "thicker descriptions of sustained structural, metrical, and non-metrical investigations of poems infused with jazz."[13] Taking up Jones's charge, this chapter first

---

[8] Lesley Wheeler, *Voicing American Poetry: Sound and Performance from the 1920s to the Present* (Ithaca: Cornell University Press, 2008), 62.

[9] Langston Hughes, "I Remember the Blues," *Missouri Reader*, ed. F. L. Mott (Columbia: University of Missouri Press, 1964), 152–53.

[10] David Chinitz, *Which Sin to Bear? Authenticity and Compromise in Langston Hughes* (Oxford: Oxford University Press, 2013), 223n28.

[11] Alexander Wehelie, *Phonographies: Grooves in Sonic Afro-Modernity* (Durham: Duke University Press, 2005), observes that Hughes tends not to "dwell on the technological aspects" (114) of his listening habits. Yet this should not be taken as Hughes's entirely rosy view of the music industry. Writing to Claude McKay in 1926, the poet lamented that "Some of the colored victrola records are unbearably vulgar, too. Not even funny or half-sad any more. Very bad, moronish, and, I'm afraid, largely Jewish business men are exploiting Negro things for all they're worth" (*Selected Letters*, 87).

[12] Hughes, *Poems, 1951–1967*, 53.

[13] Meta Jones, *The Muse Is Music: Jazz Poetry from the Harlem Renaissance to Spoken Word* (Urbana: The University of Illinois Press, 2011), 87. Other important studies of African-American prosody include Charles Hartman, *Jazz Text: Voice and Improvisation in Poetry, Jazz, and Song* (Princeton:

examines Hughes's first two collections of poems, *The Weary Blues* (1926) and *Fine Clothes to the Jew* (1927), showing how their scenes of live performance implicate themselves in the media discourses of sound recording and print. The second, longer section considers the last book of poetry Hughes published, *Ask Your Mama: 12 Moods for Jazz* (1961). The most visually and bibliographically ornate of Hughes's books, *Ask Your Mama* calls attention to its bookishness and so unsettles reading habits that too easily translate the voice(s) of Hughes's poems into an idealized notion of Black collectivity. And yet the book's unique visual elements, which include liner notes, instrumental cues, and all-caps text, are also what frame the work as a kind of musical score demanding literal collective performance. At once a record of past sounds and a score for future performance, *Ask Your Mama* invites readers to reframe prosody as a collaborative, multimedial event.

The title poem of *The Weary Blues* centers on a blues musician in Harlem:

> Droning a drowsy syncopated tune,
> Rocking back and forth to a mellow croon,
>   I heard a Negro play.[14]

Inspired by this performance, the poem's speaker incorporates blues elements into his own speech, syncopating his opening line's iambic pentameter norm by substituting a trochee in the first foot:

Droning | a **drow** | sy **sync** | opat | ed **tune**

His repetitions and exclamations ("O blues!", "Sweet blues!") borrow from oral forms, and twice the speaker includes quoted material we are to understand as the actual blues lyrics heard performed in Harlem: "'Ain't got nobody in all this world, / Ain't got nobody but ma self. / I's gwine to quit ma frownin' / And put ma troubles on the shelf'" (23). Yet if "The Weary Blues" is inspired by live performance, it is in other ways markedly removed from the scene. The grammatical ambiguity of the poem's opening lines, whose dangling modifiers position not "a Negro" but "I" as the performer, blends the performing musician with the reflective poet. The following couplet produces a similar effect: "Down on Lenox Avenue the other night / By the pale dull pallor of an old

Princeton University Press, 1991), Anthony Reed, *Freedom Time: The Poetics and Politics of Black Experimental Writing* (Baltimore: Johns Hopkins University Press, 2014), and Ben Glaser, *Modernism's Metronome: Meter and Twentieth Century Poetics* (Baltimore: Johns Hopkins University Press, 2020).

[14] Langston Hughes, *The Collected Works of Langston Hughes: The Poems, 1921–1940, Vol. 1*, ed. Arnold Rampersad (Columbia: The University of Missouri Press, 2002), 23. Subsequent references to this volume are cited parenthetically and abbreviated *H*.

gas light" (23). The first line's colloquial delivery and first-hand geographical knowledge affirm the actuality of the depicted event, while the second line's conspicuous poeticisms—the spondaic "**pale dull pall**or" and "**old gas light**," with all their Symbolist resonance—remind us that this event is being produced by the text at hand. The syncopation of the opening line, similarly, which feels jazzed in context, is produced by a first-foot trochaic substitution that appears regularly in the work of Milton, Keats, and other canonical figures. And while the doubling of "He did a lazy sway . . . / He did a lazy sway . . . " (23) emulates the lineal repetitions characteristic of the blues, it also could be read as evidence of the speaker's wistful vantage point. As Jahan Ramazani observes, "This blues is already a blues for the blues, the poet mourning his professional distance from the oral, proletarian, vernacular culture that he memorializes."[15]

Lisa Hollenbach suggests that Hughes's blending of real-time performance and literary reflection in "The Weary Blues" evokes the kind of listening associated with the phonograph record. "[In] the 1920s when Hughes published his first poems," Hollenbach observes, "the distribution of music through recorded sound rather than through sheet music and live performance had only recently taken hold as a mass cultural phenomenon in the US."[16] On one hand, the phonograph record's ability to preserve and reproduce actual sounds appeared to offer listeners a portal into oral, rural, and non-technological cultural forms such as African-American blues. On the other hand, the sense of authentic cultural access the phonograph afforded was dependent on a media technology that was displacing vocal and musical sounds from their embodied origins. Hollenbach suggests that this tension underwrites the "strange portrait of listening" Hughes presents in "The Weary Blues": "The potentially endless repetition of the song . . . which continues playing even beyond the consciousness of the performer, parallels the repetitive possibilities of the recorded song while aligning the blues singer with the phonograph as the medium rather than the clear source of the blues."[17] Hollenbach concludes that, "in foregrounding listening as a socially constructed act mediated through technologies of race as well as sound, Hughes locates the authenticity of African American popular music not in its origins or authentically 'folk' performers but in its reception among the listeners who spin blues and jazz records around the world."[18]

---

[15] Jahan Ramazani, *Poetry of Mourning: The Modern Elegy from Hardy to Heaney* (Chicago: The University of Chicago Press, 1994), 145.

[16] Lisa Hollenbach, "Sono-Montage: Langston Hughes and Tony Schwartz Listen to Postwar New York," *American Literature*, 87/2 (2015): 302.

[17] Hollenbach, "Sono-Montage," 310.

[18] Hollenbach, "Sono-Montage," 304.

Hollenbach's claim could be applied as well to the experience of reading Hughes's poems in printed form, where authenticity is not a feature of the text or the voices it represents as much as a sensation produced at the scene of reading.[19] A poem like "Negro Dancers," for instance, enlists the reader in a performance of song lyrics that describe, and perhaps even initiate, a specific dance step:

> "Me an' ma baby's
> Got two mo' ways,
> Two mo' ways to do de buck!
>> Da, da,
>>> Da, da, da!
> Two mo' ways to do de buck!" (*H* 25)

Quotation marks, vernacular spellings, repetitions, and exclamations all contribute to the performative, musical atmosphere of this stanza. The next stanza, by comparison, is imagistic, reflective, and literary:

> Soft light on the tables,
> Music gay,
> Brown-skin steppers
> In a cabaret. (25)

Yet despite the languidness of "**Soft light** on the tables," the second stanza obeys a larger musical structure, the first three stressed syllables of each line establishing the pulse in order for the fourth stressed syllable to arrive, in syncopated fashion, just before the fourth beat:

1   2   3   4

Soft **light** on the **tables**, **music gay**,

1   2   3   4

Brown-skin **steppers** in a **cabaret**.[20]

---

[19] T. Austin Graham, *The Great American Songbooks: Musical Texts, Modernism, and the Value of Popular Culture* (Oxford: Oxford University Press, 2013), argues that Hughes's allusions to popular songs allowed readers to not only read his printed poems silently but, in effect, to sing along with them. Music-based Harlem Renaissance poems by Hughes and others, Graham suggests, allowed readers, "in temporary and metaphorical ways, to sing their way into and occupy a different racial identity altogether" (113).

[20] If you prefer, each line's fourth stressed syllable could be placed squarely on the fourth musical beat; but to my ear this option sounds a bit, well, square. For an analogous prosodic case, listen to the opening of Hughes's 1951 poem "Dream Boogie," *Poems, 1951–1967*, which likewise syncopates its final stressed syllables just left of beat four: "Good **morning**, **daddy**! **Ain't** you **heard** / The **boogie**-woogie **rum**ble of a **dream** deferred?" (27).

This musical prosody in turn invites a reconsideration of the musicality of the first stanza. For to a reader expecting Standard English, the vernacular spellings and elisions may well impede rather than facilitate a specific musical reading. The most markedly performative aspect of the first stanza, the scat syllables "Da, da, da," are syntactically isolated and semantically opaque in a way that, prosodically speaking, leaves much to interpretation. They call to mind the thrice-repeated "DA" in the conclusion of T. S. Eliot's *The Waste Land*, which had appeared to great fanfare just a few years earlier, and they all but name the Dada movement whose Paris branch Hughes would have been aware of during his 1923 stint as a dishwasher at Le Grand Duc in Montmartre.

This push and pull between the poetry's real-time musicality and its visual, typographical features is even more pronounced in "The Cat and the Saxophone (2 A.M.)," which attempts to capture the sonic cacophony of a jazz club by employing two distinct typefaces:

> EVERYBODY
> Half-pint,—
> Gin?
> No, make it
> LOVERS MY BABY
> Corn. You like
> Liquor,
> don't you, honey?
> BUT MY BABY
> Sure. Kiss me,
> DON'T LOVE NOBODY
> daddy.
> BUT ME. (*H*25–26)

Anticipating the typographical play of *Ask Your Mama*, the poem asks readers to parse two distinct but overlapping audio files, one rendered in all caps, the other in sentence case. The all-caps text presents lyrics from the 1924 ragtime standard "Everybody Loves My Baby" by Jack Palmer and Spencer William. The sentence-case text presents a flirtatious conversation between a man and woman at a bar. Though it is possible to scan the poem linearly for its linguistic prosody, this is presumably not what Hughes is after. "Blues is an oral poem," writes David Chinitz, "and even the most powerful blues lyric in performance is not necessarily effective when transferred to the printed page."[21]

---

[21] Chinitz, *Which Sin*, 67.

Though "The Cat and the Saxophone (2 A.M.)" is not a blues poem per se, part of its charm surely emerges from the contrast it sets up between its raucous soundscape and its relative silence on the printed page. Met with this contrast, one might be inspired to assemble the various sound media the poem enlists: at a minimum, two human speakers and a jukebox, say. Then again, one might wish to understand the poem's sounds as basically figurative or virtual, and to focus on the integrity of the poem as a visual, printed text. Lesley Wheeler advocates this approach when she argues that Hughes's blues poems, despite their clear debt to musical and acoustic forms, are "complete in textual form, as visual evocations of sound that can be, but need not be, performed."[22] Perhaps the best approach is to combine Wheeler's and Chinitz's positions, engaging Hughes's poems as printed, visual, literary objects as well as acoustic, musical, performed objects. The particular mediating forms and genres a given poem evokes will of course vary from one instance to the next; so too will the precise manner in which the poem navigates the aural-visual spectrum. What a media-oriented approach to Hughes's prosody makes evident, in other words, is quite simply its multimediated nature, its constitution by an array of overlapping sonic forms and gestures.

In the summer of 1960, the Newport Jazz Festival was abruptly cut short after a crowd of young white men, having been denied entry to the sold-out event, began rioting in the streets. Hughes, an official for the festival, marked its bitter finale with a hastily prepared "Goodbye Newport Blues," which he expanded into a draft of Ask Your Mama over the coming months. Moving from the supermarket to the halls of congress, Caribbean islands to American plantations, Hughes's book pursues a dizzying cultural odyssey, traveling in Book 1 from the United States to Ghana, Egypt, Nigeria, and Cuba in the space of just seven lines, before departing for other parts of the globe. If the book is ostentatiously multicultural, it is also unavoidably multimedial. Figuring itself as a vinyl record, the squarish book includes a set of supplemental "Liner Notes" that gloss each of its twelve preceding sections and suggest, moreover, that one can simply place the book on a turntable and it will reproduce the sounds inside. Yet while many of Ask Your Mama's visual, bibliographical features support the conceit that the book is a self-playing musical text, many of these same features work to interrupt and denaturalize the reading process. Multicolored paper and ink, abstract geometric artwork, odd typographical elements, musical scoring and marginal performance cues:

[22] Wheeler, Voicing American Poetry, 67.

these features, by drawing attention to themselves, also draw attention to the question of how exactly a reader is meant to respond to them. This audio-visual back-and-forth is captured by the "12" in the book's title, which refers variously to its number of sections, the twelve-bar blues, the twelve-note chromatic scale, and, perhaps most significantly, the Dozens, the game of vernacular one-upmanship traditional in African-American communities.[23] Like "The Cat and the Saxophone (2 A.M.)" but at a much grander scale, *Ask Your Mama* both demands and deflects performative engagement by the reader.

This dynamic perplexed and indeed annoyed many of the book's first readers. One particularly harsh response came from Dudley Fitts, who wrote in the *New York Times Book Review* that "Langston Hughes' twelve jazz pieces cannot be evaluated by any canon dealing with literary right or wrong. They are non-literary—oral, vocal, compositions to be spoken, or shouted, to the accompaniment of drum and flute and bass . . . stunt poetry; a nightclub turn."[24] In hindsight, Fitts's response is ironic on a couple of fronts. First, dismissive as it is, his review highlights many of the features (e.g. orality, mediated texture, extra-literary ambition) that later critics would praise in Hughes's book. Second, Hughes took particular pride not only in *Ask Your Mama*'s "oral, vocal" elements but also in its visual, bibliographic elements. As his Knopf editor Judith Jones recalls, Hughes "planned something different for the book, something with more color and variety than our usual sort of poetry book . . . He saw the book as different, and he wanted it to look different."[25] Writing in 1961 to Arna Bontemps, Hughes bragged: "MAMA is stunning, in fact, should win a Graphic Arts prize for format and unique design."[26] And even after the book was panned by critics Hughes stood by its appearance, writing to Jones in 1966 that it would be "wonderful" if their current book project, *The Panther and the Lash*, turned out "anywhere near as handsome as ASK YOUR MAMA."[27]

Though comprised of many overlapping media, perhaps the most decisive structural element of *Ask Your Mama* is Hughes's pairing of his main poetic text (in all caps, to the left) with its musical cues (in italics, to the right) (Figure 5.1). The opening two stanzas of Book 1, titled "Cultural Exchange," read as follows:

[23] For a detailed analysis of the Dozens' role in *Ask Your Mama*, see Larry Scanlon, "News from Heaven: Vernacular Time in Langston Hughes's *Ask Your Mama*," *Callaloo*, 25/1 (2002): 45–65.

[24] Dudley Fitts, "A Trio of Singers," *New York Times*, October 29, 1961.

[25] Arnold Rampersad, *The Life of Langston Hughes, Volume 2, 1941–1967: I Dream a World* (Oxford: Oxford University Press, 1989), 329.

[26] Hughes, *Selected Letters*, 375.

[27] Hughes, *Selected Letters*, 412.

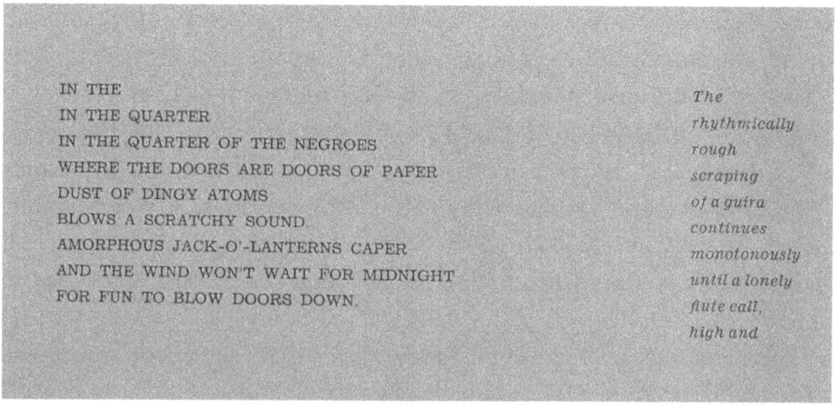

IN THE
IN THE QUARTER
IN THE QUARTER OF THE NEGROES
WHERE THE DOORS ARE DOORS OF PAPER
DUST OF DINGY ATOMS
BLOWS A SCRATCHY SOUND.
AMORPHOUS JACK-O'-LANTERNS CAPER
AND THE WIND WON'T WAIT FOR MIDNIGHT
FOR FUN TO BLOW DOORS DOWN.

The
rhythmically
rough
scraping
of a guira
continues
monotonously
until a lonely
flute call,
high and

Figure 5.1 Two-column formatting of Langston Hughes's *Ask Your Mama: 12 Moods for Jazz* (New York: Knopf, 1961), 3. Magdalen College Library, Oxford University

IN THE
IN THE QUARTER
IN THE QUARTER OF THE NEGROES
WHERE THE DOORS ARE DOORS OF PAPER
DUST OF DINGY ATOMS
BLOWS A SCRATCHY SOUND.
AMORPHOUS JACK-O'-LANTERNS CAPER
AND THE WIND WON'T WAIT FOR MIDNIGHT
FOR FUN TO BLOW DOORS DOWN.

BY THE RIVER AND THE RAILROAD
WITH FLUID FAR-OFF GOING
BOUNDARIES BIND UNBINDING
A WHIRL OF WHISTLES BLOWING
NO TRAINS OR STEAMBOATS GOING—
YET LEONTYNE'S UNPACKING.

The
rhythmically
rough
scraping
of a guira
continues
monotonously
until a lonely
flute call,
high and
far away,
merges
into piano
variations
on German
lieder[28]

What is the prosody of this passage? Confining our analysis to the left-hand verse, we can observe a generally trochaic tetrameter pattern:

In the | **quart**er | **of** the | **ne**groes
Where the | **doors** are | **doors** of | **pap**er

Kathy Schultz, applying the concept of African-American "signifying" theorized by Henry Louis Gates, suggests that Hughes's trochaic lines "[signify] on Longfellow," mocking both the prosodically lockstep metrics of the American

[28] Langston Hughes, *Ask Your Mama: 12 Moods for Jazz* (New York: Knopf, 1961), 3–4. Subsequent references to this book are cited parenthetically and abbreviated *AYM*.

fireside poet and his dubious ethnography in *The Song of Hiawatha*.[29] Compared to Longfellow's verse, Hughes's trochaic lines are indeed more varied and flexible. In the passage above, the first two lines stutter from monometer to dimeter before reaching the tetrameter norm in line 3. Other lines are anacrustic, meaning they feature added pick-up syllables, within the trochaic paradigm. End rhymes come at irregular intervals, producing moments of stanzaic coherence—such as the hint of ballad meter in the first four lines of stanza 2—that then fade away.

Yet any prosodic analysis of the left-hand verse is at all turns impinged upon by the right-hand musical cues, which themselves purport to provide rhythmic and tonal information about the work. So also, presumably, does the all-caps formatting, a feature that is not visually supplemental to the left-hand text but internal to it. Prosodic analysis of *Ask Your Mama*, in other words, inevitably entails the reader in a study not only of the poem's linguistic and metrical rhythms, but of the array of more or less supplementary media, genres, and formats that jointly embody those rhythms. What follows in the remainder of this chapter, then, is a series of glosses of *Ask Your Mama*'s constituent elements, working from relative simplicity (e.g. paper, ink) through its more complex mediating forms (e.g. marginal cues, liner notes). Though examined as discrete components, what Hughes's work demonstrates is the way these components overlap and intersect at the scene of readerly performance, sometimes complementing one another, sometimes competing in their modes of reproducing sounds and voices.

Paper

The paper in the first edition of *Ask Your Mama* is pinkish-beige, a feature that is both eye-catching and off-putting given how normative white paper is for books in general and books of literary poetry in particular. It is as if the youthful quip from "Theme for English B" ("So will my page be colored that I write?") has decades later become literally, visually true. In its semiotic spareness, the book's paper would seem to provide little data that might be brought to bear on the poem's verbal or prosodic character. But perhaps the

---

[29] Kathy Schultz, *The Afro-Modernist Epic and Literary History: Tolson, Hughes, Baraka* (New York: Palgrave, 2013), 121. See also Henry Louis Gates, *The Signifying Monkey: A Theory of African-American Literary Criticism* (Oxford: Oxford University Press, 1989), who calls *Ask Your Mama* "one of the most well-known, and one of the most subtle, representations of the dozens as a mode of discourse" (100).

page's monochromatic off-white hue works to slow or pause the reading event. Like a Mark Rothko painting, it commands attention while only minimally directing it. In this, the book's paper is one of the earliest indicators that *Ask Your Mama* is a poem about, and a poem that induces, "hesitation," a word that becomes one of its central tropes. An affective temporal sensation, hesitation is also a social and political theme of Hughes's book. Composed amidst an intensifying Civil Rights struggle and on the heels of the "Year of Africa" of 1960, when seventeen African nations gained their independence, *Ask Your Mama* is concerned throughout with both the means and impediments to a broad pan-African liberation. In Book 4, for instance, what seems an all too hesitant political process is parodied in a deeply cynical juxtaposition of technological advancement with social terror:

ON THE BIG SCREEN OF THE WELFARE CHECK	*of*
A LYNCHED TOMORROW SWAYS . . .	*fate*
WITH ALL DELIBERATE SPEED A	*begins*
LYNCHED TOMORROW SWAYS.	*to*
	(*AYM* 30)

Quoting the language of Brown v. Board of Education, which ruled that public schools must be desegregated "with all deliberate speed," Hughes's lines blend progress with regression, movement with stasis, troping an issue of political hesitation as the thematic counterpart to the book's pervasive prosodic uncertainties.

Ink

If *Ask Your Mama* contains no white paper, neither does it contain any black ink. Instead, the book uses brown and blue ink, alternating colors every two pages. Ink color, like paper color, is a feature of Hughes's book not preserved in anthologies or scholarly editions of his poetry. Yet it is an important signifying element, gaining particular resonance in relation to one of the poem's most quoted passages:

AND THEY ASKED ME RIGHT AT CHRISTMAS	TACIT
IF MY BLACKNESS, WOULD IT RUB OFF?	
I SAID, ASK YOUR MAMA.	*Figure impishly*
	(*AYM* 8)

This is the first instance of the Dozens-inspired "ask your mama" riff that recurs throughout the poem, typically as a rejoinder to white obtuseness and racism. The lines satirize the racist fear that Blackness can somehow rub off on an unsuspecting white victim, even as the sexual innuendo of the "your mama" joke suggests something of the opposite: Blackness *is* in certain respects malleable, since it is a concept produced not only by physical characteristics but by social discourse. Hughes had learned as much during his first visit to Africa: "The Africans looked at me and would not believe I was a Negro ... You see, unfortunately, I am not black ... I am brown."[30] Hughes's comment reminds the reader that the skin tones colloquially referred to as "Black" and "white" are in many cases closer to brown and pinkish-beige. The book's ink and paper color, in other words, alerts the reader to race's discursive, rather than merely visual or physical, basis.

Figure 5.2 Title page of Langston Hughes's *Ask Your Mama: 12 Moods for Jazz* (New York: Knopf, 1961). Magdalen College Library, Oxford University

Artwork

Like the book's paper, the artwork on its dust jacket—an expressive collage of red, black, blue, and green—attracts a reader's eye while stopping short of pictorial representation. Squares and other angular shapes juxtapose with circular shapes, recalling the work's broadest self-conceit as both a (square) book and a (circular) record. On the title page, this juxtaposition seems to evoke more clearly the base and horn of a gramophone (Figure 5.2). Yet even as this gramophone comes into view, the starkness of the block shapes comprising it keeps us aware of the gap between representation and suggestion and, conversely,

[30] Hughes, *The Big Sea*, 11.

between description and interpretation. Appropriate to this dynamic, *Ask Your Mama*'s original artwork was designed not by Hughes but by Knopf's in-house designer Vincent Torre. As Torre explains: "You may perhaps think that the cover design is a painting. It is not. It is done by a printing method that is almost impossible to describe to someone who is not a printer. The method is called 'blue Bristols,' which allows the designer to fill in color areas on a grid-like drawing for the printer to follow. Thus there is no piece of artwork involved that can be viewed as a complete work of art, except in the designer's imagination. This goes as well for the part titles throughout the book itself."[31] The questions of authorial agency that Torre raises are, in turn, a central thematic preoccupation of the work. In Book 6, a voice we might take as Hughes's own reflects on the fact that his rise to literary fame has turned "ME WHO USED TO BE NOBODY" into "A NAME! MY NAME—A NAME!" (*AYM* 43). And in Book 1 we find Hughes reduced to just that, one name among many that the poem rattles off:

LEONTYNE SAMMY HARRY POITIER	*against*
LOVELY LENA MARIAN LOUIS PEARLIE MAE	*blues*
GEORGE S. SCHUYLER MOLTO BENE	*fading*
COME WHAT MAY LANGSTON HUGHES	*as the*
	(4–5)

Hughes is the author of this text, but this text, the passage implies, is also the author of the poet known as Langston Hughes, who produces a body of work that in turn produces him. Speaking to the jazz critic Nat Hentoff in 1957, Hughes described collaborating with jazz musicians in terms that we might also extend into the context of writing and publishing: "The music should not only be a background to the poetry, but should comment on it. I tell the musicians—and I've worked with several different modern and traditional groups—to improvise as much as they care around what I read. Whatever they bring of themselves to the poetry is welcome to me. I merely suggest the mood of each piece as a general orientation. Then I listen to what they say in their playing, and that affects my own rhythms when I read. We listen to each other."[32] Just as Hughes's poetry is enhanced when read alongside the music of Charles Mingus and Leonard Feather, so too is it enhanced as it enters into a longer format collaborative relationship with publishers, editors, book designers, and the like.

---

[31] Vincent Torre, email correspondence with the author, August 19, 2017.
[32] Langston Hughes, qtd. in C. James Trotman, ed., *Langston Hughes: The Man, His Art, and His Continuing Influence* (New York: Routledge, 1995), 56–57.

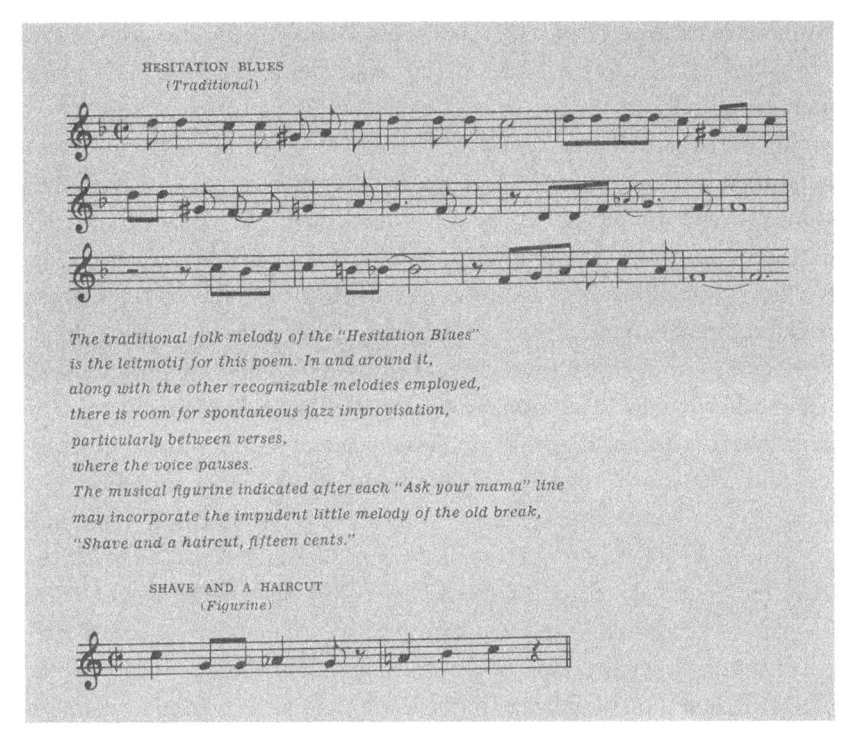

Figure 5.3 Musical scoring for "Hesitation Blues" and "Shave and a Haircut" in Langston Hughes's *Ask Your Mama: 12 Moods for Jazz* (New York: Knopf, 1961). Magdalen College Library, Oxford University

Musical Scoring

Following the book's dedication (to Louis Armstrong), Hughes presents on a single page two brief musical scores (Figure 5.3), between which he includes a paragraph of explanatory text:

> *The traditional folk melody of the "Hesitation Blues"*
> *is the leitmotif for this poem. In and around it,*
> *along with the other recognizable melodies employed,*
> *there is room for spontaneous jazz improvisation,*
> *particularly between verses,*
> *where the voice pauses.*
> *The musical figurine indicated after each "Ask your mama" line*
> *may incorporate the impudent little melody of the old break,*
> *"Shave and a haircut, fifteen cents."* (n.p.)

If other visual aspects of *Ask Your Mama*—paper, ink, artwork—bear an ambiguous relation to the work's performance demands, its musical scoring offers temporally precise instructions for audible performance. Yet by presenting the supposedly recognizable "Hesitation Blues" as sheet music rather than simply naming the tune, Hughes also raises questions of the song's mediation, provenance, and status as intellectual property. The earliest origins of "Hesitation Blues" are contested, but the song achieved broad popularity after it was published as sheet music in 1915 by Harry H. Pace and W. C. Handy under their "Home of the Blues" label. When it appears in *Ask Your Mama*, however, "Hesitation Blues" is attributed not to a single musician or publisher but to "Traditional" sources, leading A. J. Carruthers to conclude that it is unclear whether Hughes's inclusion of the song represents "a conscious attempt . . . to raise the question of the commercialization of the blues."[33] Prepublication manuscript materials suggest, however, that Hughes was indeed aware of the questions of ownership attending this song. In a set of four hand-sketched scores of "Hesitation Blues," one names Handy, one names "Traditional," and two have no attribution.[34] Earlier in his career, as a rising figure of the New Negro movement, Hughes may have oversimplified the blues' media history in the hope that, as T. Austin Graham puts it, "musical connections still existed to a vanishing culture, one that predated phonograph records, sheet music, and white involvement with the form."[35] By 1961, appearing in as audio-visually complex a work as *Ask Your Mama*, the "Hesitation Blues" attests to the multiracial and multimedial character of the blues from the moment they became a recognizable form in America.

The second musical score Hughes includes in *Ask Your Mama*, the two-bar motif titled "Shave and a Haircut," serves to further ironize desires for authentic folk origins. Virtually everyone recognizes this rhythm and melody when they hear it aloud, yet virtually nobody has encountered it on the page, so brief and essentially performative is the riff. As such, this *"impudent little melody"* may itself be more collective, fleeting, and "oral" than any blues song Hughes might have cited. And here, too, the riff's visual transcription draws attention to

[33] A. J. Carruthers, *Notational Experiments in North American Long Poems, 1961–2011: Stave Sightings* (Basingstoke: Palgrave Macmillan, 2017), 9.

[34] Langston Hughes Papers (JMJ MSS 26). Box 272, folder 4467. James Weldon Johnson Collection in the Yale Collection of American Literature, Beinecke Rare Book and Manuscript Library, Yale University.

[35] Graham, *The Great American Songbooks*, 157.

the difference between music as a sounded event and music as a textual object. For, in place of the customary rest on the downbeat of bar 2—

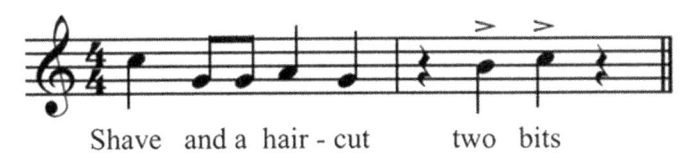

—Hughes's version includes a sounded quarter note. The change might be explained by noting that the added quarter note better accommodates the three syllables of "fifteen cents" as opposed to the two syllables of "two bits" (an archaism for twenty-five cents). On the page, as an aspect of print, this addition may seem negligible. When performed aloud, however, the difference is immediately apparent, for Hughes has turned what is traditionally a dialogic call-and-response pattern (one person sings "Shave and a Haircut," the other responds, after the downbeat rest, "two bits!") into a single-voiced musical phrase. Prepublication material again suggests the change was deliberate. One of the hand-sketched scores circles the offending quarter-note in red pencil and writes below it "rest." Another version erases the customary downbeat rest and pencils over it with a quarter note. Perhaps in acknowledgment of this audio-visual back and forth, Hughes's explanatory gloss of "Shave and a Haircut" itself contains a sly joke about the process of acoustic transcription: through a sly visual pun, the word "line" appears directly above the word "break" as the result of a couple of strategic line breaks. The impudent little melody is matched, in this instance, by some impudent typography. Notably, the "line break" pun does not appear in the *Collected Works*, which lineates Hughes's gloss slightly differently, an apt if unintentional illustration that different performances of the same text are always also remediations of that text.[36]

Marginal Cues

Of all *Ask Your Mama*'s paratexts, the most significant is the series of musical cues Hughes includes in the right-hand margin. In one of the earliest restorative readings of the work, the Hughes scholar R. Baxter Miller stakes his "claim for its excellence . . . upon the dialectic between the verbal and

[36] Hughes, *Collected Works, Vol. 3*, 85. It is a fair question whether Hughes's editor created a new line break or simply required a runover, but the book's format is wide enough to suggest the former.

musical languages."[37] This dialectic operates at multiple levels, but perhaps the most obvious point of connection between left-hand and right-hand texts is linguistic, since the musical cues are composed of words and not, say, musical notation. Moreover, while differentiated by their typefaces (all caps versus italic), the two columns of text are likewise bound together by their shared lineation. Reading from Hughes's main text and into the right-hand margin, Meta Jones suggests that the syntax of the words in the left-hand column seems at times to be modified by words in the right-hand column, an effect that blurs the distinction between poetry and music and between "margin and mainstream."[38] While this "oppositional reading practice" may contradict Hughes's intentions, Jones concedes, a repeated bibliographical pun suggests otherwise: on three separate occasions, left-hand and right-hand text is arranged so that the words "between verses" fall, precisely, between verses:

NOT OF HER OWN DOING—	*12-bar*
IN A POT OF COLLARD GREENS	*blues*
IS GENTLY STEWING.	*up strong*
	between verses
THERE, FORBID US TO REMEMBER	*until*
COMES AN AFRICAN IN MID-DECEMBER	*African*
SENT BY THE STATE DEPARTMENT	*drums*
	(AYM 4)

More than any other visual feature of *Ask Your Mama*, the two-column format works to undermine the sensation of unmediated lyric voice by entangling this voice in the mechanisms of print. The right-hand musical cues, meanwhile, far from offering dryly technical instructions to performers, are themselves often more syntactically legible and expressive (more "lyric") than the material in the left-hand column, sometimes breaking into explicitly figurative and poetic language. One cue in Book 4 reads, *"Drums alone softly merging into the ever-questioning 'Hesitation Blues' beginning slowly but gradually building to up-tempo as the metronome of fate begins to tick faster and faster then slowly retarding as the music dies"* (30–31). Another, in Book 11, reads, *"Bop blues into very modern jazz burning the air eerie like a neon swamp-fire cooled by dry ice until suddenly there is a single ear-piercing flute call ..."* (77–78).

Sonya Posmentier suggests that "[while] many critics have studied Hughes's poems ... as influenced by folk musical forms ... the path of influence is

---

[37] R. Baxter Miller, *The Art and Imagination of Langston Hughes* (Lexington: The University Press of Kentucky, 2006), 88.

[38] Jones, *The Muse Is Music*, 63.

far more circular than we often account for."[39] Analyzing the early reception history of *Fine Clothes to the Jew*, Posmentier suggests that its "musical inspirations[,] . . . the print publication and distribution of that book, the recitation aloud by [Zora Neale] Hurston of the poems, the church hymns, the 'improvising on it,' and chanting in games and singing, all constitute and create black modern poetry."[40] *Ask Your Mama* incorporates this circularity into its very form. As the blurb on the dust jacket of the first edition reads, "These are poems that demand to be read aloud, and whether or not the proper instruments are handy, the description, line by line, of the musical accompaniment which appears beside the verse is so vivid that the music can be imagined. The language derives its inspiration from the jazz, taking off at moments like a solo instrument, pounding at you like bongo drums, moving in free association" (n. p.). This is poetry ex nihilo: verse inspired by jazz imagined from text printed alongside the verse—lyric as always already remediated.

Liner Notes

The liner notes following *Ask Your Mama* are offered for the benefit of "*the Poetically Unhep*" (*AYM* 84). But far from being forthrightly explanatory, the notes operate according to the same associative, propulsive logic as the poem itself.[41] The note glossing Book 11, for instance, reads: "Because grandma lost her apron with all the answers in her pocket (perhaps consumed by fire) certain grand- and great-grandsons play music burning like dry ice against the ear" (92). Though the sentence's initial "Because" seems to promise insight into a cause-and-effect relationship, its ensuing nouns (e.g. grandma, answers, fire, music) bear little logical relation to one another, especially since the "dry ice" has been taken from an earlier marginal cue. The note glossing Book 2 obeys a similarly improvisatory logic: "In the restless Caribbean there are the same shadows as in Mississippi, where, according to *Time*, Leontyne comes

[39] Sonya Posmentier, "Lyric Reading in the Black Ethnographic Archive," *American Literature*, 30/1 (Spring 2018): 75.
[40] Posmentier, "Lyric Reading in the Black Ethnographic Archive," 75.
[41] Many readers have interpreted Hughes's Liner Notes as a parody of the self-consciously learned notes of T. S. Eliot's *Waste Land. Ask Your Mama* alludes as well to "The Love Song of J. Alfred Prufrock," *T. S. Eliot: Collected Poems, 1909–1962* (New York: Harcourt, 1991), whose protagonist's anxious deferments and social paralysis Hughes recasts under the master trope of "hesitation." Prufrock's lament over "a bald spot in the middle of my hair— / (They will say: 'How his hair is growing thin!')" (4) and the poem's culminating image of "the white hair of the waves blown back" (7) become in Hughes's poem "HAIR / BLOWING BACK IN THE WIND / (AND I NEVER HAD THAT MUCH HAIR)" (*AYM* 21).

in the back door" (86–87). As Arnold Rampersad observes, *Ask Your Mama* is "freighted with allusions," but these "[arise] for the most part not from European literary sources but instinctively, naturally, out of the heart of lived black American culture."[42] In this particular instance, however, an emphasis on the naturalness and spontaneity of Hughes's method risks obscuring his specific textual reference to the March 10, 1961 issue of *Time* magazine, whose cover story was devoted to Leontyne Price. Price was the first African American to sing a leading role at the Metropolitan Opera, and her name occurs more than any other in *Ask Your Mama*. Born and raised in Mississippi, Price was supported in her musical pursuits by a wealthy local white family named Chisolm. As the *Time* article explains, "Leontyne entered the Chisolm mansion by the back door, as she does to this day. She is free to use the front door, Mrs. Chisholm explains, but it would make the help uncomfortable."[43] Price had made her Met debut in January, and the *Time* story that Hughes's liner note cites offered an eager national readership a glimpse into her backstory and rise to fame. Hughes himself, nearing the completion of *Ask Your Mama*, must have appreciated the array of musical styles and media gathered in the opening sentences of the *Time* article: "Big Auntie sits in the parlor listening to French art songs on the phonograph. They sound, she says, 'a little like the cha cha cha.' . . . The voice in Big Auntie's phonograph belongs to one of the world's great singers: her niece, Leontyne Price."[44]

Yet if Hughes in *Ask Your Mama* allies himself with Price, the African-American soprano's chosen art form of grand opera was around 1961 leaving a rather sour taste in the poet's mouth. Hughes had recently immersed himself in what Rampersad calls "the high-toned, overwhelmingly white, elitist world of American opera" by virtue of collaborating with Jan Meyerowitz on a one-act operatic version of "Port Town."[45] Much earlier in his career, Hughes had expressed a similar frustration with middle-class Black intellectuals who looked down on popular Black musical forms in preference for Anglo-European ones. "A prominent Negro clubwoman in Philadelphia paid eleven dollars to hear Raquel Meller sing Andalusian popular songs," Hughes writes in "The Negro Artist and the Racial Mountain." "But she told me a few weeks before she would not think of going to hear 'that woman,' Clara Smith,

---

[42] Rampersad, *The Life of Langston Hughes, Volume 2*, 317–18.
[43] "A Voice Like a Flying Banner," *TIME* (March 10, 1961), 60. Hughes would have been a particularly attentive reader of *Time* following the magazine's October 3, 1960 issue, which erroneously reported a meeting between the poet and Fidel Castro.
[44] "A Voice Like a Flying Banner," 58.
[45] Rampersad, *The Life of Langston Hughes, Volume 2*, 321.

PAPER RECORDS   145

a great black artist, sing Negro folksongs."[46] Hughes, while working on *Ask Your Mama* decades later, presumably felt a similar frustration toward the success Price had achieved among white audiences in the elitist realm of opera, and while reading the *Time* article he would surely have noted the ways in which "[the] voice in Big Auntie's phonograph belongs" not only to Price but to various white-dominated spaces and media: opera houses, music labels, print magazines like *Time*. As John Lowney observes, "No one could possibly evoke the paradox of 'BOUNDARIES BIND UNBINDING' more complexly than Price, whose own life exemplified the contradictions and misperceptions of black musical celebrities."[47]

Later in the *Time* article, Hughes would have encountered a still more direct parallel to the subject matter of *Ask Your Mama*: "Often when [Price] talks about her race, it is in joking fashion. The dusky Aïda she refers to as her 'makeup-saver role.' Once a wardrobe mistress forgot and warned her about soiling her light costume with the dark Aïda makeup. Leontyne pointed to her skin and said, 'Honey, you'd be surprised; that won't come off.'"[48] The passage echoes *Ask Your Mama*'s most famous lines—

AND THEY ASKED ME RIGHT AT CHRISTMAS
IF MY BLACKNESS, WOULD IT RUB OFF?
I SAID, ASK YOUR MAMA.

—and it is tempting to imagine Hughes reading the *Time* article, encountering the Price quotation, and then incorporating it into *Ask Your Mama*. Manuscripts and typescripts suggest that Hughes had penned his lines before March 10, 1961; yet he did make one major addition to the text after this date, and this material follows immediately upon the "ASK YOUR MAMA" riff quoted above. The added material, which concludes Book 1, imagines a carnivalesque inversion of race relations in the American South:

DREAMS AND NIGHTMARES ...   *ending in high*
NIGHTMARES ... DREAMS! OH!   *shrill flute call.*
DREAMING THAT THE NEGROES   TACIT
OF THE SOUTH HAVE TAKEN OVER—
VOTED ALL THE DIXIECRATS
RIGHT OUT OF POWER—

[46] Langston Hughes, *The Collected Works of Langston Hughes: Essays on Art, Race, Politics, and World Affairs, Vol. 9*, ed. Christopher C. De Santis (Columbia: The University of Missouri Press, 2002), 33.
[47] John Lowney, *Jazz Internationalism: Literary Afro-Modernism and the Cultural Politics of Black Music* (Champaign: The University of Illinois Press, 2017), 120–21.
[48] "A Voice Like a Flying Banner," 63.

...

IN WHITE PILLARED MANSIONS
SITTING ON THEIR WIDE VERANDAS,
WEALTHY NEGROES HAVE WHITE SERVANTS,
WHITE SHARECROPPERS WORK THE BLACK PLANTATIONS,
AND COLORED CHILDREN HAVE WHITE MAMMIES:

...

HAND ME MY MINT JULEP, MAMMY.
MAKE HASTE!

*"When the Saints
Go Marching In"
(AYM 8–9)*

It is impossible to know Hughes's exact motivations, but it appears that the poet, having let his typescript sit unchanged for over a month, added this new conclusion to Book 1 in response to the *Time* article. Signifying on the image of Price "[entering] the Chisolm mansion by the back door," Hughes takes this bitter irony of Price's success story and transforms it into an alternative vision of American race relations. Uncovering this textual history gives us a somewhat different picture of Hughes from the one we are used to seeing. This Hughes is not the rising star of the Harlem Renaissance jotting "The Negro Speaks of Rivers" on the back of an envelope, but an older, cannier poet drafting and revising a work whose ironies and contradictions might match those of America in 1961.

While the first edition of *Ask Your Mama* retains a certain durability and stature, it is not the only version. Prior to print publication, Hughes performed portions of the poem at UCLA with a jazz and blues backing ensemble. Following publication, Hughes revised the work into a staged dialogue for the actors Ozzie Davis and Ruby Dee. He asked the young choreographer Alvin Ailey to turn the work into a ballet. And he asked the jazz artist Randy Weston to produce for *Ask Your Mama* a lavishly orchestrated musical score, presumably one that would fulfill the eclectic musical tastes and textures indicated by the book's marginal cues. Neither of these last two requests came to fruition, but they speak nonetheless to the strenuously multigeneric, transmedial, and collaborative terms in which Hughes understood his work. "To me jazz is a montage of a dream deferred," Hughes explained in a 1956 lecture, returning to an image from earlier in his career. "A great big dream—yet to come—and always *yet*—to become ultimately and finally true."[49] Hughes's own work, we might further

---

[49] Hughes, *Essays on Art, Race, Politics, and World Affairs*, 370.

surmise, itself becomes true insofar as it is performed and reperformed in some yet to be glimpsed future.

It therefore seems fitting to conclude by considering a version of *Ask Your Mama* produced many decades after its initial publication. Commissioned in 2009 as part of soprano Jessye Norman's three-week "Honor!" festival, this multimedia version of *Ask Your Mama* debuted at Carnegie Hall and featured an original score by the American composer Laura Karpman. Karpman was inspired to produce the work, she explains, after stumbling across a copy of Hughes's 1961 book in a used bookstore. "What attracted me to the piece," she recalls, "was not only that it was written by Langston Hughes, who I think is one of the most brilliant poets who ever lived, but in the right-hand margins of the poem, Langston says exactly how the music should sound."[50] The debut performance at Carnegie Hall included four vocalists, a symphony orchestra, drumming and rapping by The Roots, video collage, and more. "The barrage of sensations," observed a reviewer for the *New York Times*, "could be overwhelming, and not everything worked; a combination of musical and visual clichés in 'Gospel Cha-Cha' lapsed into kitsch . . . Still, it was hard not to be impressed by the audacity of Ms. Karpman's undertaking, and there were genuinely striking passages throughout."[51]

Overwhelming or not, one notable aspect of Karpman's arrangement is how closely it hews to Hughes's musical instructions. After an initial cymbal crash, a listener hears "[the] rhythmically rough scraping of a guira" described in Hughes's first marginal cue. On top of this groove, "a lonely flute call" cuts angular, minimalist patterns in the air, as an ethereal string part crescendos from below. Irregular cymbal crashes punctuate this texture until a soprano voice, at around thirty seconds, sings the first two lines of the poem: "IN THE / IN THE QUARTER." Variations on these lines repeat a full eight times before the soprano voice continues on to line 3: "IN THE QUARTER OF THE NEGROES." At line 5 ("DUST OF DINGY ATOMS") a new voice enters: Hughes's own, sampled from an unaccompanied recording of poems released by Caedmon Records in 1980. Hughes's speaking voice continues, the soprano voice repeats "IN THE QUARTER OF THE NEGROES" a few more times, and then a higher soprano voice enters to perform the final line of stanza 2 ("YET LEONTYNE'S UNPACKING"), repeating it six times. At 2:13, the track cuts abruptly to a 1933 recording of Cab Calloway's "St. James Infirmary Blues," which plays for eight seconds before Karpman's orchestration and Hughes's recorded voice return to perform the opening lines of stanza 3: "IN THE QUARTER OF THE NEGROES / WHERE THE

---

[50] "'Ask Your Mama': A Music and Poetry Premiere," *WBUR News*, March 16, 2009.
[51] Steve Smith, "Playing Langston Hughes's Jazzy Verse," *The New York Times*, March 17, 2009.

DOORKNOB LETS IN LIEDER / MORE THAN GERMAN EVER BORE." Rumbling beneath all of this are the "piano variations on German lieder," which in Karpman's version takes the form of the piano accompaniment to Franz Schubert's 1814 song "Gretchen am Spinnrade" (Gretchen at the Spinning Wheel).

This description may make the myriad sounds and voices of Karpman's arrangement seem still more opposed than the two columns of text in *Ask Your Mama*'s printed version. But whereas the two columns cannot be read simultaneously and therefore appear to exist in a dialectical or even antithetical relation, Karpman's multiple voices combine to compelling effect. Her version, moreover, resolves by necessity the various prosodic ambiguities of the print version, layering and synthesizing the work's constituent sonic elements so that the speech prosodies of the poem's left-hand text combine with the tone and pacing of the singers' voices, with technical effects such as autotuning and doubling, and with the larger harmonic and rhythmic structures of Karpman's orchestration. As a result, while Hughes's largely trochaic tetrameter lines lend themselves to the four-beat structure common in music—

1   2   3   4

Won't let | **go** un | **til** it | **thun**ders

—Karpman's polyphonic version frequently achieves a far more complex rhythmic character. When we encounter the line above, for instance, which repeats three times near the end of Book 1, Karpman's score is not in $^4/_4$ but in $^3/_4$ time (i.e. three beats per bar). By emphasizing the syllables indicated by a trochaic scansion (*Won't, go, til, thun*) while syncopating them against the $^3/_4$ time signature, the vocalists create a kind of interference effect— linguistic prosody out of kilter with musical rhythm—that resolves with the arrival of the next downbeat and the first syllable of "thunders." Undoubtedly this set of rhythmic operations is more conceptually intricate than the binaristic (i.e. stress-unstress) logic underwriting a straightforwardly iambic or trochaic rhythm. And Karpman's performance, like Hughes's book, is likewise more explicitly multigeneric and multimedial than the typical printed lyric. Yet no more or less than the printed lyric, the prosody of Karpman's *Ask Your Mama* emerges in—and as—the complex array of media that brings its language into audible being. The poem, like all poems, is indeed a record of past sounds, but also a score for performances yet to come.

Epilogue

A Transmedial Poetics

The internet retail giant Amazon sells a voice-activated "virtual assistant" named Alexa. "Using Alexa is as simple as asking a question," the company explains on its website.[1] "Just ask to play music, read the news, control your smart home, tell a joke, and more—Alexa is happy to help. It is Alexa's hardworking utility and witty personality that has led Alexa to be regarded as a member of the family." In this, Alexa is a marked improvement over, say, Edgar Allan Poe's raven, which when questioned ("*is* there balm in Gilead?") tends to keep maddeningly quiet.[2] Alexa, by contrast, listening in while perched on a bedside table or kitchen countertop, "is always getting smarter . . . The more you talk to Alexa, the more Alexa adapts to your speech patterns, vocabulary, and personal preferences, with new features continually being added."

Jonathan Culler could not have anticipated this particular form of apostrophic address when he wrote his influential 1977 essay on "Apostrophe," yet one of the remarkable things about Alexa is the degree to which the relation the device establishes with its human user resembles the relation a lyric speaker might seek in addressing an inanimate object such as a rose or urn. As Culler observes, through apostrophe

> [an] object is treated as a subject, an *I* which implies a certain type of *you* in its turn. One who successfully invokes nature is one to whom nature might, in its turn, speak . . . If asking winds to blow or seasons to stay their coming or mountains to hear one's cries is a ritualistic, practically gratuitous action, that emphasizes that voice calls in order to be calling, to dramatize its calling, to summon images of its power so as to establish its identity as poetical and prophetic voice.[3]

More and more of us are using smart speakers in just this way, hailing them as if they were subjects in the hope that they will respond, as Amazon makes

---

[1] "Alexa Brand Guidelines for Amazon Developers," Amazon, 2024, https://developer.amazon.com/en-US/alexa/branding/alexa-guidelines. Subsequent quotations of these guidelines are taken from the same webpage.

[2] Edgar Allan Poe, *Poetry, Tales, and Selected Essays*, ed. Patrick F. Quinn and G. R. Thompson (New York: The Library of America, 1984), 85.

[3] Jonathan Culler, "Apostrophe," *diacritics*, 7/4 (1977): 63.

Poetry, Sound, and the Matter of Prosody 1800–2000. Peter Miller, Oxford University Press. © Peter Miller (2025). DOI: 10.1093/9780198937210.003.0007

plain in characterizing its virtual assistant as "happy," "witty," and "hardwork-ing." Such characterizations reveal, moreover, the somewhat awkward social position of these devices, which if subject-like are also, by design, subordinate. Part of the weird pleasure of talking with Alexa comes from its eagerness to accommodate our demands, just as part of the poet's thrill in apostrophizing winds, seasons, and mountains comes from the notion that these things might actually respond to his voice.

They do not, quite. And, as Culler observes, the embarrassment a reader or observer inevitably feels *for* the lyric speaker may well be the defining feature of the trope. As Culler explains, poetic apostrophe ultimately "work[s] less to establish an *I-Thou* relation between [speaker] and [object] than to dramatize or constitute an image of self" in the eyes of an audience.[4] Thus the "prac-tically gratuitous" aspect of the lyric speaker's petitions, which do not finally bend nature to his will but serve instead to fashion an image of the poet, speak-ing. And so too the gratuitous aspect of our relationship with smart speakers, whose power to tell us the current weather, say, or dim the lights is perhaps less significant than the odd triangulation they set up between the human speaker, the device, and any onlookers witnessing the exchange. Despite advances, these artificial intelligences remain, as of this writing, charmingly artificial, routinely misconstruing simple requests, exposing their lack of lived experi-ence, and generally frustrating the human users who would have mastery over them. If apostrophic address, as Culler suggests, is the cardinal feature of lyric, as it is the activating mechanism of Alexa, this is because of how closely the figure tethers vision to myopia, incantation to cant.

How Alexa is able to understand speech, even as it stumbles, is a technical question but also clearly a prosodic one. As this book has sought to demon-strate, a broadly conceived prosodic analysis must endeavor to attend not only to rhythm and meter as rendered in print but, as the *Princeton Encyclope-dia of Poetry and Poetics* puts it, to the full range of "measurable structures of sound in language and in poetry."[5] Indeed, it is the variety and complex-ity of these structures—stress, rhythm, phrasing, intonation, volume, and so on—that makes not only the scanning of poems but the creation of artificial prosodic intelligences such a daunting project. As the authors of a 2024 arti-cle in the technology journal *Sensors* acknowledge, what may at first seem a technical challenge is also of course a cultural one:

    [4] Culler, "Apostrophe," 63.
    [5] R. Winslow, "Prosody," in Roland Greene, Stephen Cushman, Clare Cavanagh, Jahan Ramazani, and Paul Rouzer, eds., The *Princeton Encyclopedia of Poetry and Poetics* (Princeton: Princeton University Press, 2012), 1117.

Prosodic elements cross cultural and linguistic divides, but while the prosodic elements are similar, their use may not be. For example, Ekpenyong et al. defined Ibibio as a tonal language, whereby the pitch of a word changes its meaning—this is also the case for Mandarin; a common example is the word "ma," which, depending on tone, can mean mother, horse, scold, or hemp. This is in contrast to English, where pitch can turn a statement into a question, or shift emphasis between the subject and object of a spoken phrase.[6]

The highly lucrative quest to develop digital tools capable of understanding human speech may seem worlds apart from the more modest campaigns of literary studies. Amazon at one time employed as many as ten thousand people on Alexa-related projects. Traditional literary prosody, as even the *Princeton Encyclopedia* feels obliged to concede, can sometimes seem "a stony little patch of ground frequented only by eccentrics, fanatics, and pedants."[7] Yet the very gulf in prosody's perceived value should encourage us to reflect on why this may be the case. We need not abandon our humanistic commitments to ask, in other words, what might be gained by reading the history of anglophone prosody as a series of experiments in mediating and parsing speech while, at the same time, reading contemporary advances in digital voice technology as forays into the realm of poetics.

One of the most valuable by-products of recognizing prosodic analysis as a form of media theory will be the opening of new analytical terrain between so-called literary poetry and the range of popular, topical, non-print-based, musical, experimental, and otherwise alternative poetries against which literary poetry has defined itself. I have tried to suggest as much, in the preceding chapters, by taking seriously various popular remediations of my featured poets' work. Here, let me approach the issue from the other direction, considering a contemporary form of popular poetry—rap and hip-hop—that has sometimes been seen as decidedly non-poetic, yet which perhaps more than any other form illustrates the mutual entanglement of prosody and sound technology in an age of modern media.

Rap traces its origins to the late 1970s, when young people in the Bronx, most of them Black and Latino, began experimenting with new ways of mediating sound. Seeking a form of entertainment suitable for outdoor block parties

---

[6] J. Kane, M. N. Johnstone, and P. Szewczyk, "Voice Synthesis Improvement by Machine Learning of Natural Prosody," *Sensors*, 24/5 (2024): 1624.

[7] T. V. F. Brogan, "Prosody," in Alex Preminger, T. V. F. Brogan, Frank J. Warnke, O. B. Hardison, and Earl Miner, eds., *New Princeton Encyclopedia of Poetry and Poetics* (Princeton: Princeton University Press, 1993), 992.

and other informal social gatherings, these artists drew on existing musical and acoustic techniques—record turntabling and scratching, sampling, beatboxing—while adding to them another element: a performed vocal line, often highly rhythmic and densely rhymed. The central figure in these performances was the Master of Ceremonies, or MC, whose facility as both a technician and a wordsmith would become the measure of his craft. These artists were transforming poetry for an age of new media, but they were also, counterintuitively, returning the genre to some of its earliest cultural roots. As the rap scholar Adam Bradley explains, "Rather than resembling the dominant contemporary form of free verse . . . rap bears a stronger affinity to some of poetry's oldest forms, such as the strong-stress meter of *Beowulf* and the ballad stanzas of the bardic past."[8] Rap's creative fusion of new and old media, electronics and aurality, has proven wildly successful. "Thanks to the engines of global commerce," Bradley observes, "rap is now the most widely disseminated poetry in the history of the world."[9]

Yet precisely because of its rhythmic and acoustic richness, rap's signature effects remain largely opaque on the printed or digitized page. Prosodic features such as vocal tone and pacing, wordplay based on idiosyncrasies of pronunciation, and most of all the complex interplay of music and speech rhythms can only be guessed at when rap lyrics are approached as a visual text. Consider, for instance, the opening line of Tupac Shakur's 1995 song "If I Die 2Nite," which plays into certain rap stereotypes while defying others:

They say pussy and paper is poetry, power and pistols[10]

After the first two syllables, the line divides neatly into dactyls, each cued by a strongly alliterative /p/ sound, and so can be scanned as a line of hexameter:

They say | **puss**y and | **pa**per is | **po**etry, | **pow**er and | **pis**tols

But this is not quite how Tupac structures his line, which he published not on the "paper" he associates with poetry but on an album that by the end of the year had sold over two million copies. "If I Die 2Nite" is written in $^4/_4$ time, and in performance Tupac syncopates his line's hexameter linguistic prosody against the four-beat musical norm typical of popular song:

1	2	3	4

They say **puss** y and **pa** per is **po** et ry **pow** er and **pis** tols

[8] Adam Bradley, *Book of Rhymes: The Poetics of Hip Hop* (New York: Civitas Books, 2017), xvi.
[9] Bradley, *Book of Rhymes*, xiii.
[10] Tupac, "If I Die 2Nite," track 2 on *Me Against the World* (Interscope Records, 1995).

That is, by lining up his speech syllables precisely with the sixteenth-note subdivision of the song's drum track, while at the same time preserving his sentence's naturally dactylic (e.g. triplet) stress pattern, Tupac produces a three-over-four effect, a polyrhythm that might be graphed something like this:

Music Beats	1				2				3				4			
Syllable Beats	/p/			/p/			/p/			/p/			/p/			

The effect illustrates what Bradley calls the "dual rhythmic relationship" at the heart of rap: the layering of speech rhythms on top of music rhythms, from which emerges a host of prosodic possibilities unavailable to a strictly linguistically defined text.[11] The opening line of "If I Die 2Nite" occupies just three seconds of airtime and, remarkably, is more prosodically regular than much of the rest of the song. Mapping its entire prosodic shape would, at the present rate, fill about one hundred pages and require more charts and graphs than most publishers would be willing to print.

Another notable prosodic feature appears even before Tupac has performed his opening line. In the first few seconds of the track, before the drum beat and instruments have entered, an unaccompanied voice that is not Tupac's recites two lines of what sounds like ballad meter:

> A coward dies a thousand deaths,
> A soldier dies but once.[12]

The lines serve as a kind of acoustic epigraph, introducing the theme of militant machismo that Tupac himself takes up a few moments later. But their presumed reference point (e.g. violence on the streets of New York or Los Angeles) is not entirely what it seems. For the lines are a revision of text from Shakespeare's *Julius Caesar*:

> Cowards die many times before their deaths;
> The valiant never taste of death but once.[13]

What motivated Tupac to transform Shakespeare's blank verse into ballad meter is difficult to say. What can be said is that by increasing the lines' syntactic and prosodic parallelism ("A coward dies" / "A soldier dies"), regularizing

---

[11] Bradley, *Book of Rhymes*, 6. In fact Tupac's rhythm is still more complex, as he performs "They say" as pick-up notes not to beat 1, but beat 4, further decoupling his syntax from the head of the musical bar. I have grudgingly simplified Tupac's prosody for the sake of argumentative clarity.

[12] Tupac, "If I Die 2Nite."

[13] William Shakespeare, *Julius Caesar*, ed. Barbara A. Mowat and Paul Werstine (New York: Washington Square Press, 1993), 77.

their iambic pattern, and repackaging them within a traditional 4/3/4/3 ballad meter, Tupac amplifies the kinds of acoustic-poetic traits that rap values
generally, and in the process makes Shakespeare's blank verse appear comparatively prosaic. Recapitulating a dynamic we saw in Wordsworth's poetry,
Tupac balladizes Caesar's lyric utterance, weakening the sensation of spontaneous poetic speech by editing it into four-beat lines. If one history of modern
poetry observes an ineluctable shift away from meter, rhyme, and communitarian acoustics, Tupac's revision of Shakespeare opens onto an alternative,
complementary history—a history that, this book has suggested, was there all
along.

For the lyricization of poetry is at all turns haunted by the mediatization
of sound, a fact that a genre like rap—vigorously rhythmic, eminently popular, technologically advanced—can help make retrospectively clear. Rap's
strongest literary precursors are decidedly those modes of poetic expression
that the Romantic lyric supposedly supplanted: the poised formalism of Pope
or the ballad collection of Bishop Percy, both of whom rode a burgeoning print
culture to make their archaic materials feel characteristically modern. These
pre-Romantic artists, like today's rappers, made no pretense of being surrepti-
tiously "overheard" but presented their artistry as the consummate realization
of taste. Thus the dismay, in the following century, of the rhyme-loving for-
malists Poe and Byron when confronted with the new Romantic orthodoxy.
And thus the novelty, in the last decade, of a sub-genre known as "emo rap,"
whose practitioners' anxious inward turn is all the more stirring for having
emerged from the brash performativity of its parent genre. As scholars and
educators, we need not replace Wordsworth with Tupac, or books with smart
speakers, but we would do well to put these figures in conversation with one
another—to explore the ways in which our assumptions about the nature of
poetic sound betray still deeper assumptions about the nature of poetic media.
Doing so, let me suggest in closing, will require us to pursue four related
goals.

First, we must expand the object of prosodic analysis. This means attending to sound effects beyond meter and rhythm. But it also, more importantly,
means expanding prosody beyond language and into the realm of media,
incorporating into our analysis the books, manuscripts, billboards, gramophone records, journals, songs, and television shows in which poetic language
lives. This book has focused on canonical figures to offer a proof of concept
from inside, as it were, but developing a media-oriented prosody will also
entail attending to genres, media, and formats seemingly outside the purview
of literary studies. Mike Chasar's work on popular poetries offers one model

for how this might proceed. In his virtuoso reading of a series of poetry-emblazoned billboards erected by the Burma-Shave Company at mid-century, for instance, Chasar underscores the degree to which prosodic form arrives as a function of specific media formats, genre conventions, advertising strategies, sense experiences, and even miles per hour:

> [The] most striking aspect of the process of signification in the Burma-Shave poems is not the innovative prosody of the individual billboard but how that prosody is constantly counterpointed against a second, more familiar form: the rhyme and meter of the traditional ballad. From the time the poems started rhyming, the standard five-line jingle (plus the product name in line 6) almost always extended a four-line ballad stanza over the space of five signs. If the poems unfolded visually—short lines appearing as free verse or prose until clearly made into poetry by the rhyme in line 5—then they unfolded aurally as well, following a popular form that motorists knew by ear. The resulting tension between how the poems look (free verse) and how they sound (a ballad rhyming *abcb*) creates a structural dialectic producing a verse form perpetually engaged in self-examination. The two prosodic systems do not exist side by side but on top of, within, and even at odds with each other, each erecting hurdles for the other during enunciation—a sort of palimpsest in which each system is continuously erased and rewritten by the other.[14]

It is a mistake to call Chasar's work cultural studies if by "cultural studies" we mean to designate some sphere of non- or extra-literary inquiry. The point of Chasar's work, like that of this book, is to open for analysis the tacit alliance of print technology with academic criticism in the production of poetic genre. Such a program might seem to require a demotion or replacement of traditional prosodic concepts with new modern ones; but to my mind these concepts may in fact become more valuable, in the sense that we now have the capability to explore how well they map onto—and are themselves transformed by—prosodic forms that exist beyond the book.

Second, we must adjust our sense of who and what prosodic analysis is for. The lively online discussion of rap prosodies makes plain the limits of a narrative in which prosody is conceived as primarily Victorian (in historical terms) or academic (in methodological terms). The most "liked" comment on the YouTube page for the rapper Common's 2005 song "The Corner" reads:

---

[14] Mike Chasar, "The Business of Rhyming: Burma-Shave Poetry and Popular Culture," *PMLA*, 125/1 (2010): 39. See also Chasar's books *Everyday Reading: Poetry and Popular Culture in Modern America* (New York: Columbia University Press, 2012) and *Poetry Unbound: Poems and New Media from the Magic Lantern to Instagram* (New York: Columbia University Press, 2020).

"This song is fucking legendary. Pay attention to the rhyme schemes in each of the verses. Verse 1: All 1 syllable rhymes with the same vowel sound, Verse 2: is 2 syllable rhymes and Verse 3: is 3 syllable rhymes. Common is one of the most skilled lyricists to ever live."[15] Listening to the opening lines of each of Common's three verses, one sees what this commenter means:

Verse 1	Memories on **corn**ers with the **fo's** and the **mo's**
	Walk to the **store** for the **rose**, talkin' straight**for**ward to **hoes**
Verse 2	**Street lights** and **deep nights**, cats tryin' to **eat right**
	Ridin' no-**seat-bikes**, with work to **feed hypes**
Verse 3	Black church **services, murderers**, Arabs servin' **burgers as**
	Cats with gold **permanents** move they bags as **herbalists**[16]

Another commenter hears Verse 1 slightly differently: "First verse are more than one syllable if you consider more than the last word, for instance 'got uncles that SMOKE and put BLOW up their NOSE, they're COPING with LOWS, the wind is COLD and it BLOWS' so in reality he's doing 2–3 syllable rhymes in the rhyme scheme in the first verse."[17] And a third commenter points out the role assonance and consonance play in binding Common's lines together: "Can't forget the 1st verse ends in O's, 2nd verse ends in E-I's, 3rd ends in Er's."[18] Though the premises of traditional accentual-syllabic prosody do not hold up well in the context of popular song, it is clear that these listeners are debating something like the basis and boundaries of Common's poetic feet. Whereas the first commenter thinks in terms of single syllables, the second commenter encourages thinking in syllable groups. My own impulse is to describe these groups in terms of a generally dactylic triple meter—

Walk to the | **store** for the | **rose**, | **talkin'** straight | **forward** to | **hoes**

—and to describe Verses 2 and 3 by using terms like spondees and feminine endings. But it ultimately matters less *how* we describe these prosodic phenomena than that we describe them at all. A media-oriented prosody will be characterized by its diversity of methods, motives, and participants.

[15] Funkypotato14, comment on Common, "The Corner ft. The Last Poets," YouTube Video, 4:04, October 8, 2009, https://www.youtube.com/watch?v=6mnKNr2Tiq8&ab_channel=CommonVEVO.
[16] Common, "The Corner," track 2 on *Be* (Geffen Records, 2005).
[17] user-vh8pn1uf9g, comment on Common, "The Corner."
[18] tonydegregorio4895, comment on Common, "The Corner."

Third, we must reimagine what is meant by historical poetics. Today, most scholarship in historical poetics characterizes the passage of time as something that destabilizes or obscures some earlier formal or generic coherence, whose recovery in turn becomes the task of the critic. This book, by contrast, while drawing on insights and methods from historical poetics, has tried to approach poetic form as something that is transformed and remediated over time. My objective, therefore, has not been to recreate the literary or cultural discourses of, say, Dickinson's Amherst or Hughes's Harlem but to characterize the shifting media conditions in which their poetry's sounds signify. I have done so because it allows, to my mind, a truer calibration of the purposes and methods of prosodic analysis. Were we somehow able to thoroughly document Dickinson's original prosodic intentions for her work, it does not follow that a twenty-first-century reader should, or even could, realize those intentions. But neither does it follow that a reader should be contented simply with "Dickinson's words," since her words are inevitably tangled up, more or less obviously, in her media. Methodologically, then, prosodic analysis must attend to a poem's historical media as well as its language; but because the purpose of prosodic analysis is enunciative as well as historical, it must remain true as well to the modern reader's verbal capacities and aesthetic priorities. This greater tolerance of readerly idiosyncrasy may, in turn, have pedagogical benefits. One of the undergraduate poetry courses I teach focuses on contemporary retellings of canonical works, from Derek Walcott's Caribbean epic *Omeros*, to Seamus Heaney's translation of the Old English poem *Beowulf*, to Patience Agbabi's remix of Chaucer, *Telling Tales*. My goal for the course is to show students that the canon is valuable because it is malleable, open to revision, generic as well as cultural, by writers from backgrounds (e.g. West Indian, North Irish, British-Nigerian) quite different from those ostensibly celebrated by works such as the *Odyssey* or *The Canterbury Tales*. Indeed, for these contemporary poets, the very remoteness of Homer, Chaucer, and the *Beowulf* poet is what licenses creative repurposing in the present. Thus Walcott's frustration, for instance, with historicist readings of *Omeros* that place his poem in a "chronological" rather than "simultaneous" relation to Homer's works.[19] For him, as for Heaney and Agbabi, historical poetics means reconfiguring, rather than recovering, the literary past.

---

[19] Derek Walcott, "Reflections on *Omeros*," *South Atlantic Quarterly*, 96/2 (1997): 240. See also Seamus Heaney, "Introduction" to *Beowulf: A New Verse Translation* (New York: Norton, 2000), who feels that *Beowulf* "lives in its own continuous present, equal to our knowledge of reality in the present time" (ix), and Patience Agbabi, *Telling Tales* (London: Canongate, 2014), whose Acknowledgments page "[thanks] Geoffrey Chaucer for creating a literary work that defies time and space" (n.p.).

Fourth, we must reaffirm our discipline's commitment to textual criticism and philology, updating these modes of inquiry for the twenty-first century. As we move deeper into an age of media, literary scholars will need to gain proficiency in not only interpreting texts but stewarding, preserving, and indeed transforming them, attending to the ways that language lives and moves through material forms, from books to phonograph records to Twitter posts and beyond. We must do this not because poetry is today multimediated whereas in the past it was printed, but because the challenge of writing sound is perennial. Against the backdrop of the various intrinsic, hermeneutic critical models of the twentieth century—from Saussurian structuralism to New Criticism to the Theory-informed approaches of century's end—the printed lyric's visual stasis could be taken as an emblem of well-wrought coherence or, alternatively, an artful façade in need of deconstruction. The very stability of the text, in other words, licensed a host of critical reading practices otherwise quite different from one another. If the past century witnessed, as Roland Barthes put it, a move from work to text, the next century may need to move in turn from text to document and, especially where prosody is concerned, to score.[20] "It was an epic where every line was erased // yet freshly written in sheets of exploding surf," writes Walcott near the end of *Omeros*, characterizing his own revisionary ambitions as well as the larger historical process whereby Homer is rewritten by each new age, moving from bardic origins to Renaissance print shops, from Pope's couplets to Milman Parry's phonograph records, and on to versions in our own time by figures like Walcott and Emily Wilson.[21] If the poetry we inherit from the past continues to speak to us, that is because it speaks through us, through the most advanced and the most mundane language technologies we bring to it. No small wonder, and no great cause for concern, if the sounds of this poetry, as one poet put it, should seem at once far off, and near.

---

[20] See Roland Barthes, "From Work to Text," in *Image Music Text*, trans. Stephen Heath (London: Fontana Press, 1977), 155–64.

[21] Derek Walcott, *Omeros* (New York: Farrar, Straus and Giroux, 1991), 296.

Bibliography

"A Voice Like a Flying Banner," *TIME* (March 10, 1961).

Abrams, M. H. *Natural Supernaturalism: Tradition and Revolution in Romantic Literature* (New York: Norton, 1971).

Abrams, M. H. "Structure and Style in the Greater Romantic Lyric." In *The Correspondent Breeze: Essays on English Romanticism* (New York: W. W. Norton, 1984), 76–108.

Addison, Joseph. *Spectator* 85, The Spectator Project: A Hypermedia Research Archive of Eighteenth-Century Periodicals, http://www2.scc.rutgers.edu/spectator/project.html.

Adorno, Theodor. "The Form of the Phonograph Record," trans. Thomas Levin, *October*, 55 (1990): 56–61.

Agbabi, Patience. *Telling Tales* (London: Canongate, 2014).

"Alexa Brand Guidelines for Amazon Developers," Amazon, 2024, https://developer. amazon.com/en-US/alexa/branding/alexa-guidelines.

Altieri, Charles. *Painterly Abstraction in Modernist American Poetry* (University Park: The Pennsylvania State University Press, 1989).

Anderson, Charles. *Emily Dickinson's Poetry: Stairway of Surprise* (New York: Holt, Rinehart and Winston, 1960).

Aruffo, Christopher. "Reconsidering Poe's 'Rationale of Verse'," *Poe Studies*, 44/1 (2011): 69–88.

"'Ask Your Mama': A Music and Poetry Premiere," *WBUR News*, March 16, 2009.

Attridge, Derek. "The Rhythms of the English Dolnik." In Ben Glaser and Jonathan Culler, eds., *Critical Rhythm: The Poetics of a Literary Life Form* (Fordham University Press, 2019), 153–73.

Baldwin, Neil. *Edison: Inventing the Century* (Chicago: University of Chicago Press, 1995).

Barthes, Roland. *Image Music Text*, trans. Stephen Heath (London: Fontana Press, 1977).

Beavers, Herman. "Dead Rocks and Sleeping Men: Aurality in the Aesthetic of Langston Hughes," *The Langston Hughes Review*, 11/1 (Spring 1992): 1–5.

Benjamin, Walter. *The Work of Art in the Age of Its Technological Reproducibility, and Other Writings on Media* (Cambridge: Harvard University Press, 2008).

Bewell, Alan. *Wordsworth and the Enlightenment: Nature, Man, and Society in the Experimental Poetry* (New Haven: Yale University Press, 1989).

Beyoncé, "All Night," track 11 on *Lemonade* (Columbia Records, 2016).

Bloom, Harold, ed. *Edgar Allan Poe's "The Tell-Tale Heart" and Other Stories* (New York: Infobase, 2009).

Bornstein, George. *Material Modernism: The Politics of the Page* (Cambridge: Cambridge University Press, 2001).

Bradley, Adam. *Book of Rhymes: The Poetics of Hip Hop* (New York: Civitas Books, 2017).

Brady, Erika. *A Spiral Way: How the Phonograph Changed Ethnography* (Jackson: University Press of Mississippi, 1999).

Brogan, T. V. F. "Prosody." In Alex Preminger, T. V. F. Brogan, Frank J. Warnke, O. B. Hardison, and Earl Miner, eds., *New Princeton Encyclopedia of Poetry and Poetics* (Princeton: Princeton University Press, 1993), 982–94.

Brown, Margery E. *A Man of No Taste Whatsoever: Joseph Pocklington 1736–1817* (AuthorHouse, 2010).

Browning, Robert. *Robert Browning: Selected Poems,* ed. Daniel Karlin (London: Penguin Books, 1989).

Browning, Robert. "How They Brought the Good News from Ghent to Aix," track 2 on *The Spoken Word, Poets: Historic Recordings of Poets Born in the Nineteenth Century* (British Library Board, 2003).

Buchan, David D. *The Ballad and the Folk: Studies in the Balladry and the Society of the North-East of Scotland* (Aberdeen: Aberdeen University Press, 1966).

Burney, Charles. Unsigned review, *Monthly Review,* 29 (June 1799), rprt. in Robert Woof, ed., *William Wordsworth: The Critical Heritage, Volume I: 1793–1820* (New York: Routledge, 2001), 74–78.

Burt, Stephanie [Stephen]. "What Is This Thing Called Lyric?" *Modern Philology,* 113/3 (2016): 422–40.

Cameron, Sharon. *Choosing Not Choosing: Dickinson's Fascicles* (Chicago: The University of Chicago Press, 1993).

Camlot, Jason. *Phonopoetics: The Making of Early Literary Recordings* (Stanford: Stanford University Press, 2019).

Carroll, Lewis. "A-Sitting on a Gate." In Mary Wilder Tileston, ed., *The Child's Harvest of Verse* (Boston: Little, Brown and Co., 1910), 269–72.

Caruthers, A. J. *Notational Experiments in North American Long Poems, 1961–2011: Stave Sightings* (Basingstoke: Palgrave Macmillan, 2017).

Chandler, James. *An Archaeology of Sympathy: The Sentimental Mode in Literature and Cinema* (Chicago: University of Chicago Press, 2013).

Chasar, Mike. "The Business of Rhyming: Burma-Shave Poetry and Popular Culture," *PMLA,* 125/1 (2010): 29–47.

Chasar, Mike. *Everyday Reading: Poetry and Popular Culture in Modern America* (New York: Columbia University Press, 2012).

Chasar, Mike. *Poetry Unbound: Poems and New Media from the Magic Lantern to Instagram* (New York: Columbia University Press, 2020).

Chinitz, David. *Which Sin to Bear? Authenticity and Compromise in Langston Hughes* (Oxford: Oxford University Press, 2013).

Chubb, Edwin Watts. *Stories of Authors British and American* (New York: The Macmillan Company, 1926).

Clark, J. Scott. *A Practical Rhetoric for Instruction in English Composition and Revision in Colleges and Intermediate Schools* (New York: Henry Holt, 1886).

Coleridge, Samuel Taylor. *Biographia Literaria: Or, Biographical Sketches of My Literary Life and Opinions* (New York: Leavitt, Lord, 1834).

Common, "The Corner", track 2 on *Be* (Geffen Records, 2005).

Crystal, David. *A Dictionary of Linguistics & Phonetics, 5th Edition* (New York: Blackwell, 2003).

Culler, Jonathan. "Apostrophe," *diacritics,* 7/4 (1977): 59–69.

Culler, Jonathan. *Theory of the Lyric* (Cambridge: Harvard University Press, 2015).

Derrida, Jacques. *Glas*, trans. John P. Leavey, Jr. and Richard Rand (Lincoln: University of Nebraska Press, 1986).

Dickie, Margaret. "Dickinson in Context," *American Literary History*, 7/2 (Summer 1995): 320–33.

Dickinson, Emily. *Further Poems of Emily Dickinson*, ed. Martha Dickinson Bianchi and Alfred Leete Hampson (Boston: Little Brown & Co., 1929).

Dickinson, Emily. *The Poems of Emily Dickinson: Including Variant Readings Critically Compared with All Known Manuscripts*, ed. Thomas Johnson (Cambridge: Harvard University Press, 1955).

Dickinson, Emily. *The Manuscript Books of Emily Dickinson*, ed. Ralph Franklin, vol. 1 (Cambridge: Harvard University Press, 1981).

Dickinson, Emily. *The Master Letters of Emily Dickinson*, ed. R. W. Franklin (Amherst: Amherst University Press, 1986).

Dickinson, Emily. *The Poems of Emily Dickinson: Reading Edition*, ed. Ralph Franklin (Cambridge: Harvard University Press, 1998).

Dickinson, Emily. *The Poems of Emily Dickinson: Variorum Edition*, ed. Ralph Franklin, vol. 1 (Cambridge: Harvard University Press, 1998).

Easthope, Antony. *Poetry as Discourse* (London: Routledge, 1983).

Edison, Thomas. "The Phonograph and Its Future," *The North American Review*, 126/262 (May–June 1878): 527–36.

Edison, Thomas. "The Perfected Phonograph," *The North American Review*, 146/379 (January 1888): 641–50.

Eliot, T. S. "From Poe to Valéry," *The Hudson Review*, 2/3 (Autumn 1949): 327–42.

Eliot, T. S. *T. S. Eliot: Collected Poems, 1909–1962* (New York: Harcourt, 1991).

Feld, Steven. "Aesthetics as Iconicity of Style, or 'Lift-up-over Sounding': Getting into the Kaluli Groove," *Yearbook for Traditional Music*, 20 (1988): 74–113.

Fitts, Dudley. "A Trio of Singers," *New York Times*, October 29, 1961.

Flint, Kate. *The Transatlantic Indian, 1776–1930* (Princeton: Princeton University Press, 2009).

Fotheringham, John. *Wordsworth's "Prelude" as a Study of Education* (London: Horace Marshall & Son, 1899).

Fox, Charles James. Letter to Wordsworth, May 25, 1801, rprt. in Robert Woof, ed., *William Wordsworth: The Critical Heritage, Volume I: 1793–1820* (New York: Routledge, 2001), 106.

Franklin, Ralph. *The Editing of Emily Dickinson: A Reconsideration* (Madison: The University of Wisconsin Press, 1967).

Furr, Derek. *Recorded Poetry and Poetic Reception from Edna Millay to the Circle of Robert Lowell* (New York: Palgrave Macmillan, 2008).

Gates, Henry Louis. *The Signifying Monkey: A Theory of African-American Literary Criticism* (Oxford: Oxford University Press, 1989).

Gill, Stephen. *Wordsworth: The Prelude* (Oxford: Oxford University Press, 1991).

Gitelman, Lisa. *Scripts, Grooves, and Writing Machines: Representing Technology in the Edison Era* (Stanford: Stanford University Press, 1999).

Glaser, Ben. *Modernism's Metronome: Meter and Twentieth-Century Poetics* (Baltimore: Johns Hopkins University Press, 2020).

Golston, Michael. *Rhythm and Race in Modernist Poetry and Science: Pound, Yeats, Williams, and Modern Sciences of Rhythm* (New York: Columbia University Press, 2007).

Graham, T. Austin. *The Great American Songbooks: Musical Texts, Modernism, and the Value of Popular Culture* (Oxford: Oxford University Press, 2013).

Green, David Gordon. "Because I could not stop," Season 1, Episode 1 of *Dickinson*, Apple TV+, 34:00, November 1, 2019, tv.apple.com/us/show/Dickinson.

Green, David Gordon. "I have never seen 'Volcanoes'," Season 1, Episode 2 of *Dickinson*, Apple TV+, 27:00, November 1, 2019, tv.apple.com/us/show/Dickinson.

Guillory, John. "Genesis of the Media Concept," *Critical Inquiry*, 36/2 (2010): 321–62.

Guyau, Jean-Marie. Qtd. in Friedrich Kittler, *Gramophone, Film, Typewriter*, trans. Geoffrey Winthrop-Young and Michael Wutz (Stanford: Stanford University Press, 1999), 30–33.

Hall, Jason David, ed. *Meter Matters: Verse Cultures of the Long Nineteenth Century* (Athens: Ohio University Press, 2011).

Hall, Jason David. *Nineteenth-Century Verse and Technology: Machines of Meter* (London: Palgrave, 2017).

Hartman, Charles. *Free Verse: An Essay on Prosody* (Evanston: Northwestern University Press, 1980).

Hartman, Charles. *Jazz Text: Voice and Improvisation in Poetry, Jazz, and Song* (Princeton: Princeton University Press, 1991).

Hartman, Geoffrey. *Wordsworth's Poetry 1787–1814* (New Haven: Yale University Press, 1964).

Hartman, Geoffrey. *The Unremarkable Wordsworth* (Minneapolis: The University of Minnesota Press, 1987).

Heaney, Seamus. *Beowulf: A New Verse Translation* (New York: Norton, 2000).

Higginson, Thomas Wentworth. Letter to his wife, August 16, 1870, *The Letters of Emily Dickinson*, ed. Thomas Johnson, vol. 1 (Cambridge: Harvard University Press, 1958), 473–74.

Hollenbach, Lisa. "Sono-Montage: Langston Hughes and Tony Schwartz Listen to Postwar New York," *American Literature*, 87/2 (2015): 275–302.

"How We Gave a Phonograph Party" (New York: National Phonograph Company, 1899). In Timothy D. Taylor, Mark Katz, and Tony Grajeda, eds., *Music, Sound, and Technology in America: A Documentary History of Early Phonograph, Cinema, and Radio* (Durham: Duke University Press, 2012), 48–51.

Howe, Susan. *My Emily Dickinson* (New York: New Directions, 1985).

Howe, Susan. *The Birth-mark: Unsettling the Wilderness in American Literary History* (Middleton: Wesleyan University Press, 1993).

Hughes, Langston. *Ask Your Mama: 12 Moods for Jazz* (New York: Knopf, 1961).

Hughes, Langston. "I Remember the Blues." In F. L. Mott, ed., *Missouri Reader* (Columbia: University of Missouri Press, 1964), 152-55.

Hughes, Langston. *The Big Sea: An Autobiography* (New York: Hill and Wang, 1993).

Hughes, Langston. *The Collected Works of Langston Hughes: The Poems, 1921–1940, Vol. 1*, ed. Arnold Rampersad (Columbia: The University of Missouri Press, 2002).

Hughes, Langston. *The Collected Works of Langston Hughes: The Poems, 1951–1967, Vol. 3*, ed. Arnold Rampersad (Columbia: The University of Missouri Press, 2002).

Hughes, Langston. *The Collected Works of Langston Hughes: Essays on Art, Race, Politics, and World Affairs, Vol. 9*, ed. Christopher C. De Santis (Columbia: The University of Missouri Press, 2002).

Hughes, Langston. *Selected Letters of Langston Hughes*, ed. Arnold Rampersad and David Roessel (New York: Knopf, 2015).

Hughes, Langston. "Hesitation Blues." Langston Hughes Papers (JWJ MSS 26). James Weldon Johnson Collection in the Yale Collection of American Literature, Beinecke Rare Book and Manuscript Library, Yale University.

Jackson, Virginia. *Dickinson's Misery: A Theory of Lyric Reading* (Princeton University Press, 2005).

Jackson, Virginia. "Lyric." In Roland Greene, Stephen Cushman, Clare Cavanagh, Jahan Ramazani, and Paul Rouzer, eds., *Princeton Encyclopedia of Poetry and Poetics* (Princeton: Princeton University Press, 2012), 826–34.

Jacobus, Mary. *Tradition and Experiment in Wordsworth's "Lyrical Ballads" (1798)* (Oxford: Clarendon Press, 1976).

Jarvis, Simon. "Prosody as Cognition," *Critical Quarterly*, 40/4 (1998): 3–15.

Jarvis, Simon. *Wordsworth's Philosophic Song* (Cambridge: Cambridge University Press, 2006).

Jones, Meta. *The Muse Is Music: Jazz Poetry from the Harlem Renaissance to Spoken Word* (Urbana: The University of Illinois Press, 2011).

Joyce, James. *Ulysses* (New York: Vintage Books, 1986).

Kane, J., M. N. Johnstone, and P. Szewczyk. "Voice Synthesis Improvement by Machine Learning of Natural Prosody," *Sensors*, 24/5 (2024): 1624.

Kennedy, J. Gerald, and Jerome McGann, eds. *Poe and the Remapping of Antebellum Print Culture* (Baton Rouge: Louisiana State University Press, 2012).

Kenner, Hugh. *The Pound Era* (Berkeley: The University of California Press, 1971).

Kenner, Hugh. "Notes on Amateur Emendations." In Lawrence Rainey, ed., *A Poem Containing History* (Ann Arbor: University of Michigan Press, 1997), 21–29.

Kim, Sabine. *Acoustic Entanglements: Sound and Aesthetic Practice* (Heidelberg: Universitatsverlag Winter, 2017).

Kittler, Friedrich. *Gramophone, Film, Typewriter*, trans. Geoffrey Winthrop-Young and Michael Wutz (Stanford: Stanford University Press, 1999).

Kylstra, Peter H. "The Use of the Early Phonograph in Phonetic Research," *Phonographic Bulletin*, 17 (1977): 3–12.

Lanier, Sidney. *The Science of English Verse* (New York: Charles Scribner's Sons, 1880).

Levine, Stuart and Susan F. Levine, Introduction to "The Rationale of Verse". In Levine and Levine, eds., *Edgar Allan Poe: Critical Theory, the Major Documents* (Springfield: University of Illinois Press, 2009), 77–80.

Levine, Caroline. *Forms: Whole, Rhythm, Hierarchy, Network* (Princeton: Princeton University Press, 2015).

Levinson, Marjorie. *Wordsworth's Great Period Poems: Four Essays* (Cambridge: Cambridge University Press, 1986).

Liu, Alan. *Wordsworth: The Sense of History* (Stanford: Stanford University Press, 1989).

Loeffelholz, Mary. "'We send the Wave to find the Wave': Dickinson's Wave-Particle Duality," *Dickinson Electronic Archives*, https://www.emilydickinson.org/emily-dickinson-lyrical-ecologies-forays-into-the-field/we-send-the-wave-to-find-the-wave-dickinson-s-wave-particle-duality.

Lord, Albert. *The Singer of Tales*, ed. Stephen Mitchell and Gregory Nagy (Cambridge: Harvard University Press, 2000).

Lowney, John. *Jazz Internationalism: Literary Afro-Modernism and the Cultural Politics of Black Music* (Champaign: The University of Illinois Press, 2017).

MacArthur, Marit. "Monotony, the Churches of Poetry Reading, and Sound Studies," *PMLA*, 131/1 (January 2016): 38–63.

Mallarmé, Stéphane. "Notes on the Poems of Poe." In Jean Alexander, ed., *Affidavits of Genius: Edgar Allan Poe and the French Critics, 1847–1924* (Port Washington: Kennikat Press, 1971), 215–18.

Manson, Michael. "'The Thews of Hymn': Dickinson's Metrical Grammar." In Martha Nell Smith and Mary Loeffelholz, eds., *A Companion to Emily Dickinson* (Oxford: Wiley Blackwell, 2014), 368–90.

Martin, Meredith. *The Rise and Fall of Meter: Poetry and English National Culture, 1860–1930* (Princeton: Princeton University Press, 2012).

Martin, Meredith. "'Imperfectly Civilized': Ballads, Nations, and Histories of Form," *English Literary History*, 82/2 (2015): 345–63.

McGann, Jerome. *The Textual Condition* (Princeton: Princeton University Press, 1991).

McGann, Jerome. *Black Riders: The Visible Language of Modernism* (Princeton: Princeton University Press, 1993).

McGann, Jerome. *Radiant Textuality: Literary Studies after the World Wide Web* (New York: Palgrave, 2001).

McGann, Jerome. *Byron and the Poetics of Adversity* (Cambridge: Cambridge University Press, 2023).

McGill, Meredith. *American Literature and the Culture of Reprinting, 1834–1853* (Philadelphia: University of Pennsylvania Press, 2003).

McGill, Meredith L. "What Is a Ballad? Reading for Genre, Format, and Medium," *Nineteenth-Century Literature*, 71/2 (2016): 156–75.

McKenzie, D. F. *Bibliography and the Sociology of Texts* (Cambridge: Cambridge University Press, 1999).

McLane, Maureen. *Balladeering, Minstrelsy, and the Making of British Romantic Poetry* (Cambridge: Cambridge University Press, 2011).

McLuhan, Marshall. *The Gutenberg Galaxy: The Making of Typographic Man* (Toronto: University of Toronto Press, 2011).

Mill, John Stuart. *Dissertations and Discussions: Political, Philosophical, and Historical*, vol. 1 (London: John W. Parker and Son, 1859).

Mill, John Stuart. *Essays on Poetry*, ed. F. Parvin Sharpless (Columbia: University of South Carolina Press, 1976).

Miller, R. Baxter. *The Art and Imagination of Langston Hughes* (Lexington: The University Press of Kentucky, 2006).

Mooney, Margaret S. *Composition-Rhetoric from Literature: For High Schools, Academies and Normal Schools* (New York: Brandow Printing Company, 1903).

Morgan, Victoria. *Emily Dickinson and Hymn Culture: Tradition and Experience* (London: Routledge, 2016).

Newman, Ian. "Moderation in the *Lyrical Ballads*: Wordsworth and the Ballad Debates of the 1790s," *Studies in Romanticism*, 55/2 (Summer 2016): 185–210.

Nichols, P. "Modernism." In Roland Greene, Stephen Cushman, Clare Cavanagh, Jahan Ramazani, and Paul Rouzer, eds., *Princeton Encyclopedia of Poetry & Poetics* (Princeton: Princeton University Press, 2012), 889–94.

Ochs, Phil. "The Bells," track 7 on *All the News That's Fit to Sing* (Elektra, 1964).

O'Donnell, Brennen. *The Passion of Meter: A Study of Wordsworth's Metrical Art* (Kent: Kent State University Press, 1995).

Ong, Walter. *Orality and Literacy* (New York: Routledge, 2002).

Pahl, Dennis. "De-Composing Poe's 'Philosophy,'" *Texas Studies in Literature and Language*, 38/1 (Spring 1996): 1–25.

Passon, Stacie. "I'm Nobody! Who are you?" Season 2, Episode 8 of *Dickinson*, Apple TV+, 32:00, February 12, 2021, tv.apple.com/us/show/Dickinson.

Patmore, Coventry. *Essay on English Metrical Law*, ed. Mary Augustine Roth (Washington: The Catholic University of America Press, 1961).

Pepperberg, Irene. "Grey Parrots Do Not Always 'Parrot': The Roles of Imitation and Phonological Awareness in the Creation of New Labels from Existing Vocalizations," *Language Sciences*, 29 (2007): 1–13.

Perloff, Marjorie. *The Futurist Moment: Avant-Garde, Avant Guerre, and the Language of Rupture* (Chicago: The University of Chicago Press, 1986).

Poe, Edgar Allan. *The Narrative of Arthur Gordon Pym* (London: Wiley & Putnam, 1838).

Poe, Edgar Allan. *Poetry, Tales, and Selected Essays*, ed. Patrick F. Quinn and G. R. Thompson (New York: The Library of America, 1984).

Poe, Edgar Allan. "The Philosophy of Composition." In Stuart Levine and Susan F. Levine, eds., *Edgar Allan Poe: Critical Theory, the Major Documents* (Springfield: University of Illinois Press, 2009), 60–76.

Poe, Edgar Allan. "The Poetic Principle." In Stuart Levine and Susan F. Levine, eds., *Edgar Allan Poe: Critical Theory, the Major Documents* (Springfield: University of Illinois Press, 2009), 178–211.

Poe, Edgar Allan. "The Rationale of Verse." In Stuart Levine and Susan F. Levine, eds., *Edgar Allan Poe: Critical Theory, the Major Documents* (Springfield: University of Illinois Press, 2009), 80–143.

Posmentier, Sonya. "Lyric Reading in the Black Ethnographic Archive," *American Literature*, 30/1 (Spring 2018): 55–84.

Pound, Ezra. *Gaudier-Brzeska: A Memoir* (New York: John Lane, 1916).

Pound, Ezra. "Three Cantos," *Poetry*, 10/4 (July 1917): 180–88.

Pound, Ezra. *Instigations of Ezra Pound* (New York: Boni and Liveright, 1920).

Pound, Ezra. "The Island of Paris: A Letter," *Dial*, 69/5 (October 1920): 635–39.

Pound, Ezra. *Antheil and the Treatise on Harmony* (Chicago: Pascal Covici, 1927).

Pound, Ezra. "E. E. Cummings Alive," *New English Weekly*, 6/10 (1934): 210–11.

Pound, Ezra. *Literary Essays of Ezra Pound* (New York: New Directions, 1935).

Pound, Ezra. *Selected Poems of Ezra Pound* (New York: New Directions, 1957).

Pound, Ezra. "Ezra Pound: Readings and Recollections." With D. G. Bridson, recorded April 1959.

Pound, Ezra. *Guide to Kulchur* (New York: New Directions, 1970).

Pound, Ezra. *Ezra Pound and Music: The Complete Criticism*, ed. R. Murray Schafer (New York: New Directions, 1977).

Pound, Ezra. *The Cantos* (New York: New Directions, 1996).

Pound, Ezra. *ABC of Reading* (New York: New Directions, 2010).

Pound, Ezra. "Dissertation on Rhythm." Ezra Pound Papers (YCAL MSS 43). American Literature Collection, Beinecke Rare Book and Manuscript Library, Yale University.

Pound, Ezra and George Antheil. Score to *Le Testament de Villon*. Ezra Pound Papers (YCAL MSS 43). American Literature Collection, Beinecke Rare Book and Manuscript Library, Yale University.

Pratt, Russell. "There Is Nothing Quite Like Ezra Pound's Opera," *The New Yorker* (April 29, 2017).

Prins, Yopie. "Robert Browning, Transported by Meter." In Meredith L. McGill, ed., *The Traffic in Poems: Nineteenth-century Poetry and Transatlantic Exchange* (New Brunswick: Rutgers University Press, 2008), 205–30.

Quinn, Arthur H., and Edward H. O'Neill, eds. *The Complete Poems and Stories of Edgar Allan Poe*, vol. 2 (New York: Knopf, 1946).

Quinn, Arthur Hobson. *Edgar Allan Poe: A Critical Biography* (Baltimore: The Johns Hopkins University Press, 1998).

Rainey, Lawrence. *Ezra Pound and the Monument of Culture: Text, History, and the Malatesta Cantos* (Chicago: The University of Chicago Press, 1991).

Ramazani, Jahan. *Poetry of Mourning: The Modern Elegy from Hardy to Heaney* (Chicago: The University of Chicago Press, 1994).

Ramazani, Jahan. *Poetry in a Global Age* (Chicago: The University of Chicago Press, 2020).

Rampersad, Arnold. "Langston Hughes's Fine Clothes to the Jew," *Callaloo*, 26 (Winter 1986): 144–58.

Rampersad, Arnold. *The Life of Langston Hughes, Volume 2, 1941–1967: I Dream a World* (Oxford: Oxford University Press, 1989).

Reed, Anthony. *Freedom Time: The Poetics and Politics of Black Experimental Writing* (Baltimore: Johns Hopkins University Press, 2014).

Richards, Eliza. *Gender and the Poetics of Reception in Poe's Circle* (Cambridge: Cambridge University Press, 2004).

Richards, Eliza. "Poe's Lyrical Media: The Raven's Returns." In J. Gerald Kennedy and Jerome McGann, eds., *Poe and the Remapping of Antebellum Print Culture* (Baton Rouge: Louisiana State University Press, 2012), 200–24.

Riding, Laura. "The Facts in the Case of Monsieur Poe." In Laura Heffernan and Jane Malcolm, eds., *Contemporaries and Snobs* (Tuscaloosa: University of Alabama Press, 2014), 86–112.

Rudy, Jason. *Electric Meters: Victorian Physiological Poetics* (Athens: Ohio University Press, 2009).

Rush, Rebecca. *The Fetters of Rhyme: Liberty and Poetic Form in Early Modern England* (Princeton: Princeton University Press, 2021).

Saintsbury, George. *A History of English Prosody: From the Twelfth Century to the Present Day*, 3 vols. (London: Macmillan and Co., 1910).

Scanlon, Larry. "News from Heaven: Vernacular Time in Langston Hughes's *Ask Your Mama*," *Callaloo* 25.1 (2002): 45–65.

Schuessler, Jennifer. "A 21st-Century Emily Dickinson Finds a Home in the Archives," *New York Times*, December 10, 2021.

Schultz, Kathy. *The Afro-Modernist Epic and Literary History: Tolson, Hughes, Baraka* (New York: Palgrave, 2013).

Scott, Édouard-Léon. Qtd. in Jonathan Sterne, *The Audible Past: Cultural Origins of Sound Reproduction* (Durham: Duke University Press, 2003), 46.

Shakespeare, William. *Julius Caesar*, ed. Barbara A. Mowat and Paul Werstine (New York: Washington Square Press, 1993).

Shelton, Lynn. "Alone, I cannot be," Season 1, Episode 1 of *Dickinson*, Apple TV+, 28:00, November 1, 2019, tv.apple.com/us/show/Dickinson.

Shoptaw, John. "Listening to Dickinson," *Representations*, 86/1 (Spring 2004): 20–52.

Silverman, David. "Treehouse of Horror," *The Simpsons*, Season 2, Episode 3, Fox, 30:00, October 25, 1990.

Smith, Alena. "Alena Smith on the Media," Apple TV+, 2:00, January 8, 2021, tv.apple.com/us/show/Dickinson.

Smith, Steve. "Playing Langston Hughes's Jazzy Verse," *The New York Times*, March 17, 2009.

Southey, Robert. Unsigned review, *Critical Review* (October 1798), rprt. in Robert Woof, ed., *William Wordsworth: The Critical Heritage, Volume I: 1793–1820* (New York: Routledge, 2001), 65–68.

Spenser, Edmund. "Amoretti 75." In Margaret Ferguson, Tim Kendall, and Mary Jo Salter, eds., *The Norton Anthology of Poetry, Sixth Edition* (New York: Norton & Co., 2018), 202.

Stedman, Edmund C. and George Edward Woodberry, eds., *The Works of Edgar Allan Poe*, vol. 6 (Chicago: Stone and Kimball, 1895).

Steele, Joshua. *Prosodia Rationalis: Or, an Essay Towards Establishing the Melody and Measure of Speech, to be Expressend and Perpetuated by Peculiar Symbols* (London: J. Nichols, 1789).

Sterne, Jonathan. *The Audible Past: Cultural Origins of Sound Reproduction* (Durham: Duke University Press, 2003).

Stewart, Garrett. *Reading Voices: Literature and the Phonotext* (Berkeley: The University of California Press, 1990).

Stoddart, John. *British Critic* 17 (February 1801), rprt. in Robert Woof, ed., *William Wordsworth: The Critical Heritage, Volume I: 1793–1820* (New York: Routledge, 2001), 138–43.

Storer, Christopher. "Fame is a fickle food," Season 2, Episode 2 of *Dickinson*, Apple TV+, 25:00, January 8, 2021, tv.apple.com/us/show/Dickinson.

Swift, Taylor. "The Last Great American Dynasty," track 3 on *folklore* (Republic Records, 2020).

Swift, Taylor. "The Lakes", track 17 on *folklore* (Republic Records, 2020).

Tanselle, G. Thomas. "The Textual Criticism of Visual and Aural Works," *Studies in Bibliography*, 57/1 (2005): 1–37.

Taruskin, Richard. *Text and Act: Essays on Music and Performance* (Oxford: Oxford University Press, 1995).

Tiffany, Daniel. *My Silver Planet: A Secret History of Poetry and Kitsch* (Baltimore: Johns Hopkins University Press, 2014).

Tracy, Steven. *Langston Hughes and the Blues* (Urbana: The University of Illinois Press, 1988).

Trotman, C. James, ed., *Langston Hughes: The Man, His Art, and His Continuing Influence* (New York: Routledge, 1995).

Tucker, Herbert F. *Epic: Britain's Heroic Muse, 1790–1910* (Oxford: Oxford University Press, 2008).

Tucker, Herbert F. "Unsettled Scores: Meter and Play in Two Music Poems by Browning," *Critical Inquiry*, 41 (Autumn 2014): 24–52.

Tucker, Herbert F. "Dramatic Monologue and the Overhearing of Lyric." In Virginia Jackson and Yopie Prins, eds., *The Lyric Theory Reader* (Baltimore: Johns Hopkins University Press, 2014), 144–58.

Tucker, Herbert F. "Balladry in Motion," *The Wordsworth Circle*, 52/1 (Winter 2021): 34–49.

Tupac, "If I Die 2Nite", track 2 on *Me Against the World* (Interscope Records, 1995).

Vendler, Helen. "*Tintern Abbey*: Two Assaults," *The Bucknell Review*, 36/1 (1992): 173–90.

Vergil, Polydore. *On Discovery*, ed. and trans. Brian P. Copenhaver (Cambridge: Harvard University Press, 2002).

Vincent, David. *Literacy and Popular Culture: England 1750–1914* (Cambridge: Cambridge University Press, 1993).

Wagner, Roy. *The Invention of Culture* (Chicago: University of Chicago Press, 1981).

Walcott, Derek. *Omeros* (New York: Farrar, Straus and Giroux, 1991).

Walcott, Derek. "Reflections on *Omeros*," *South Atlantic Quarterly*, 96/2 (1997): 229–46.

Wehelie, Alexander. *Phonographies: Grooves in Sonic Afro-Modernity* (Durham: Duke University Press, 2005).

Weisbuch, Robert. *Emily Dickinson's Poetry* (Chicago: The University of Chicago Press, 1975).

Weiskott, Eric. *Meter and Modernity in English Verse, 1350–1650* (Philadelphia: University of Pennsylvania Press, 2021).

Wheeler, Lesley. *Voicing American Poetry: Sound and Performance from the 1920s to the Present* (Ithaca: Cornell University Press, 2008).

Williams, Raymond. *Culture and Society, 1780–1950* (New York: Columbia University Press, 1983).

Winslow, R. "Prosody." In Roland Greene, Stephen Cushman, Clare Cavanagh, Jahan Ramazani, and Paul Rouzer, eds., *Princeton Encyclopedia of Poetry and Poetics* (Princeton: Princeton University Press, 2012), 1117–120.

Winters, Yvor. "Edgar Allan Poe: A Crisis in the History of American Obscurantism," *American Literature*, 8/4 (January 1937): 379–402.

Wolfson, Susan J. "Wordsworth's Craft." In Stephen Gill, ed., *The Cambridge Companion to Wordsworth* (Cambridge: Cambridge University Press, 2003), 108–24.

Wordsworth, William. *The Prelude: 1799, 1805, 1850*, ed. Jonathan Wordsworth, M. H. Abrams, and Stephen Gill (New York: Norton, 1979).

Wordsworth, William. 1804 Letter to John Thelwall. Qtd. in Brennen O'Donnell, *The Passion of Meter: A Study of Wordsworth's Metrical Art* (Kent: Kent State University Press, 1995), 179–80.

Wordsworth, William, and Samuel Taylor Coleridge. *Lyrical Ballads: 1798 and 1802*, ed. Fiona Stafford (Oxford: Oxford University Press, 2013).

Wylder, Edith Perry. *The Last Face: Emily Dickinson's Manuscripts* (Albuquerque: University of New Mexico Press, 1971).

Wylder, Edith. "Emily Dickinson's Punctuation: The Controversy Revisited," *American Literary Realism*, 36/3 (Spring 2004): 206–24.

Index